To-
Bill,
Best Wishes -
Robert Emerson
Sept. 2002

DANCING WITH DEVILS

DANCING WITH DEVILS

Robert D. Emerson

VANTAGE PRESS
New York

FIRST EDITION

Published by Vantage Press, Inc.
516 West 34th Street, New York, New York 10001

Manufactured in the United States of America
ISBN: 0-533-12539-1

Library of Congress Catalog Card No.: 97-91038

0 9 8 7 6 5 4 3 2 1

To Vicky, who endured the hardships of a lawman's wife
and whose love and support made this book possible

Author's Note

The names of most of the subjects of investigations, suspects, witnesses, police officers, and some fellow agents have been changed to protect their privacy. Dates and times in this book are accurate. The conversations are as I remember them and should not be considered verbatim. Many of the law enforcement personnel have passed away, but I shall forever remember them for their dedication to a way of life known only to a few . . . a lawman's life.

Prologue

It was just before midnight, December 18, 1967, just seven short days before Patty Guthrie would have enjoyed only her fourth Christmas on this earth. A cold rain was slowly falling, but the thicket afforded some protection. I was on my knees as I brushed back pine needles and saw freshly disturbed soil. Having failed to bring a shovel to the scene, I dug gently with my hands into the soft, wet earth to a depth of about two feet before they touched the lifeless form of four-year-old Patty. Carefully, the soil was moved aside to disclose the doll-like features of a beautiful child lying on her back as if asleep. I gently lifted Patty from her grave and placed her small body on a canvas stretcher. The area had been illuminated by flashlights held by officers who witnessed death often and thought they had become hardened to it. As I looked around, there was not a dry eye among them.

How and why was I involved in this nightmarish hell in a remote section of Wayne County, North Carolina? It's a story I'll try to tell as best I can from what has been told to me, what I remember, and notes I have retained over the years. It's the best I can do.

DANCING WITH DEVILS

1

Siler City is located in the western part of Chatham County and is very near the geographical center of the state of North Carolina. Few people outside of North Carolina had ever heard of it until it was referred to several times in the old *Andy Griffith Show* TV series as a neighboring community to Mayberry. The current population is approximately 5,000, but when I was born there on Memorial Day, 1933, there were only about 1800 residents, most of whom were employed in local textile and furniture factories. For the past thirty years I have resided in Cary, North Carolina, which is a suburb of Raleigh and is in Wake County, forty miles due east of Siler City. My hometown has changed little over the years and the increase in population is mainly the result of the corporate limits of the town being expanded during the late 1950's.

My father, John W. Emerson, Jr., was reared on a large tobacco farm near Durham, North Carolina. After graduating from high school he attended North Carolina State College, where he studied mechanical engineering. In the mid-1920's he moved with his father, John W. Emerson, Sr., to Siler City, where he operated the Chevrolet agency for several years. My grandmother, Mollie King Emerson, died when my father was only five years old.

I guess the best thing that ever happened as far as I am concerned is, after moving to Siler City, my father met and later married my mother, Nannie Maude Dunlap. She was the daughter of John H. Dunlap and Mary Lea Buie Dunlap. The town of Bonlee was founded by her father when he started a lumber business there in 1884. Bonlee is located about five miles south of Siler City. My parents were married in 1926 and in 1929, just a few months before the collapse of the stock market and the start of the Great Depression, my older brother, John Hudson Emerson, was born. My grandfather lived in the home with my parents and, since there were already two Johns in the house, they called my brother by his middle name, Hudson. Four years later, on a beautiful spring day with flags flying to honor our fallen servicemen, my mother brought me into this world at 8:20 pm with the assistance of Dr. Ronald C. Gyles.

The family now consisted of my parents, Hudson, myself, and, of course, my grandfather, a grand old gentlemen who was born in 1860. He remembered "Yankee" troops coming to his home in southern Chatham County looking for horses towards the end of the Civil War. Grandpa was a man of action and adventure as he went to Texas in 1882 to work with the A.T.&K. Railroad. He was said to be the only employee who could jump from a slow-moving work car, lift a keg of railroad spikes, and throw the keg onto the same car. Grandpa later became involved in logging operations along the Mexican border and later was a cowboy on one of the last cattle drives from Texas to Abilene, Kansas. While in the West, Grandpa brushed elbows with cattle barons, cowboys, gamblers, gunmen, and outlaws. He saw Geronimo after his capture, met and became friends with Frank James, and saw three men hanged at one time—and assisted the sheriff by lifting one man whose feet were touching the ground so the rope could be shortened. Grandpa stayed in the West until his return to North Carolina in about 1900; however, he brought back with him scars on his upper lip resulting from a saloon brawl. This caused him to keep a mustache for the rest of his life. He also returned with a bullet embedded in his body, which was still there when he died in 1948. Grandpa lived with us until his death, and I feel privileged to have grown up in a household where I could listen to his stories and picture in my mind some of his experiences. Grandpa is a legend around Siler City as he continued to be active in construction work until shortly before his death. He kept one or more horses, usually they were wild and mean and no one else could handle them, and he would hitch one to his buggy for his daily excursion to town. Grandpa would usually tie his horse to the bumper of a parked car and then jaywalk from one corner to another diagonally across the main intersection. The horse and buggy were not his only means of transportation, he always kept my mother supplied with a nice automobile as he loved speed and travel. Grandpa feared no man and pretty well did as he pleased. He could not have cared less what the opinions of others were of himself. He was not wealthy, but lived very comfortably on an inheritance from his brother, Isaac Emerson, who invented that great hangover and headache remedy, Bromo-Seltzer. Grandpa influenced me a great deal and in later years I had many anxious moments and was apprehensive on many occasions when arresting killers, bank robbers, rapists, arsonists, armed robbers, and others who lived outside the law. But, like Grandpa, I didn't fear them.

I wish I could have known my Grandpa Dunlap, as he was quite a character. He accumulated a fortune in the lumber business with operations in both North and South Carolina. He paid for a high school to be built in Bonlee, the town he founded, and also donated the lumber for the construction of a nearby church. His financial assistance to many people was done discreetly with no thought given to repayment. In 1908, he built and was president of his own railroad, which ran from Bonlee to Bennett, a distance of ten miles. Passengers, freight, and lumber were transported between the two communities. It was customary in those days for railroad executives to exchange passes with one another. One out-of-state executive questioned the wisdom of exchanging passes with the president of the Bonlee & Western because of its short length. Grandpa Dunlap said to the pompous gentlemen, "My railroad may not be as long as yours, but it's just as damned wide." When the Great Depression hit in October 1929, he lost everything in just a matter of weeks and less than three months later died from an apparent stroke. My grandmother continued to live at home in Bonlee until 1954, when she passed away while I was in Korea.

Well within the town limits, in a quiet neighborhood directly behind the elementary school, still stands the three bedroom bungalow where I was born. By this time my father had abandoned the Chevrolet dealership, as times were hard and people were not interested in new automobiles, but were struggling to buy the necessities of life. He had gone into the service station business and later became a Pure Oil distributor. He was the most influential person in my life and the person I most admired.

I differed from my dad physically, as I tended to take after the Dunlap side of the family in appearance and mannerisms. I was small in stature but quick and agile. My dad stood six feet tall and weighed an even 200 pounds until shortly before his death in 1974. He had broad rounded shoulders and dark wavy hair that was always neatly trimmed. A powerful man with extremely large hands, which in years to come restrained many a fleeing felon, ladies considered him handsome.

A smile from Dad did not come easily, but when it did, it was with sincerity and would brighten any room. As he was a very serious person, frowns came much more often. His feelings and emotions were difficult to hide and a glance at his face would immediately disclose his mood. Dad was a deacon in the Baptist Church, a Sunday school teacher, a mason, a Southern Democrat and an absolute teetotaler. He despised alcohol in any form and had little patience with those who would partake of it. His stand against alcoholic beverages later became well known in Chatham County and throughout much of North Carolina. Dad had one vice that would eventually contribute to his death: he was a very heavy smoker.

2

In 1938, a most unusual agreement was reached by my parents and a local physician and his wife. They agreed to swap homes! Our newly acquired residence was a spacious two-story, ten-room, brick-and-frame home located a mile west of Siler City. It had been constructed in the 1920's, and was situated directly atop the highest hill in the county. It had a carport, a separate garage, a patio, a tenant house, a vineyard, an orchard, a barn, a wood house, and a smokehouse. It was surrounded by thirty-five acres of pasture and fields bordered by forests of tall pines and hardwoods. From the front porch, the beacon lights at the Greensboro airport, thirty-five miles to the north, could be seen at night. This is where I grew up, played in the vast yard, worked in the fields, hunted in the woods, and looked after my pony and cared for various pets including dogs, cats, a tame crow, a squirrel, pigeons, and rabbits. A year after moving to our new home, my younger brother, Thomas Jackson Emerson, was born. Except for the four years he was away at school, Tommy has remained in the Siler City area and after my parents' death moved into the family home where he raised his family. He and his wife reside there today.

In later years, I learned from my mother that what had prompted the move to the country was that my Dad didn't want his sons to grow up in town. He wanted them not only to experience the work ethic of farm life, but also to enjoy nature by being a part of it. For his sons there were daily chores to perform from the time we were small until we left home for college. During the summers we went shirtless except for our weekly pilgrimages to the First Baptist Church for Sunday school and preaching. Our bodies toughened, but our minds were clear and our thoughts pure. There were no gray areas. Things were either right or wrong, good or bad, clean or dirty.

In 1940, my Dad was appointed by the County Commissioners as Register of Deeds for Chatham County to complete the unexpired term of the incumbent who had passed away. He was later elected to this office for two consecutive four-year terms. Being Register of Deeds required a daily commute by automobile to the county seat of Pittsboro, located sixteen miles east of Siler City. He didn't know it at the time, but the commute was to continue for the next 28 years. Dad's office was located in a beautiful old courthouse that was constructed in the center of town in 1881. Pittsboro is smaller in size than Siler City, and today has a population less than 2,000.

The war years were not as unpleasant for the Emersons as they were for many other families, as much of what we needed was produced on our small farm. Milk and butter were in plentiful supply from our cow as were fruits and vegetables from the orchard, vineyard, and garden. We had a large flock of chickens, so eggs were always available, as were tender pullets for frying. We raised our own hogs and the smokehouse was nearly always full of country hams, fatback, chitterlings, souse meat, and sausage. Three or four beehives furnished more honey than we could use.

Late in the afternoons, Dad would arrive home from Pittsboro and would usually work around the farm until dark. He bought a small Allis Chambers tractor that was equipped with lights and, when necessary, would allow him to plow or disc fields until late at night. However, all was not work as Dad was a sportsman who loved to hunt and fish. He had friends with whom he made occasional overnight fishing trips, but the sport he loved most of all was turkey hunting. During hunting season, hardly a holiday or a Saturday passed that he and his best friend, the local dentist, weren't roaming the hills of Chatham in an effort to bring back one of those elusive birds. They were both renowned hunters and both got their share of turkeys. When I was ten, my Dad allowed me to start accompanying him on short hunts. I was not allowed to carry a gun at this young age, but after a year of following in his footsteps and learning from his instructions on safe handling of firearms, I received my first gun at Christmas 1944. It was a single-barrel, .410 gauge shotgun, which I have to this day. Of course, it was too small for turkeys, but I can attest to the fact that it has accounted for lots of small game and many copperhead snakes, which we frequently encountered on the farm.

As Hudson got into his teens, his interest turned to team sports, especially football. He excelled at the game and was co-captain of the local high school team his senior year. This was 1946, and I was 13 years old, just starting the eighth grade, and weighing considerably less than 100 pounds. Hudson dared me to come out for the team and that was enough to possess me to do so. The coach had a uniform cut down to fit me, and I made every practice and dressed for all the games. That year, I played short periods in three games when our team ran up big scores against the opposition. I scrimmaged against and played against veterans from World War II who had returned to school to obtain high school diplomas. I suffered only minor scrapes and bruises and went on to play for four more years, earning a starting position the last two years. My younger brother, Tommy, also turned out to be a fine football player, earning Most Valuable Player honors his senior year of high school. I not only played high school football, but basketball and baseball as well. Baseball was my game, and play it I could! I pitched for the high school team, the American Legion team, area semi-pro teams, and several years later for a semi-pro team in Butte, Montana. I'd pitch today if I could get rid of my bursitis and find a league for those over sixty.

3

Life changed completely for the Emerson family in July 1949 when my Dad was again appointed by the County Commissioners to fill the unexpired term of another county official. The Chatham County Sheriff had resigned to accept a position with the state government in Raleigh and Dad was asked to pin on the badge. He did so and was re-elected to the position for five consecutive four-year terms, resigning in 1967 because of his declining health. He held the office longer than any Chatham sheriff who preceded him. He became a legend among North Carolina sheriffs for the long hours he kept, the miles he drove, the crimes he solved, and the aggressive and courageous actions he took against those who violated the law. When law enforcement officers in North Carolina gather today for conventions, funerals, seminars, or just to "pick a pig," his deeds and exploits are told and re-told.

If ever a man was born to be a lawman, it was my Dad. There was no more hunting, no more fishing, and no more farming. He immediately dedicated and devoted his entire life to enforcing the laws of the United States and North Carolina within the boundaries of the 707 square miles of Chatham County.

When Dad assumed office in 1949, he had three full-time field deputies, a full-time jailer who was also a sworn deputy, and two part time deputies who worked on a fee basis for serving civil actions, criminal warrants, and other legal documents. He and his men were on call twenty-four hours a day, seven days a week. They accepted these long hours and low pay (overtime was unheard of) without complaint.

In 1949, North Carolina operated Alcohol Beverage Control Stores (ABC stores) in those counties where the voters had so approved. Chatham had repeatedly voted against ABC stores and was a dry county as far as liquor was concerned, as it could not legally be sold there. However, beer could be sold at licensed establishments for consumption on premises only. What this boiled down to was that there were legal "beer joints" operating throughout the county that also were discreetly selling "government liquor" transported in from neighboring counties and/or "white liquor" manufactured in nearby stills. There were also illegal liquor houses operating where "government liquor" or "white liquor" could be bought by the drink, jar, or case. Whiskey stills for the manufacture of illegal liquor, also known as "white lightning" or "moonshine," were located in remote wooded areas of the county or in barns, chicken houses, or other places where they could be cleverly concealed.

Shortly after assuming office, Dad declared war on the bootleggers and the following year headed the "dry forces" who won a referendum on the beer and liquor issue. The voters responded by voting for the county to be completely dry with no legal sales of alcoholic beverages of any kind. The war began in earnest with Dad and his deputies, assisted by state and federal officers, raiding and destroying stills throughout the county and identifying and apprehending those who made, sold, transported, or participated in any manner in illegal activities relating to alcohol.

Our home became known to officers far and wide as "Christian Hill" as that is where many raids were planned by Dad and other officers around our dining room table late into the night. In cooler months, they were well-supplied with hot, strong coffee freshly prepared by my mother. In summer, sweet iced tea was served. Except for my Dad, the other officers always hid their cars behind the house in the barn lot so that bootleggers checking by the residence wouldn't know a raid was in the making. State and federal officers from outside the county would spread their sleeping bags on our large front porch and grab a few hours' sleep before leaving on the raids well before dawn. My mother never allowed them to leave without a hearty breakfast. I can recall many a morning well before daylight when a dozen or so officers were around that dining room table stuffing themselves with eggs, country ham, sausage, black molasses and biscuits. These men were about to raid stills and liquor houses, set up roadblocks for transport drivers, and start surveillance

9

that might last for hours or days. These men looked to Dad for guidance and leadership and he damned sure gave it to them, as he never sent a man where he wouldn't go himself.

4

Shortly after Dad became sheriff, he started classes at the North Carolina Institute of Government in Chapel Hill regarding the duties and responsibilities of a county sheriff and how the office should be properly operated. He also attended numerous schools and seminars relating to law enforcement and saw to it that his deputies were well-trained as to new procedures and techniques.

The North Carolina State Bureau of Investigation (SBI) is a state law enforcement agency whose responsibility is to assist local law enforcement authorities in investigating violations of state statutes when requested to do so by local officials, such as police chiefs, district attorneys, or sheriffs. The SBI also provides technical assistance to local officers, such as helping in crime scene searches, performing ballistics, tool marks, and document examinations, as well as photography and furnishing fingerprint expertise. They also have a chemical laboratory for drug analysis, blood work, paint and soil comparisons, and numerous other examinations.

Within a matter of weeks from the time he took office, Dad was at the SBI headquarters in Raleigh (only thirty-five miles from his office) on a regular basis. He became acquainted with the technicians by their first names. He was there to learn how to conduct his own crime scene searches, his own latent fingerprint examinations, and his own photography, and how to collect, preserve, and maintain the chain of custody of evidence. He learned, and I learned from him.

During the summer of 1949, I rode with and accompanied Dad nearly everywhere he went. I'll bet there weren't any other 16-year-olds who could dust for fingerprints, photograph and lift them, or pour plaster casts of footprint or tire impressions. I could also correctly use the Sheriff's Office two-way radio equipment and had the nearly 100 ten codes committed to memory.

I alluded earlier to the war Dad declared on the illegal liquor business. Well, that wasn't the only war he declared, as he seemed to take every crime committed in the county as a personal challenge. He worked night and day without letting up when a major felony occurred, and he expected the same from his deputies. They responded without complaint as they were proud to be associated with Dad, and all were just as loyal to him as he was to them.

Dad didn't encourage me to become interested in law enforcement and, in fact, attempted to discourage me as he knew the pay was inadequate, the hours long, and the risks high. When he saw I was not to be deterred, he then wanted me to excel in law enforcement as he would have wanted me to do so in any other profession. Many years and many crimes later, I now strongly believe that those officers that do excel in their profession are those who have a "calling" for it just as a minister has a "calling" to spread the word of God.

I believe I had already received my "calling," but it was really cemented on a hot summer morning in 1949 when I was barely sixteen years old. A high school teacher, who also owned a large farm a few miles from Siler City, came to "Christian Hill" at about 8:00 P.M. the previous evening. He was a short, balding, rotund man with a beet-red complexion that displayed the veins of his face. Even though he didn't teach at the school I attended, I knew of his ferocious temper. He was fit to be tied and too excited to sit when Dad offered him one of the front porch rockers.

"Sheriff, they got a damned still on my land and I want it off my property and the sons of bitches who put it there in jail."

It took awhile, but Dad got him quieted down and learned that a couple of hours earlier the teacher was looking for a lost dog on the back side of his farm when he discovered a whiskey still that appeared to be operational but unattended. He had slipped quietly away and drove directly to our house. Dad instructed him to go on home and that he and his deputies would arrive at his house about daylight the next morning, and he could accompany them and point out the still's location. Dad also explained that the mash probably had not fermented long enough and was not ready to be distilled. This would account for the still being unattended. He further explained that either he or one of his deputies could slip up to the still, check the mash,

12

and determine when it would be ready for distilling. They could then return when the still was operational and hopefully catch the operators in the act. Dad said he would bring the deputies just in case the still was running the next day or in the event the operators were there bringing in supplies.

After the teacher left, I begged and pleaded to go along the next morning, and since there wasn't much chance of any action, Dad finally agreed to it. He contacted three of his deputies and they arrived at "Christian Hill" well before daylight the next morning. We all consumed a scrumptious breakfast prepared by my mother. I had slept little as I was excited to be embarking on my first trip to a still. We drove in two automobiles to the teacher's farm, arriving shortly after sunup. He was ready and waiting and just as upset as he had been the previous evening.

We walked behind a barn, through a pasture, and across a broom straw field to an old logging road. We followed it to a small stream that emerged from dense woods. The teacher informed us the still was about a quarter of a mile in the woods beside the stream. Before we entered the woods, Dad instructed the teacher and me to keep absolutely silent and not to disturb any foliage or leave any tracks. The most experienced deputy, one with many years of service and whom the other deputies called "Pappy," led the way, followed by Dad. We were in single file with me at the rear. We cautiously followed the creek for about twenty minutes when we heard faint voices and other unidentifiable sounds a hundred or so yards ahead of us. The teacher became very inflamed and his face turned beet red. He was finally able to whisper that the sounds were from the location of the still.

Dad selected the youngest deputy, who was as fast as a deer and would fight a circle saw if Dad had asked him to, to be the "flush man." His job was to work his way undetected around to the other side of the still and then to slip up to it as close as possible without being seen or heard. He was to charge in the last few yards, calling out his identity and hopefully apprehending one or more of the operators before they could flee. The other operators would likely flee away from him in the direction of Dad and the other two deputies, who were stationed about seventy-five yards downstream.

Dad placed "Pappy" and the teacher about forty yards across

the creek and the other deputy about forty yards up the hill in the opposite direction. Dad and I concealed ourselves behind a large oak beside a game path that ran parallel to the stream. We waited without a sound for what seemed to me to be an hour, but was probably only about twenty minutes.

Finally, there was a great deal of commotion from upstream and I could hear the young deputy shout, "Deputy Sheriff, halt!" A few seconds later two men came "hell bent for leather" down the game path directly toward Dad and me. One was a middle-aged white man wearing overalls and carrying a shotgun. The other was much younger, unarmed, and black.

Dad whispered to me, "If they split, you take the Negro."

When they were about ten yards away and rapidly bearing down on us, Dad stepped from behind the tree and said in a booming voice, "Sheriff Emerson, halt!"

As he had predicted, they split. The white man tried to jump the creek, but failed and was easily apprehended by Dad. The Negro veered slightly away from the creek and sped past me. I took off after him and after about fifty yards caught up with him, as he had run a considerable distance before I took up the chase. Once I overtook him I didn't know what to do. I knew I didn't have arrest powers, and didn't know what he would do if I tackled him. The situation resolved itself as he soon became winded and just fell to his knees, exhausted. I eased up to him, but he regained his feet and got behind an enormous holly tree. As I would go around one side of the tree, he would go to the other. This went on for a couple of minutes, and then I heard laughing from behind me. I turned and saw the deputy who had been stationed up the hill. He had witnessed the chase and the Negro and me playing "ring around the rosy." He finally stopped laughing and came over and cuffed the Negro, who seemed relieved to be in custody.

We followed the path beside the stream and soon came to the still that "Pappy" said was of "right good size." Sitting on a barrel to greet us was the young deputy who had been the "flush man." He wore a wide grin and said to Dad, "Look who I found here." Handcuffed and sitting on the ground near him was a rough, unshaven white man who appeared to be in his early fifties.

14

Dad looked at him, knowing him to be the owner of the still, and said, "Henry, when are you going to give it up?"

With a stained-tooth smile, Henry replied, "When the cows come home Sheriff, when they all come home."

Dad and the deputies spent the better part of the morning photographing and dynamiting the still as the handcuffed operators sat nearby and watched, joking occasionally with the officers, but saying nothing to the teacher as they could easily sense his anger. He had held his temper as long as he possibly could. Finally, he went to where the still's owner was seated on the ground and "laid a cussing on him," using words I am sure he had never used before and would probably never use again.

As for the shotgun being at the still site, "Pappy" explained to me that the owners of many stills post a guard or "crow" several hundred yards from the still along the most accessible route to it. If officers approached, the "crow" would fire a shot into the air to alert those working at the still so they could flee in safety. If the "crow" was apprehended he could claim he was hunting and would be so far away from the still that he could not be charged in connection with it. Dad and "Pappy" figured the operator Dad apprehended with the shotgun was the "crow," who had not gone out to his position when the raid took place.

That summer morning was only the beginning, as over the years countless adventures were to follow. But it was the day the "law enforcement bug" took hold of me, never to turn me loose.

Chatham County, NC, Whiskey Still–1949. Author, age 16, is pictured on far right. His father, Sheriff John W. Emerson, Jr., is second from left.

5

That summer of 1949 passed swiftly, and in September I returned to high school for my junior year. I became a starter in the only three sports offered at Siler City High: football, basketball, and baseball. I enjoyed the social activities of a sixteen-year-old, which consisted of bonfires, hayrides, drive-in movies, and dating; but I was always home by the 11:00 P.M. curfew set by Dad, as his philosophy was that anyone out after that hour was up to nothing good.

In the spring of 1950, the Siler City American Legion Post sponsored their first-ever American Legion baseball team. I experienced my finest moment in sports when I pitched and won the opening game before a huge hometown crowd.

Much of that summer was devoted to continuing my unofficial lawman training, as I constantly accompanied Dad or his deputies on all types of criminal investigations from homicides and armed robberies to liquor raids. I vividly recall being in the Sheriff's Office on a Friday afternoon and hearing a report broadcast over the Highway Patrol radio of a Negro escapee from the North Carolina Prison Department. He had escaped while on a work detail near Raleigh and the report went on to give his physical description and hometown, which was in the western part of the state. I thought to myself that if he attempted the most direct route home, he would have to pass through Pittsboro and then Siler City. The next morning I had to drive my mother's automobile to Pittsboro, but I don't recall for what reason. My classmate and best friend since grammar school, Jack Pritchard, went along for the ride. A few miles from Pittsboro I saw a person hitchhiking toward Siler City. His description matched that of the escapee, and he was even wearing green fatigues like prison dungarees. My heart jumped into my throat and in a voice I had difficulty controlling, I said to Jack, "How would you like to catch an escaped convict?"

His response was pretty simple and to the point. "Are you crazy as hell?"

I told Jack what I had heard on the radio and that I thought the man we had just passed was the escapee. I also told him I was going to turn around and offer him a ride, and when he was in the car I was all of a sudden going to pretend to discover I had left my wallet at the station where we had gassed in the small town a few miles back. This would give us an excuse to turn around and I could drive right up to the Sheriff's Office in Pittsboro to make our delivery. My discussion with Jack was about a mile from the hitchhiker, where I had stopped at a side road. Jack was not very enthusiastic with my plan and asked if I knew for what type crime the convict was sentenced. I replied that I didn't know what specific crime he was convicted of, but the broadcast had said he was a misdemeanant, which meant it was a minor offense with a maximum penalty of two years. Jack replied that there probably wasn't enough evidence to convict him of killing and mutilating the bodies of young white boys who picked him up; however, he reluctantly agreed to go along with my scheme. As we approached the hitchhiker, my palms became sweaty and my legs began to twitch, which made controlling the accelerator difficult. I carefully braked to a stop and a very dark-skinned young man in his early twenties with a friendly smile hopped right into the backseat. I told him with a trembling voice that we were going to Charlotte, and he said that would be just fine. About half a mile down the road, I loudly announced in a voice that didn't appear to be my own that I had left my wallet at the station where we gassed in the little town a few miles behind us. I quickly turned around and said I was going back for it. I didn't hear any objections from the backseat and couldn't understand what Jack was mumbling under his breath. A quick trip was made to Pittsboro directly to the Sheriff's Office. "Pappy" happened to be coming out of the courthouse and he came over to the car and took our guest into custody and within a few minutes determined he was indeed the escapee. I was overjoyed with my first apprehension; however, Dad was less than delighted and lightly reprimanded me for the chance I took, but I could tell he was also somewhat proud of my accomplishment. The "law enforcement bug" had bitten a little deeper.

About the time I graduated from high school, my parents and I had a very serious disagreement. College was not of interest to me, as I had my sights set on a law enforcement career and wanted it with all my heart as soon as possible. A three-year wait to age twenty-one seemed an eternity, but in my young, immature mind there was a solution. The Korean War was in progress, and I wanted to be there, as it would be a temporary substitute for the war against crime. After a three-year enlistment in the army, a law enforcement career could begin. My parents strongly objected, as they wanted me to start college at the beginning of the fall semester. Hudson had just graduated from North Carolina State (Dad's alma mater), and was commissioned a second lieutenant through the Army ROTC program. Dad talked to me as only a father can, and informed me that one of the things he and my mother wanted most in life was to see all three of their sons graduate from college. He also explained to me that they wanted us to serve our country, but felt they would worry less with only one of us at a time on active duty. I couldn't bring myself to disappoint my parents, and believed it would have broken their hearts if I had gone against their wishes and declined to continue my education.

In September 1951, I matriculated at North Carolina State College in Raleigh. Higher education and I didn't get along from the very start, but enjoyment was found by being completely on my own without a curfew. Attending class and studying are two ingredients necessary to successfully further one's education, and I wasn't too attentive to either. Average grades were maintained for a semester, but for the next year and a half my grades "went to hell in a handbasket." The only courses I excelled in were physical education and Army ROTC. My life was extremely confused, and I couldn't keep my mind off my dream of being a lawman. I also felt guilty being in school while others my age were fighting and dying in Korea. I began to consider myself a slacker, as I really didn't want to be in college and yet by being there I was temporarily excused from military service. My feelings toward the other students were not the same, as they were interested in their studies and were there to obtain an education in their chosen fields.

My only accomplishment my freshman year was to win the

intramural boxing championship in my weight division. I had never before boxed in a ring, but in growing up we always had boxing gloves at home and Hudson regularly used me as a punching bag. My "manager" was my good friend, Jack, from high school. He didn't know "doodly squat" about boxing, and on the night of the championship fight gave me these instructions: "When he hits you, hit him back." It must have been good advice, as I scored a knockdown and a unanimous decision. My son now has the medal I won that cold December night.

I went to summer school after my freshman year in an effort to improve my grade point average. I even took an elective course in criminology, but soon decided the professor was a wimp who would be too frightened to raid a liquor house or struggle to handcuff a drunk. I dropped out of his class with a mark of incomplete.

Things got even worse during my sophomore year, as my grade point average continued to drop. By the end of the year I was on academic probation, which called for another round of summer school. I was obviously depressed, and apparently a faculty member sensed it to be serious and Dad was summoned to the campus for a meeting with one of the deans. After the meeting, Dad and I had a man-to-man talk in which I related to him that I wasn't interested in college or the educational opportunities it afforded. I explained to him that I had learned that I could volunteer for the draft and would only have to serve on active duty for two years. Surprisingly, he readily agreed it would probably be in my best interests, and my education could be continued after military service. In the summer of 1953, I gave up my student deferment and volunteered to be drafted into the United States Army.

6

After my pre-induction physical, I was informed that it would be about five weeks before I would actually be drafted. I was still extremely distraught over my poor performance at college and felt as though my parents were exceedingly disappointed with me. If they were, they concealed it well, as there appeared to be no change toward me in their treatment or attitude. In fact, I still continued my "lawman training" as an unofficial deputy, and in many ways Dad and I became even closer. Perhaps he sensed my dismay.

After being home from school for a few days, I attended a baseball game played by the local semi-pro team. There were a number of girls about my own age in a group and they chatted and laughed amongst themselves, paying little attention to the activities on the field. One stood out from the others, as she was a striking brunette with short hair, a friendly smile, full red lips, and a shapely figure. I knew most of the girls in the group, but not the attractive brunette, who apparently had detected the glances I was casting her way. As the game progressed, one of the girls I knew went to the concession stand where I intercepted her and made an inquiry about the young lady whom I wanted desperately to meet. She offered to introduce me, and suggested I drop by at the end of the game.

As the game neared its conclusion, I casually walked over and spoke to the girls in the group whom I knew. My co-conspirator then said to me, "Here is someone I would like for you to meet." She introduced us, and I learned her name was Vicky Moore and quickly decided she was just as pretty up close as she was from a distance. I also learned she lived at home with her parents in the nearby community of Bear Creek and worked as a secretary at a Siler City insurance agency. Vicky and I were instantly attracted to each other, and after a few minutes of small talk I suggested lunch together the next day. She accepted the invitation and for the next five weeks we dated several nights a week, getting more and more serious. We had met each other's families, gone to movies, ball games, shopping, cookouts, parties, and did countless other things together in the few short weeks before my induction. Meeting Vicky had been the catalyst to offset my depression, and her warmth and understanding was a source of strength.

On August 10, 1953, I was drafted into the United States Army. After being sworn in at Raleigh with several hundred other draftees, we were transported in buses to Fort Jackson, South Carolina, to commence basic training. I hated leaving Vicky and my family, but nevertheless had a feeling of pride as I was now a member of our armed forces.

Basic training was a piece of cake for me, as I was in superb physical condition and had just completed two years of Army ROTC. While others struggled with the manual of arms, marching, push-ups, chin-ups, and other fundamental military matters, I cruised along without difficulty. Of course, I had to do my share of KP and guard duty in order to earn, after four weeks, my thirty-six hour weekend passes. Since I was only 150 miles from home, when I received a pass I could make it to Siler City by late Saturday afternoon and see Vicky that night. Sunday afternoons I would return to Fort Jackson.

In late October 1953, I completed basic infantry training and was transferred to Fort Lee, Virginia, for specialized training at the Army Quartermaster School. Fort Lee was also about 150 miles from Siler City, so weekend trips home continued. I was saddled with guard duty on Thanksgiving, but managed a five-day pass for Christmas. Hudson and his wife, Joyce, were also home for Christmas from Fort Belvoir, Virginia. Tommy was just a freshman in high school and was in awe of his two brothers in uniform. The three of us spent a lot of time together, but my evenings were with Vicky and her family. It was truly a Merry Christmas for all of us.

My training at Fort Lee was completed in early January 1954, and I received orders for Korea with a ten-day delay en route. The ten days were spent at home, with Vicky and I becoming more and more devoted to each other. A cease-fire was in existence in Korea, but there was a possibility fighting could resume at any time. With this in mind, we made the decision not to become officially engaged, but to wait until my Korean tour of sixteen months was over and see if we still felt the same. On the night of January 23rd, I said good-bye to Vicky and her family and drove from her home to mine with a feeling of loneliness I had never before experienced.

That night a heavy snow fell, making highway travel nearly impossible. I was scheduled on a flight on the 24th from Raleigh to Seattle, Washington, where I was to report to Fort Lewis. A call to the airport disclosed all flights were cancelled indefinitely; however, I was informed the nearest airport where flights were on a near normal schedule and where I could fly on a direct flight to Seattle was National Airport in Washington, DC.

Appropriate changes in my flight schedule were made, and Dad put chains on his automobile and, after an emotional good-bye with my mother, he drove me to Raleigh. I shook hands with Dad at the depot and boarded a train for Washington. It was a long overnight trip and a day coach was all that was available. I arrived at Washington early the following morning with no more than two hours sleep. A few hours later, I boarded a four-motor, propeller-driven aircraft for the first flight of my life. I arrived at Seattle that night completely exhausted. I checked into a nice hotel and fell into a deep sleep. Upon awakening the next morning, I discovered that a large building directly across the street from my room was completely destroyed by fire during the night. I had slept undisturbed by the sirens and all the other commotions.

After reporting in at Fort Lewis, I was in the Replacement Depot until February 18, when thousands of others and I sailed on a troop ship from Seattle. It was a long, cold voyage to Sasabo, Japan, where we debarked and were quartered at another Replacement Depot for a few days. Several hundred of us were then transported on a much smaller ship, and on March 4 we landed at Pusan, Korea. My wish to be in Korea had been fulfilled.

7

I was assigned to the headquarters motor pool of the Korean Civil Assistance Command (KCAC) and was placed in charge of petroleum, oil, and lubricants (POL) for about 100 headquarters vehicles, consisting of jeeps, three-quarter-ton weapon carriers, two-and-a-half-ton trucks, and several wreckers. KCAC was made up of United States Military and United Nation civilian personnel and was charged with the responsibility of assisting the Republic of Korea in reconstruction and rehabilitation. This apparently accounted for Korean civilians being employed by KCAC to perform many duties normally done by GI's, such as driving vehicles assigned to the motor pool.

When I first arrived in Korea the headquarters for KCAC was in Pusan, but several weeks later we moved to Seoul to a compound that had previously been a school of some type. My duties consisted mainly of keeping the motor pool supplied with fuel for the vehicles, which required daily trips in a 1000 gallon gasoline tanker truck to a POL dump a few miles from Seoul. After returning to headquarters with the fuel, our vehicles would be filled as needed by Korean civilians who worked at the motor pool. This daily routine became boring for me after a few months, and I had a great deal of time to drive around and explore Seoul, Inchon, Yongdungpo, and other well-known places. During these excursions, my law enforcement background came into play as I explored the black market areas of these cities and noted the incredible amount of American merchandise for sale, such as cigarettes, candy, toothpaste, cameras, razors, fountain pens, watches, c-rations, etc. Then one day what should have been obvious to me from the beginning, suddenly was very clear. What I realized was what I hauled every day was gasoline, and it was one of the most difficult products for civilians to legally obtain. It therefore seemed logical to me that if it was that scarce, then it would be of great demand on the black market. I rushed back to the motor pool and started pulling vehicle records. These records contained the amount of fuel each vehicle had received, but no one had ever figured the miles per gallon for the vehicles. Simple arithmetic disclosed we had jeeps averaging less than five miles per gallon and two and one-half-ton trucks less than two miles per gallon! Physical security of the compound was adequate and each vehicle leaving the compound was searched at the security gate. This indicated to me that gasoline was being siphoned from the vehicles when they were on trips outside the compound. There was a pool of Korean civilian drivers assigned to headquarters, but these drivers were not assigned to specific vehicles. As trips were scheduled, a GI dispatcher would select the type vehicle to be used and it would be driven by the next driver on a rotation list. Within a period of a week, one vehicle may have been driven by as many as ten to fifteen drivers. This meant vehicle records were of no value in determining possible gasoline theft suspects. I prepared a written report on my findings and suspicions and presented it to the motor pool officer, Captain Cummings. He immediately perceived the seriousness of the problem and asked if I had recommendations. I suggested that since I had plenty of excess time I should work through the dispatchers, who would know when vehicles would be leaving the compound and their destinations, and discreetly undertake the surveillance of various vehicles at random. The Captain readily agreed and ordered that I terminate the employment of any driver caught stealing gasoline and furnish to him the names of all drivers terminated and the details of each incident so appropriate Korean civilian authorities could be notified.

Commencing in June 1954 and continuing for the next six months, periodic surveillance was conducted of the vehicles assigned to KCAC. During this time I caught literally dozens of drivers siphoning from our vehicles. When the surveillance first began, it was not uncommon for me to spot several drivers stealing in a single day or night. As the investigation continued, the thefts diminished, as driving for KCAC was a very desirable job in a country whose economy was in shambles. Being fired for stealing gasoline was just not worth the risk.

After six months of investigation, the fuel consumption figure for KCAC had been cut in half and the miles per gallon for our vehicles was back to normal. My efforts to curtail the gasoline thefts did not go unnoticed, as I was quickly promoted to private first class, a few months later to corporal, and then to staff sergeant. I also received a personal letter of commendation from Brigadier General M. C. Walter.

While in Korea, I had ample opportunities to consider my future. Vicky and I had corresponded regularly, and there was one thing that I was darned sure of, and that was we would spend the future together. I also had made the decision to earn a college degree, which would help me to obtain employment with a federal law enforcement agency.

During the spring of 1955, I wrote to the Registrar at North Carolina State College and obtained certification that I was accepted at that institution for the summer term beginning in June. I delivered this certification to the KCAC Personnel Officer and requested an early release from active duty to resume my college studies. The request was granted, and in mid-May I departed from Inchon on a troop ship for Seattle. A troop train took us from Seattle across America to Fort Jackson, South Carolina, where I was released from active duty on June 2, 1955.

8

I spent a week at home with my family and Vicky and then started summer school. At that time, North Carolina State was a technical institution consisting of three main schools: Engineering, Textiles, and Agriculture. I had already spent two years in the School of Agriculture, and didn't want that time and the credits I had earned to go to waste. I therefore chose to major in Rural Sociology, which I thought would be of value in a law enforcement career.

During the week I attended classes and studied, but weekends were for Vicky and the family. In late June, Vicky and I, with the blessings of both our families, became engaged and planned an August wedding. I completed the summer term with very good grades and the next two weeks passed quickly as the big day approached. Our wedding was a beautiful affair that took place in a small country church where Vicky was a member and where my mother had attended as a child. After a brief honeymoon, we rented a nice duplex in Raleigh near the campus. Vicky was fortunate enough to obtain employment in the claims department of a large insurance company. With her salary and the money I received from the GI Bill, we lived comfortably. During the day, Vicky worked and I went to class, but at night we both studied as she helped me with my homework. The next year and a half were unforgettably happy times for us as we made friends with other married couples whose husbands were struggling through school on the GI Bill. We were very proud of my grades as each semester I made the Dean's List.

Weekends would find Vicky and me at my home in Siler City, where I continued to help Dad and his deputies carry out their duties. On one of those warm Saturday nights I had my first physical confrontation. It took place during the raid on a known liquor and gambling house. Deputies Poole, Simmons, and I were with Dad in his car. The plan was for Dad to drive to the front of the building and he and Simmons would enter quickly through

27

the front door. Poole was to go around the left side of the building and I was to go around the right side. The two of us were to meet at the back door and enter through it. Dad and Simmons made their entry as planned as Poole and I rushed around the building. What I didn't know at the time, but later learned from Poole, was that as he started around the building he ran right into the middle of a gambling game in progress. It was so hot inside that the game had moved outside. With Poole's unexpected entry into the game, those participating or spectating, or who just happened to be in the area, fled as if confronted by the devil himself. As I rounded the rear corner of the building, several of those fleeing nearly ran over me. I grabbed for one closest to me but missed and the chase was on. I was still in good shape from being in the service, and overtook him without much effort and made a nice open-field tackle. I didn't have any idea as to what he had done, if anything, or why I had run him down. I told him we had to go back, but he jerked away from the grip I had on his arm, and that's when he learned why deputies carry three-cell instead of two-cell flashlights. I popped him on the head with the three-cell and it apparently got his attention. We then marched in step back to the liquor house. Poole had apprehended the house card game dealer, and Dad and Simmons had seized several half-gallon jars of moonshine and had arrested the proprietor. The man I brought in had only been a participant in the card game. For the next few years, Poole would remind me of the night I was caught in the middle of a stampede that he caused. For many years to come, when working difficult homicide cases, armed robbery investigations, or other complicated matters, I would think back as to how simple it was to raid a Chatham County liquor house.

9

The summer schools I had attended qualified me to graduate from college a semester ahead of schedule, which was in January 1957. As graduation day approached, I started exploring the possibility of obtaining employment in my chosen profession of law enforcement. I wanted more than anything on earth to become a Federal Agent. In December, I took the examination offered by the United States Treasury Department with hopes of being appointed to the Secret Service, Border Patrol, Alcohol Tobacco Tax Unit or some other investigative agency. The FBI wasn't even considered, as at the time they were only accepting applicants with accounting or law degrees. I still had eighteen months remaining on the GI Bill, and Dad talked to me about going to law school. He offered to assist me financially if I would do so, but having already waited nearly eight long years to start my career, I elected to bypass the opportunity. In future years I had brief second thoughts about this decision, but they didn't last long as attorneys and I clashed often and sometimes sharply. Big Glen, who stood six feet six inches and weighed 275 pounds, was a deputy sheriff in a rural county in eastern North Carolina. Several times I heard him say he would rather his boy to be a safe cracker than a damned lawyer.

A few days before my scheduled graduation, an executive with the insurance company where Vicky worked invited us to his home for dinner. We were puzzled as her contact with him had been very limited and I only knew him by reputation. After a delicious meal with him and his family, we all went into a very formal living room where we chatted casually for a short time. The children then excused themselves and, to our surprise, so did his wife. I was then subjected to a mild interrogation as to what my long-term plans were, why I wanted to be a Federal Agent, what my thoughts were about the Korean War, and numerous other topics. An occasional question would be directed to Vicky. When it apparently became obvious the two of us were becoming annoyed, our host gave us a very warm smile and explained that he was a Captain in the United States Naval Reserve and was assigned to the Office of Naval Intelligence (ONI). He further explained that ONI was an extremely secret part of the Navy and was made up of both civilian and military personnel. He advised that the military operations of ONI such as cryptanalysis, enemy ship movements, et ceteras were handled by active duty Navy personnel, and that ONI employed civilian Special Agents as investigators whose responsibilities included intelligence and counterintelligence work as well as criminal investigations involving crimes aboard ships and on Navy and Marine Corps bases. He stated most criminal investigations involved violations of the Uniform Code of Military Justice (UCMJ) by military personnel and were adjudicated in military courts.

Our host continued by saying that he had taken the liberty to inform ONI of my scheduled graduation and of my interest in being a Federal Agent. He said ONI had expressed an interest in talking to me and that if I liked he would arrange for me to be interviewed. It was all I could do to maintain my composure and didn't even recognize my own voice when I asked him to please make the arrangements.

10

Less than a week later, after I had passed all my exams and just a couple of days before graduation, I received a telephone call from an individual who identified himself as Tom Fentress, a Special Agent with the Office of Naval Intelligence. He stated he was in the Raleigh area and would like to come by after dinner and meet Vicky and me. I said we would be home all evening and for him to come by at his convenience. As I started to give him directions to our residence, he stopped me in mid-sentence and said, "I already know where you live."

Dinner was hardly touched by Vicky or me as we both were thrilled at the prospect of meeting Special Agent Tom Fentress. We discussed what we needed to do to impress him and how we might get him to understand my obsession to be a Federal Agent. We finally reached the decision to just be ourselves and act as though he was just another GI Bill student dropping by for an after-dinner visit.

Upon responding to our doorbell promptly at 7:00 P.M., I was confronted with not one but two gentlemen dressed in conservative business suits. The older of the two, who appeared to be in his early forties, introduced himself as Tom Fentress and displayed to me credentials that identified him as a Special Agent with the Office of Naval Intelligence. From being around law enforcement officers I had heard some of their stories about gaining entry to establishments by flashing their credentials and identifying themselves as health inspectors, fire inspectors, insurance adjusters, or some other type of official. They had laughed about how most people only glance at credentials, do not closely examine them, and just assume the person is whatever he says he is. With this in mind, I carefully studied Tom's credentials, but noticed that he never released custody of them to me as he retained them in a firm grip during my inspection. Never to surrender control of your credentials was something I would later be taught.

Tom introduced the second man as Special Agent George Masgeson, and he also displayed credentials, which I examined. The two were invited into the living room where I introduced them to Vicky. As they exchanged pleasantries with her, I scrutinized both men. Tom was about six feet and a solid two hundred pounds with closely cropped brown hair. He possessed a deep, authoritative voice and a ruddy complexion. His most striking feature were the hardest set of gray eyes I had ever seen.

George was in his late thirties and was about five feet ten inches tall and weighed about 180 pounds. He had sandy hair that grew low on his forehead, starting a few inches above his bushy eyebrows. Like Tom's, his hair was closely cropped. George carried a brown leather briefcase, which I was to later learn was standard issue for ONI agents. As we were all seated, George removed a legal pad from the briefcase and for the next hour made notes as Tom interviewed me, asking Vicky questions from time to time. Questions and conversation topics ranged from sports to my feelings about communism, my military activities in Korea, and how Vicky and I spent our leisure time. One question related to my opinion of homosexuals entering the military and what I thought should be done if they were discovered serving in the armed forces. I could detect that this was a very sensitive issue with Tom, and George was poised to make notes of my answer.

I gave the question careful consideration and said to myself, "These men are interested in the security of the United States, so why ask me about homosexuals unless they are somehow involved with security?" It then dawned on me that homosexuals would be a poor security risk, as they could be blackmailed.

With this in mind, I answered Tom's questions by replying, "If they are admitted homosexuals, I don't think they should be allowed to become members of the armed forces. If they conceal their homosexuality and enter service and are subsequently detected to be gay, then I think they should be discharged, but not honorably. If they participate in homosexual acts, I believe they should be prosecuted and dishonorably discharged."

My answer to the homosexual question and to his other questions apparently were satisfactory with Tom, as he went on to tell Vicky and me a great deal about ONI. He revealed to us that he was a Supervising Agent for the Sixth Naval District with headquarters at Charleston, South Carolina; that the Sixth Naval District was made up of seven southeastern states consisting of Florida, Georgia, Alabama, Mississippi, Tennessee, South Carolina and part of North Carolina. He said civilian ONI agents were stationed at major cities in the seven states but that the largest concentration of agents were at the Navy and Marine Corps bases in the district. He told of the agent responsibilities of conducting criminal investigations and investigations involving National Security. Tom emphasized how ONI operated in secrecy while some other government agencies pursued publicity. He told how agents never identified themselves except when necessary and routinely claimed their occupation to be a "Naval Research Analyst," even on tax forms and other documents. For inquisitive friends and neighbors, they would say their research duties were classified. Tom advised that the starting salary for agents was $4,800 per year with the standard twenty years law enforcement retirement program.

Tom informed me that an agent position would be available in a few months and, if I was interested, I could apply for it, and that if I passed a stringent background investigation, I would then be interviewed by a screening board of officers and Special Agents at the Sixth Naval District Headquarters at Charleston. If I successfully passed the board, I would become a Special Agent and undergo six months of on the job training at Charleston and then a four week basic investigative school at the Pentagon in Arlington, Virginia. He stated I would then probably be assigned as a resident agent at Durham, North Carolina.

There was no decision to make, as Vicky and I were both ecstatic over the opportunity for me to apply for a Special Agent's position. The possibility of being stationed at Durham just added to our happiness. I told Tom I certainly would like to apply and no sooner had I said so when George removed an application from his briefcase and handed it to me. He also handed me a very lengthy and detailed Personal History Statement (PHS) that I needed to complete. Tom asked me to look over the PHS and waited patiently while I did so. When I finished, he asked me if there were any questions that I didn't understand or if there were any questions the answers to which might eliminate me as an applicant? I replied in the negative, and he then asked if there was anything a complete background investigation would uncover that needed to be explained? I again answered in the negative. The application and PHS were left with me to be completed and mailed to the District Intelligence Office at the United States Naval Base at Charleston.

Vicky and I felt confident I would be called to Charleston for an interview, as there was nothing derogatory in either of our backgrounds; however, we realized it might not be for several months. On January 28, 1957, I received my college diploma, and a few days later obtained a part-time job on the staff of the Sergeant at Arms of the North Carolina State Senate. Vicky continued her job at the insurance company. I turned down several employment opportunities that didn't appeal to me and anxiously waited to hear from ONI. When we arrived home from work each day, I would make a mad dash to the mailbox only to be disappointed, day after day. Finally, in late March, I received notification to appear in April before a screening board at the District Intelligence Office, Building #5, United States Naval Base, Charleston, South Carolina.

On the designated date in mid-April 1957, I presented myself before the board. It was composed of Tom and his Assistant Supervising Agent, Dave Planton, Special Agent Clint Lane, a Security Analyst named Chucknow, and two Naval officers in uniform (a Commander and a Lieutenant). For approximately two hours I was examined, cross examined, badgered, and harassed. When it was over I was mentally exhausted, but felt as though I had done well. I drank strong Navy coffee in an anteroom while I waited.

In less than ten minutes, Tom entered and said, while shaking my hand, "We would like for you to go to work the first of May."

Through what must have been the biggest smile of my life, I replied, "I'll be here."

Tom located a duplex for rent in Mount Pleasant, which is a small town just across the Cooper River from Charleston. Tom and his family lived a block away, and across the street from them lived Special Agent Clint Lane and his family. Vicky and I moved into the duplex in late April, and on May 1, 1957, just twenty-nine days short of my twenty-fourth birthday, I was sworn in as a Federal agent. Eight years of hoping and waiting had finally come to an end. What would the future hold? There would be thirty years of background investigations, robberies, rapes, frauds, murders, a contract killing for $200—on credit— and several brushes with death.

11

For my first three weeks with Naval Intelligence I was confined to the offices of Tom or his assistant, Dave Planton. There I studied Navy protocol, the structure of ONI, reviewed investigative reports, and learned what my duties, responsibilities, and personal privileges were as a Special Agent with ONI. The duties and responsibilities were many, and privileges few; however, I must admit that I enjoyed the salutes rendered to me by Marine guards when I displayed my credentials each day for admission to the Charleston Naval Base. I also thoroughly enjoyed lunches at the officers' club.

In addition to credentials, I had also been issued a large gold badge pinned in a black leather case. Tom, Dave, and the other agents all carried their badges in the front pockets of their trousers with the badge cases fastened to keychains attached to their belts. Credentials were carried in the shirt pocket and secured to it by a spring clip. I was told that if an agent lost either his credentials or badge he may as well submit his resignation. The clip was issued with the credentials, but the keychain had to be purchased. I soon sported one. I quickly determined that I could look at an agent and immediately know if he was right or left handed. The keychain was the giveaway. Agents seldom carried handguns, but when they did, the badge would be located on the side opposite their "gun hand." This was so the badge could be displayed in the "weak hand," while the other could draw the weapon if necessary.

I never heard of an agent who lost his badge or credentials, but one had a very close call while boarding a ship at Charleston. As he pulled his credentials from his pocket to identify himself to the Officer of the Deck, they slipped from his hand and fell to the water between the ship and the pier. The agent was said to have made a beautiful dive, hitting the water a split-second after his credentials and recovering them before they sank. Some agents were so fearful of losing their credentials that they would place a hundred dollar bill in the leather folder behind their credentials with a note attached instructing the person finding same to keep the money and call the telephone number listed in the note. Of course, it would be the agent's home number, and you can be sure his wife had been informed of what to do should she receive a call about his credentials.

The standard issue weapon for ONI Special Agents was a Smith & Wesson .38 caliber revolver with a four-inch barrel. Shortly after I learned of my acceptance with ONI, Dad presented me with a .38 caliber Colt revolver made with an alloy frame and a two-inch barrel. It was very light and easily concealed, and, with Tom's permission, I declined the standard issue weapon and was allowed to carry my personal handgun. It was to serve me well for the next thirty years, being on or near my person at all times.

12

During my indoctrination period I learned that I was to live a life above reproach in every respect and was to keep a very low profile in the community. Other agents and their families also had to maintain these standards, so we tended to shut out the rest of the world and live and socialize in our own ONI community. The men worked together and played together—golf, softball, hunting, and fishing—and they and their families were together a great deal of the time. They were even closer in times of illness or other crisis. Penny poker games were common, as were beach cookouts and occasional dinners at the officers' club.

Tom's assistant, Dave, was eight years older than me, and he and his wife, Vonnie, were a fine young couple. Vonnie and Vicky became close friends, as did Dave and me. Dave was very intelligent and gifted with the ability to not only express himself orally, but do so exceedingly well in writing. In my thirty-odd years in the investigative business I never met another investigator with a better personality or a better understanding of human behavior. In later years, ONI became the Naval Investigative Service (NIS) and Dave became one of their top officials as well as an Admiral in the Naval Reserve.

After my initial indoctrination, I was assigned to train under the supervision of Special Agent Clint Lane. This meant that for the next two months, when Clint was on duty, I was to be his shadow. I was to learn how to conduct investigations by observing him as he went about his duties, and he was to teach me the "investigative ropes" by answering my questions and explaining to me the investigative steps he was taking. Clint was in his early forties, short, and starting a middle-aged spread. He had thin, reddish hair and a wide, friendly smile. His overall appearance was similar to that of President Eisenhower. Clint was a chain smoker, and, once a cigarette was between his lips, it wasn't removed until he was ready to light another. The ashes would just get longer and longer, finally falling off and usually leaving his shirt and tie speckled gray. He was a grand fellow with a heart of gold. I later learned he was an expert with electronics and was used on cases requiring the planting of listening devices. At other times he did "security sweeps" to make sure there were no hidden listening devices in certain areas that had to be secure.

Clint lived only two blocks from me, and each working day at exactly 7:30 A.M. he would arrive at my home in the unmarked Chevrolet sedan assigned to him. ONI vehicles could not be distinguished from regular civilian vehicles, except that close examination would reveal a radio antenna mounted in the proper place, but no commercial radio inside the car. Hidden in the glove compartment was a two way radio on the ONI private frequency.

Since Clint was my training agent, for the next two months he only received background investigations instead of other assignments. I learned that these cases were the bread and butter investigations for ONI, and were primarily the only cases worked by agents stationed in locations where there were no Naval or Marine Corps installations, such as my prospective duty station of Durham, North Carolina. Background investigations were conducted on civilians who made applications for sensitive positions within the Navy Department, and on Navy or Marine Corps personnel being considered for positions requiring security clearances. Also, backgrounds had to be brought up-to-date from time to time on personnel who had already been granted security clearances.

From Clint I learned how to conduct background investigations by doing criminal and credit checks, verifying date and place of birth, confirming education and previous employments, making neighborhood inquiries, interviewing references, and developing other sources who had known the subject of the investigation. Time and time again Clint would tell me that background investigations were not glamorous or exciting, but necessary for national security. He taught me how to put the information developed by the investigation into proper report form, containing no recommendations, but only facts to be forwarded to the command requesting the investigation. After two months with Clint, I was conducting background checks without supervision.

13

In my third month with ONI I was being assigned background investigations on a regular basis; however, my other training continued. It consisted mostly of sitting in as a witness on interrogations conducted by Tom and Dave. An interview was the questioning of a friendly source, such as a police officer, former employer, character reference, et cetera. An interrogation was the questioning of a subject thought to be withholding or hiding the truth. Tom and Dave were the two best interrogators in the Sixth Naval District and both were polygraph (lie detector) operators, which added to their effectiveness. They had to be good, as most of the suspects they interrogated were those from whom other agents had failed to obtain admissions or confessions. At times they would interrogate together, and at other times only one of them would conduct the interrogation. When they were together, I would observe from an adjoining room through a two-way mirror. When only one conducted the interrogation, I would sit in only as a witness, as my instructions were not to ask any questions and to remain silent during the interrogation. I did this on a regular basis for over a year before I ever asked my first question. During this time, it was a privilege to watch two masters at work. Tom's method was the tough, rough-talking demanding type and was not out of character for him. Dave's approach was to be smooth, pleasant, and sympathetic with the subject being questioned regardless of the crime involved. After a few months of witnessing interrogations by Tom and Dave, it became obvious to me that there were two types of offenses that accounted for most of the interrogations and polygraph time. These were cases involving larceny of personal property and homosexual investigations. Of course, there were sprinklings of other cases, such as rapes, assaults, robberies, fraud, and even sabotage. Not the James Bond sort of sabotage, with cloak-and-dagger espionage agents, but a marine or sailor who, out of anger or some other reason, would secretly damage government property. I specifically recall one case involving a lovesick sailor whose ship was ready for sea duty after being dry-docked at the Charleston Shipyard. The sailor wasn't ready to leave the barmaid he had fallen for, so he purposely contaminated the ship's fuel supply, resulting in extensive damage to the engines. What I don't recall is how many years he was sentenced to at his court-martial.

To this day, I consider the interrogations observed by me and conducted by Tom and Dave to be the one thing that helped me more than any other in my career.

After six months at Charleston, I was sent to a four-week ONI basic investigative school along with about twenty other agents from around the country. The school was at the Pentagon, but we were quartered across the river at the Anacostia Naval Base. The school was well run, with instructors who were experts in their various fields. Most of the courses were easy for me, as I had already been well-schooled by Dad in crime scene searches, dusting for latent fingerprints, making plaster casts and other basics relating to investigations. Most of the other students had not been exposed to a law enforcement environment before joining ONI and, therefore, had to quickly absorb what I had learned over the years. The courses most interesting to me were on how to conduct surveillances and how to make surreptitious entries or "black bag jobs." About the latter, I'll say no more.

Towards the end of school, the class was divided into four-man teams for practice surveillance exercises in downtown Washington. The persons to be surveilled were young active duty officers assigned to ONI, but dressed in civilian clothing. They knew they were to be under surveillance, and were scheduled to be at certain locations at 10:00 A.M. Their physical descriptions and color and clothing type were given to the teams, along with their 10:00 A.M. locations. The exercises were to terminate at 3:00 P.M., but any team losing their subject was to immediately return to the training room. What we were not told was that the young officers had played this game before, and took great delight in taking evasive actions to lose the team and bring cocky new agents down a notch or two. The team I was assigned to picked up our subject at exactly 10:00 A.M. and despite his obvious efforts to shake us, we somehow managed to keep him under surveillance until 3:00 P.M. When we arrived back at the training room, we discovered that two teams had returned before lunch and two shortly after lunch. Our team was the only one to keep our subject under surveillance the entire time and maintain an accurate log of his movements. To our surprise, he came into the training room and could not identify any member of our team. He also acknowledged that he could not detect that he was being followed.

I returned to Charleston with expectations of being transferred to the resident agency at Durham, North Carolina. A few days passed before Tom received the results of my performance at the basic school. He called me into his office and informed me that my desire to participate in criminal investigations had not gone unnoticed, and that he and Dave were both of the opinion I would soon be bored working a steady diet of background investigations in central and eastern North Carolina. Tom gave me the choice of transferring to Durham or remaining in Charleston where I would continue to work background investigations, participate in criminal investigations, and assist in training new agents as they were then being hired with regularity. He also informed me that if I elected to remain in Charleston, I would travel extensively throughout the Sixth Naval District, helping various resident agents who were behind in their work. Tom suggested that I discuss the choices with Vicky and let him know of our decision within a few days. That night I told Vicky of my talk with Tom, and informed her of the decision we had to make. It took all of ten minutes. We both loved Charleston and had many close ONI friends there, and we both thought it best for my career to remain at Sixth Naval District Headquarters.

14

For the next year, I would usually be away for two or three weeks, and then back in Charleston for a week or two. I traveled to various resident agencies in all seven states that made up the district, and worked only past due background investigations (each case had an assigned due date). All the agents welcomed my appearance, as I was there to help reduce their backlog of delinquent cases. As soon as I arrived in town, I would check in at the local resident agency, which was usually at the Naval Reserve Center. The resident agent (the senior agent if it was more than a one-man office) would be there to meet with me and give me a stack of cases, and road and city maps. Within a few hours I would be on my way, usually to the most remote area covered by the resident agency. This brings to mind a humorous story that happened to the resident agent at Columbia, South Carolina. His area included the mountainous northwestern portion of South Carolina, near the Georgia and Tennessee borders. He was there working a background investigation on a subject who had previously lived in the area, but not for several years. He talked to the local sheriff, who did not recall the person, but suggested that an old man who lived just outside town might recall him or his family. The agent made his way to the man's cabin as directed by the sheriff. A knock on the door was answered by a tall, thin man in his mid-seventies with a scraggly beard and bib overalls and a dirty felt hat. As he had done thousands of times before, the agent displayed his credentials, but, before he could identify himself, the man said, "Son, I can't read a word."

The agent reached into his pocket, pulled out his badge, and said, "The sheriff sent me here, I'm a Federal Agent with . . ."

Before he could say "The Office of Naval Intelligence," the old fellow raised both hands in the air and said, "It took you thirty years to do it, but you finally caught up with me. I'll not give you any trouble."

Shaken, but thinking fast, the agent said, "Yes, and you

might as well tell me about it." What the old man then revealed was that, over thirty years ago, he had gotten mad at a neighbor and, one night while drunk, had deliberately set fire to the neighbor's barn and burned it to the ground. The old man had worried all those years, expecting to be arrested any day. The agent assured the old man he was not there to arrest him and, without another word, made his way back to the Sheriff's Office where he told the sheriff what had happened.

The sheriff grinned and said, "So that's why he has always been so nervous around me. He's been a good citizen and the statue of limitations expired years ago. I'll go out there and put his mind at ease."

After returning from assignments away from Charleston, I would dictate reports, work backgrounds in the Charleston area, and continue to witness interrogations by Tom and Dave. During the fall of 1958, after observing interrogations for nearly eighteen months, an extraordinary thing occurred, for which I have no explanation. Dave was interrogating a young sailor and I was present in my usual passive role as a witness. The interrogation had been underway for a couple of hours and Dave had done his best, but the subject would just not "break." I don't recall the details of the case, other than it involved larceny and that the subject being questioned was from North Carolina. I could sense Dave was about to terminate the interrogation, when all of a sudden I spontaneously started talking to the young man. It seemed as though I was transformed into a different person; one whom I had never before known. I used evangelistic abilities I didn't know I was capable of, and begged and pleaded for the truth. The young sailor, whom we considered a "hard case," broke down completely and not only confessed to the larceny case, but to other crimes of which we were not even aware. After the shore patrol had taken the sailor away, Dave complimented me on a job well done, and didn't mention the fact that I had interjected myself into "his investigation." From that day on, I never again participated in an interrogation in a passive manner. I knew I had a power few possessed, and that was the ability to obtain the truth from those reluctant to tell it without the use of threats, promises, or duress.

A few days after my "awakening," criminal cases started

being assigned to me and within a year I was promoted to Assistant Senior Resident Agent at Charleston. I was not only working all types of investigations, but also assisting in the training of many new agents who were in Charleston for their first six months with ONI. Instead of sitting in on Tom and Dave's interrogations, they were assigning new agents to sit in and witness mine.

15

Vicky and I had grown close to Dave and Vonnie Planton, and we visited them quite often. They lived west of the Ashley River and just a few blocks from the Charleston Municipal Golf Course. The Plantons had four children, all under the age of ten, so it was much easier for us to visit them than for them to get a sitter and drive to our apartment. Dave enjoyed playing golf, and many times he and I went to the golf course where he introduced me to the game. Golf would usually be followed by grilling hamburgers with the Plantons, and later Dave and I would make a quick run to the Krispy Kreme for doughnuts.

Vicky and I envied the warmth and love in the Planton home, and after two years in the duplex were ready for a place of our own. We chose to look west of the Ashley and finally picked a three-bedroom brick home in a subdivision a few miles from Dave and Vonnie. We closed on it in April 1959. The subdivision was made up of mostly young couples with children. Cookouts and other community activities were common. To our surprise, we discovered that Chuck and Rachel Harrison, who lived across the street from us, were longtime friends of the Plantons. Chuck was a sales representative for a major oil company and traveled a great deal. Vicky and Rachel became the very best of friends, and together they visited Vonnie frequently. I played softball for the subdivision team and Vicky attended all the games, as did most of the other wives. We were happy and proud of our home. Many new agents were passing through Charleston, and I can't recall a single one whom we didn't have to dinner at least once.

In December 1959, Vicky disclosed to me that we could expect an addition to our family. We were both overjoyed and anxiously looked forward to the event. On June 23, 1960, Vicky delivered a seven-pound little bundle of joy. We named her Gloria Rose. Tom and Dave sat with me during the long hours Vicky was in labor. That's how close we were in ONI.

16

I have written a great deal about background investigations. The vast majority of these cases revealed the subjects of the investigations to be individuals of high integrity, loyal to the United States government, and possessed of commendable personal traits. One reason for this was that a preliminary screening was done on individuals considered for access to classified information or positions of trust. This eliminated subjects known to have alcohol or drug dependencies, serious financial difficulties, and other problems, such as gambling or whoremongering. Even though our investigations were on people considered to be the elite, we nevertheless uncovered much information that greatly surprised the commands requesting the backgrounds.

I recall a case I worked in a Georgia city of about 25,000 inhabitants. The investigation was to bring up to date a Top Secret security clearance on a prominent attorney in that city who held the rank of Lieutenant Commander in the Naval Reserve. His military specialty was highly classified, as it was not on any of the paperwork I had with me. A routine criminal check was negative, and a credit check was favorable. Three of the job references were interviewed, and all highly recommended him for a position of trust; however, the last reference obviously got carried away and referred to him in a very effeminate manner as one of the sweetest men he had ever known. This remark, coupled with the fact that the attorney was a bachelor who reportedly lived alone in a quiet subdivision, aroused my suspicions. A neighborhood investigation revealed the lawyer was no ladies' man, as a couple of nosey neighbors told of young men arriving and departing from his residence at odd hours. Neither had ever seen any female visitors there. The following morning I decided to check with the local vice officers to see if they knew the attorney and, if not, if they had a gay informer whom they could contact. The two officers who worked vice were both in court so, while waiting for them to return to the station, I called the motel where I was staying to see if I had any messages.

The desk clerk said, "Only one, call your office."

When Tom got on the line, he said, "Go by the office of Lieutenant Commander Wilson, he's got something for you."

When Tom gave you an order, he expected it to be carried out without hesitation. I knew better than to ask any questions, and even if I dared there wasn't time, as Tom immediately hung up. I was still a very young agent in awe of attorneys. Of course, this would change in a few years. I didn't like meeting the lawyer on his home court, but made my way to his office, arriving shortly before noon. It was located near the courthouse in the heart of the city and was in an old southern mansion, which had been renovated for office space. Other attorneys were also in the building, but his was the first office on the right of the main entrance and consisted of a large reception room with two rooms leading off from it. I was extremely apprehensive when I identified myself to the receptionist. She smiled warmly and said that Mr. Wilson (not his real name) was expecting me. She got up and gently tapped on the door to the room directly behind her desk. She stepped inside, but immediately came out and said that he was ready to see me. I entered, and across the highly-polished hardwood floor was a huge walnut desk, behind which sat a fine-looking man in his mid-thirties. He stood, smiled and introduced himself as I displayed my credentials to him. He had the physique of a professional linebacker and the good looks of a movie star. I accepted a chair across the desk from him. There was no idle chit-chat, and he came straight to the point.

He said, "I understand you have been bringing my security clearance up to date with a background investigation." I replied that I had. He then handed me a neatly folded sheet of paper, which I unfolded and slowly read. It was addressed to the District Intelligence Officer, Sixth Naval District, Charleston, South Carolina, and was a letter in which Lieutenant Commander Wilson resigned his commission.

Continuing, he said that he understood the letter would terminate the investigation, and I replied that it would. He appeared to be in thought for a moment, and then said, "Mr. Emerson, I'm gay and I was born and raised in this city. Few people know I'm a homosexual, and I prefer to keep it that way." I

49

stood, put the letter in my briefcase, and assured him they would not hear it from ONI. His reply was, "No, I'm sure they will not."

When I returned to Charleston, I asked Tom why he hadn't told me about the letter the lawyer had for me. His reply was, "I wanted to see how you would handle it." As I started to leave Tom's office, he said, "By the way, when he was on active duty he was one of us. That's why his letter of resignation was addressed to the District Intelligence Officer."

17

I should have told this story earlier, but I just couldn't bring myself to write about it. Now that I have a little courage, here goes.

It is the most humiliating thing that happened to me in over thirty years as an investigator. It, too, concerned an attorney and a background investigation. It was the summer of 1957, and I had recently completed my training under Clint's supervision and was just starting to do background investigations on my own. I was assigned an investigation on a very high-ranking civilian official of the Charleston Naval Shipyard. The references on his Personal History Statement were all well-known Charlestonians, but one stood out from the others. He was not only a reference, but a neighbor as well. I knew an interview with him would kill two birds with one stone, as I could count him as a reference and a neighborhood source. He was one of Charleston's most well-known attorneys, a prestigious civic leader and a force behind the scenes in South Carolina politics. When he was not on the front page of the Charleston *News & Courier*, he could be found either in the political or society pages. He was descended from a long line of Charleston barristers whose interests were not only in the law, but also included vast real estate and farming operations. I wanted to meet this man, and I wanted to interview him. A telephone call to his office receptionist resulted in a 9:00 A.M. appointment for me later in the week. The night before the scheduled interview, I brushed off my best suit and shined my wingtips as though I was preparing for inspection. The next morning I ate breakfast in my t-shirt so as not to spill anything on the freshly ironed white shirt Vicky had prepared. I picked out a conservative tie, and off to work I went. I drove to Broad Street near Charleston's battery, and located a parking space a couple of blocks from the attorney's office. It was a beautiful morning, and tourists were already on the streets as I casually walked the short distance for my 9:00 A.M. appointment. His office was in a rather small building just off Broad

Street, but he was the only occupant, which actually made it very spacious for an attorney practicing alone. When I presented myself to his receptionist at 8:55 A.M., she said he would be with me shortly. I declined her offer of coffee or tea. As I waited, I glanced at the portraits lining one wall of the room. They were of Generals Lee, Jackson, Hood, and other Confederate officers, some of whom were probably ancestors of the attorney. Another wall contained paintings of the South Carolina low country. I fully expected at anytime to see Rhett Butler and Scarlet O'Hara emerge from behind one of the closed doors leading from the reception area. At precisely 9:00 A.M., the receptionist, without any visible means of being prompted, said, "He's ready to see you now."

She opened one of the closed doors and led me into a short hallway whose walls were lined with Civil War scenes. She opened a door at the end of the hall and motioned for me to enter. As I did so, it was like stepping into a museum. I immediately noticed that the royal blue carpet in the hallway changed to a plush snow-white carpet that covered his entire office from wall to wall. The room was very large. A red leather sofa was against the wall, and three red leather chairs were in front of his over-sized desk. The middle chair faced him directly, and the other two were at slight angles. Beautiful mahogany bookshelves ran from the floor to the top of the ten-foot ceiling and completely circled the room. They contained volumes and volumes of law books, history books, photographs of well-known dignitaries, politicians, sports personalities, and military people. Various mementoes and family photographs were on his enormous desk. Civil War artifacts were placed neatly on tables and stands throughout the room.

The attorney introduced himself and carefully examined my credentials as I explained why I was there. He indicated I should have a seat and said, "Yes, I have known George since childhood. We grew up together and graduated together at the Citadel."

I had taken a seat in one of the chairs facing him at a slight angle. I removed a legal pad from my briefcase and crossed my left leg over my right to stabilize the pad when I noticed it! Cold, damp sweat popped out on my forehead, my mouth went dry, and my stomach turned over. I wanted to get up and flee. I wanted to scream, "Why me?" The smell was instantly nauseating and the sight nearly unbearable. There, on the bottom of my freshly shined left shoe, was the remains of dog excrement. Let's not mince words. Back in Chatham County, we didn't say chicken excrement or bull excrement. We told it like it was. There was dogshit between the heel and sole of my shoe, and it had actually oozed over the sole to the shiny leather. It was not old dogshit, but fresh, with the texture of creamy peanut butter. The stench was horrible. I didn't know what to do! I faked a cough and in so doing deliberately turned my head to the side, giving me the opportunity to glance over my shoulder toward the door. No pun intended, but the attorney, as do most of them, had diarrhea of the mouth, and just kept talking about his friend George. He damned well didn't know what I did. There, for anyone with any powers of observation to see, was the unmistakable evidence of where I had walked across the beautiful snow-white carpet. I could see the brown splotches of dogshit each time my left shoe had come in contact with the carpet. My God, it must have been a Great Dane! What to do now? It just didn't seem like the Federal Agent type thing to do to interrupt counsel and say, "Pardon me, sir, but it appears I have tracked dogshit across your expensive white carpet." Questions flashed through my mind so fast I couldn't answer them myself. Can it be cleaned? Who will pay? Can you be drummed out of ONI for tracking dogshit through a lawyer's office? The attorney kept talking and I kept sweating. I didn't hear what he was saying, and certainly wasn't making any notes; however, I made up my mind what to do. I was not going to mention the problem unless he did, and then I would plead for mercy. As the lawyer droned on, I started wrestling with another dilemma. When I got ready to leave, should I make a new path of dogshit or try to stay on the existing path and step only on areas already soiled? I made my decision. When the lawyer quit talking, I was going to thank him for his time, shake his hand, and make my exit without looking down. I figured if he saw what was on his carpet he could shoot me in the back as I attempted to make my way out and it would probably be ruled justifiable homicide. The lawyer ended his oration and asked if I needed anything else. I was tempted to say that some tissue would do nicely; however, I replied in a shaky voice that he had been most helpful and nothing else would be needed. I did an about face and left without glancing down, but as I walked through the reception room, I noticed brown splotches on the oriental rug directly in front of the chair where I had my five-minute wait.

I drove directly home. Vicky had gone to the grocery store. I changed shoes and then drove to the Naval Base. On the way I decided to tell Tom the whole story. The most I had to lose was to be fired and return to Chatham County in disgrace. Tom and Dave were both in Tom's office, and I was motioned inside. I immediately blurted out what had happened. Tom's hard gray eyes got larger and larger. He didn't have much of a sense of humor, but he started snickering behind the hand he had placed over his mouth. Dave didn't even try to hide his laughter and soon both were doubled over the desk with tears running down their cheeks.

After several minutes, Tom became somewhat composed and apparently sensed my concern. Still grinning, he finally was able to mutter, "Don't worry about it. I've known that son of a bitch for years, and anytime you can hand him some shit, you've done a good day's work."

Years later, when I told this story to Big Glen, the eastern North Carolina deputy who disliked lawyers, his only response was: "They should have given you a damned promotion."

18

After about three years with ONI, I seldom worked background investigations, as criminal assignments kept me busy most of the time. However, when a backlog of backgrounds would build up in the Charleston office, I would help out, as would Dave and sometimes even Tom. On one such occasion, I started to bring up to date a Top Secret security clearance on a civilian engineer employed at the Charleston Naval Shipyard. His name was William Henry Maxton. He had been there for approximately ten years, and had no difficulty passing his initial Top Secret clearance. I looked over his Personal History Statement and noted that Maxton was forty years of age, married, and lived in downtown Charleston. He was originally from Georgia, and was educated in that state. Of course, investigative leads in Georgia had previously been covered, and would not have to be updated as he had lived in Charleston since the first investigation. I only had to do criminal and credit checks and talk to two or three references and a couple of neighbors.

The first thing to do was to go by the Charleston Police Department and check Maxton through their files. I only located a stop sign violation, which had occurred a few weeks earlier. From a copy of the citation, his date of birth, address, and other personal data were determined to be consistent with the information on his Personal History Statement. My next stop was the Charleston County Police Department. I located another citation for an unsafe moving violation involving a minor motor vehicle accident. Maxton's date of birth and other personal data were again verified from the citation and the accident report. However, both documents listed his home address as the scene of the fender bender in which he was involved, which was at a North Charleston location. The accident had taken place a week after the stop sign violation, and information on the accident report reflected he backed out of his driveway into the path of an approaching vehicle. I wasn't alarmed at finding a second home address, as perhaps he had moved to the North Charleston address after his latest Personal History Statement was completed. Another thought that crossed my mind was that the traffic officer who investigated the accident had simply made a mistake and had written down the accident address instead of Maxton's home address. I checked the date Maxton signed his Personal History Statement and noted it to be a few days before the stop sign violation. If he had moved, this would require that neighbors be interviewed at both locations. I also noted the accident had happened at 7:30 A.M. on a Wednesday morning, which would have been about the time he would have been leaving home for work. Copies of the citation and accident report were obtained, and then I walked down the hall to the radio room. A glance at the accident report disclosed the name of the officer who had completed it. I identified myself to the dispatcher and asked if the officer who investigated the accident was on duty. The dispatcher said that he was, and, at my request, contacted him by radio and asked him to meet me at a North Charleston coffee shop that was a favorite of law enforcement officers, as it never closed, the coffee was always hot and strong, and the owner was a retired highway patrolman. Thirty minutes later I was having coffee with officer Jim Belton. After exchanging pleasantries, copies of the accident report and citation were displayed to him.

He examined both and said, "Why the hell is ONI interested in this? The man was backing out of his driveway and a car parked at the curb obstructed his view. As he eased into the street the bumper of a passing pickup caught his rear bumper—end of story."

I explained that I was doing a background investigation on Maxton and there were some questions as to his residence address. Belton said he didn't recall what address appeared on his driver's license, and that those addresses weren't reliable anyway because of all the military and other transit personnel in the area. Belton stated he always made it a point to put in his reports and citations the actual addresses where individuals were living at the time of the incidents.

Belton explained this by saying that if they failed to appear in court or pay the citation, they wouldn't be hard to find. He continued, "Maxton told me he was living at the address, which I wrote on the citation and accident report. I distinctly remember how mad he was at his neighbor for parking his car at the curb, which blocked his view of traffic. He said he had been telling him for over a year that it could cause an accident and that his wife had nearly gotten hit a couple of times."

I picked up the tab for the coffee, thanked officer Belton, and sat in my car thinking. I could feel it, I was on to something but didn't know what. But I was darned sure going to find out. I reached in the backseat and retrieved a current telephone directory for the greater Charleston area. I located the name and number of William H. Maxton at the downtown Charleston address, but nothing to indicate a Maxton at the North Charleston address. I walked over to a nearby telephone booth. A call to an ONI confidential source at the local telephone company disclosed a W. Henry Maxton had an unlisted number at the North Charleston address for the past eighteen months. Inquiries at offices of local utility companies revealed that for the past eighteen months, water and electricity at the North Charleston address had been in the name of W. Henry Maxton.

About mid-afternoon, I arrived back at the office and briefed Tom on what I had learned about Maxton. He called in Dave and Mr. Chucknow, the security analyst. The four of us discussed the matter for over an hour, but failed to come up with a logical explanation as to what, if anything, Maxton was up to. Mr. Chucknow finally suggested that since Maxton would know that his security clearance was being updated, to go ahead and contact a neighbor or two at the downtown address listed on his Personal History Statement. After that, we could decide what our next move would be.

The following morning, I drove to the downtown address, which was just off King Street in the Historic District. I rang the bell of the home next door to Maxton and an attractive lady in her fifties opened the thick wooden door, but kept the screen door closed. I identified myself to her and informed her I was conducting a background investigation on her neighbor, Mr. Maxton. She asked if he was in trouble, and I explained the investigation was for a routine security clearance. She invited me inside and led me to a small sun room containing an abundance of houseplants. In response to my questions, she said she had known Mr. and Mrs. Maxton for the entire ten years they had lived next door. She stated they were childless and socialized very little, keeping mostly to themselves. She knew him to be some sort of official at the Shipyard, but stated that he didn't discuss his work. She reported the Maxtons seldom had visitors and that she did not know anything about their backgrounds except that both were originally from Georgia. She talked of Mrs. Maxton's interest in art and said that a great deal of her time was spent painting, and that on nice days Mrs. Maxton would paint on the rear patio and she would walk over and talk to her. She then commented that at times Mrs. Maxton appeared to be rather lonely, as Mr. Maxton's job had, for the last year or so, required him to be out of town on Tuesday, Wednesday, and Thursday nights. My pulse rate increased as I told the nice lady a little white lie when I said that I may have met the Maxtons at a reception at the Naval Base and asked her to describe Mrs. Maxton.

She said, "Oh, she's a pretty little brunette in her late thirties or early forties who won't weigh a hundred pounds soaking wet."

I thanked the lady for her cooperation and requested her to keep our conversation in confidence. I then had to control myself to keep from running to my car. One thing I knew for sure, as an engineer at the Shipyard, Maxton's duties would not necessitate him being away from home three nights a week.

I drove directly to the Charleston County Police Station and went directly to the radio room. I told the dispatcher it was urgent that I meet with officer Belton as soon as possible. Fifteen minutes later, I sat in his cruiser at the coffee shop. I asked if he had met Mrs. Maxton when he investigated her husband's automobile accident. He replied that he was not introduced to her, but Maxton told him she was his wife when she came out of the house to examine the damage to the car. Anxiously, I asked what she looked like.

Belton thought for a moment and replied, "A long, tall blonde in her late twenties with a good figure, but who appeared to have a lot of mileage."

My parting comment to Belton was: "You just made my day!"

Forty-five minutes later, I was in conference with Tom, Dave, and Mr. Chucknow. After digesting the latest information, Mr. Chucknow smiled and said, "Gentlemen, it's obvious we have a man maintaining two households. He probably just has a mistress, but let's find out the whole story."

Tom instructed me to pick one of the new agents and brief him on what information we had regarding Maxton. Tom said he then wanted us to obtain the license number and description of Maxton's automobile, and for us to determine at which residence it was located at midnight and 6:00 A.M. for the next week. One of us could check at midnight and the other at 6:00 A.M., and neither would lose too much sleep.

I picked a young agent named Johnny Howard. He listened attentively to my briefing, and when I finished, said, "Maxton must be a glutton for punishment. It's difficult as hell to keep one woman happy."

Johnny and I drove over to the office of the Naval Base Police Department. Their main responsibility was traffic control on the Naval Base, which included the Shipyard. Personal vehicles of military and civilians who were assigned or worked at either installation had to be registered with them before they were allowed to be driven on the base. We determined the make, model, and license number of Maxton's vehicle and noted it to be the same as what appeared on the accident report completed by officer Belton. We also learned that because of his position, Maxton had an assigned parking place, which we soon located. We got a good look at his dark blue Buick.

Not being an early-morning person, I elected to make the midnight checks on our subject and let Johnny do the 6:00 A.M. checks. I would make the first check that night, which was a Friday. After watching TV much later than usual, I cranked up the government automobile and drove to downtown Charleston. It was a minute or two before midnight when I drove slowly past Maxton's downtown address. The home was completely dark, and his car was in the driveway. The same was true for Saturday, Sunday, and Monday nights. Johnny had also noted that Maxton's vehicle was in the driveway at the downtown address at 6:00 A.M. each of those mornings.

On Tuesday night, I checked the downtown address at 11:40

P.M. and the vehicle was not there. I drove directly to the North Charleston address, arriving about fifteen minutes later. There in the driveway was Maxton's vehicle. It was there Wednesday and Thursday nights and Johnny had located it there Wednesday, Thursday, and Friday mornings.

Later that Friday morning, I briefed Tom on the results of our surveillance. He said, "You talk to the bastard and listen to what he has to say. I'll make arrangements through the Shipyard Commander for him to be here at 1:00 P.M. on Monday. Let Johnny be your witness."

Johnny and I were waiting in the interrogation room at the designated time when Tom opened the door and introduced us to William Henry Maxton. Maxton sat across the desk from us, and, after Tom left, Johnny and I displayed our credentials to him. Maxton was the exact opposite of what I expected. He appeared to be fifty instead of forty and was about five feet six inches, and weighed no more than one hundred and twenty pounds. He was nearly bald, had a very fair complexion, and wore glasses with extremely thick lens and wire frames.

I went into a detailed explanation of how ONI conducted background investigations on persons needing security clearances and periodically brought up to date investigations on persons already having security clearances. I told Maxton that while bringing his background up to date we became aware of his situation and therefore he was placed under surveillance, that we knew of the two households he was maintaining, and we quoted the two addresses to him.

Before I could ask the first question, tears started down Maxton's cheeks and he began to sob. After a few minutes, he gained some control of himself and in a quivering voice shocked me to the core when he said, "I should have known in this day and age that I couldn't get by with having two wives."

I glanced at Johnny and noted a look of surprise on his face. If he had glanced at me, I am sure he would have found the same. Both of us had expected a married man with a mistress. Neither had anticipated a case of bigamy. I recovered rather quickly and said, "I don't think there is much you can tell us we don't already know, but go ahead and tell us anyway."

Maxton then related a bizarre story that held Johnny and

me spellbound. He told of growing up in a very small Georgia town and being the only child of a wealthy family. His family and the family of his wife, Shirley Mae Maxton, were not only neighbors, but very close friends as well. From early childhood, he and Shirley Mae were constantly together and as they progressed to their teens both families assumed and expected them to marry. Maxton advised he and Shirley Mae were very fond of each other, but their relationship was strictly platonic. They were more like brother and sister than sweethearts. Maxton said that by the time they finished high school and went off to college, not only did their families expect them to marry, but so did the entire community.

Continuing, Maxton furnished the following additional details:

After graduating from college, neither wanted to be the one to back away from what was expected of them, so they were united in holy matrimony in a beautiful church wedding. It came as no surprise that his wife didn't want children and didn't like the way they were conceived. They moved to Atlanta, where he worked for an engineering firm for eight years, before he accepted employment at the Charleston Shipyard. He believed a move to Charleston, a city they had visited on vacation and which they both loved, would make them both happier, as neither of them liked Atlanta. Life was more pleasant for them in Charleston, but Shirley Mae was still unresponsive to his needs. At work, he had heard other men talk of a house of prostitution located in a small town about fifty miles north of Charleston. After he and Shirley Mae had been in Charleston for nearly five years, he started frequenting the establishment on the average of once a month. He tried different girls, but finally settled for one named Sarah Jean Lamb. She not only satisfied him sexually, but appeared to understand him. She was a good listener and sympathetic to his problems.

For several months he concealed his trips to the house of prostitution from Shirley Mae, but finally he broke down and told her. To his astonishment, she was not angry or upset, but said she was happy for him. Shirley Mae was content with her painting, books, and occasional visits back to their hometown. His parents had both passed away and his inheritance had made him well off financially.

Maxton stopped and lit a cigarette, inhaling deeply. He didn't even appear aware of Johnny and I being in the room. However, he continued his story:

Sarah Jean was from a small town in Tennessee and a high school dropout. She came to Charleston to be with her boyfriend whose ship was home-ported there. She found him shacked up with a waitress. Heartbroken and without money to return home, she started working the bars and eventually made her way to the house of prostitution. What she wanted more than anything was a place of her own. He came up with a plan to buy a small home in North Charleston and move Sarah Jean there where he could be with her more often in their own place. Sarah Jean was excited over the prospect and agreed to the move on two conditions: That she be allowed to work the bars on weekends, and that he marry her! Of course, she knew he was already married, but insisted that it did not matter to her. When he told Shirley Mae of his plan and of Sarah Jean's two conditions, she again did not get angry or emotionally upset. Her response was to go ahead and marry her, as it wouldn't be legal anyway.

Maxton said he had married Sarah Jean in a civil ceremony about two years earlier in Dillon County, South Carolina. He bought and furnished the small home in North Charleston, and a few weeks later Sarah Jean moved in. Since that time, he had spent Tuesday, Wednesday, and Thursday nights with her and the other nights at home with Shirley Mae.

Johnny and I listened considerately to Maxton's story. He finished with, "I'm glad my double life is over."

I responded with, "Mr. Maxton, bigamy is a crime in the state of South Carolina and if a person knowingly aids or abets in bigamy that person too is guilty of a crime. This would definitely include Sarah Jean, and maybe even Shirley Mae."

Maxton thought for a few moments and then looked up with red-stained eyes. He said, "Gentlemen, if I am free to leave I'm not even going back to the office. I am going to call my boss and resign over the telephone to avoid being fired."

I informed Maxton that we had no authority to detain him, nor any desire to do so, and that our responsibility would end when the Shipyard Commander received our report, and, since there was evidence of a crime(s), the local District Attorney would be briefed. After Maxton left, I told Tom what had taken place. His only comment was: "I'll be damned."

To complete this story, Maxton called in his resignation and, within a few days, he and Shirley Mae returned to Georgia and Sarah Jean went back to Tennessee. The District Attorney didn't seek indictments against anyone.

Years later, when I told Big Glen of this case, his comment was: "It wouldn't have done any good to have indicted any of them. They were all crazy as hell and could have gotten off on insanity pleas."

19

A Memorandum of Understanding signed by the Department of Defense and the Justice Department said the FBI would have jurisdiction in criminal cases if any civilian personnel were involved either as suspects or victims. This Memorandum stated military authorities would have jurisdiction if all involved were military personnel. The only exception to this rule was that military authorities would have jurisdiction if the victim was a military dependent and the crime took place on a military base and was committed by a military person. The restrictions of the Memorandum awarded jurisdiction to the FBI in most cases, as seldom were all military personnel and/or their dependents involved in serious felonies; however, there were exceptions.

I recall a case that I investigated in 1960. There was a United States Air Force base located at Charleston, which was a rather large facility, but lacked a base hospital. Airmen, or their dependents, requiring hospitalization were sent to the United States Naval Hospital located at the Charleston Naval Base. The wife of an airman was hospitalized there for about a week with a nervous disorder. Upon release, she confided to her husband that she was not sure, but she believed that while under sedation someone had had sexual intercourse with her. Her suspicions were made known to the Office of Special Investigations (OSI), which was the Air Force equivalent to ONI. Agents from OSI took a statement from the young woman and a copy of it was later made available to me, with a request for investigation. I met with the OSI agents and immediately sensed they were skeptical of her story because she could not say when the incident took place or with whom. She could not give a description of the person who may have had relations with her and could only describe the incident in vague terms and could not explain her inability to resist.

At my request, I was granted an interview with the young

lady who, to my surprise, was black. She appeared very sincere when I talked to her, and unhesitatingly told of experiencing severe unexplained nervous disorders from time to time. She was not at all certain that someone had had sexual relations with her during the week she was hospitalized, but she thought she remembered it more or less as one could recall bits and pieces of a dream. The one thing she kept repeating was that she apparently was powerless to resist. There was no physical evidence to substantiate her story, but the earnest manner in which she related it persuaded me she was being truthful. Her explanation as to why she had not reported her suspicions to hospital authorities was that she was there to be treated for a nervous condition, and to make allegations that she could not support might have resulted in the doctors prolonging her hospital stay, as they may have had doubts about her mental condition. Not once did the airman's wife inject race into the situation.

An interview with her doctor disclosed that the alleged victim suffered from depression and was being treated with various medications. He steadfastly maintained none of the drugs would cause her to hallucinate and further advised that she had no history of mental delusions.

Inquiry at the hospital established the dates of her confinement and also revealed she had been assigned to a private room. If someone had relations with her, it seemed reasonable to assume it would be at a time when there was little activity at the hospital and at a time when the perpetrator would have the opportunity. Taking these factors into consideration, I determined there were several different male hospital attendants on late duty in the wing where she was confined and who had access to her room. I elected to interview each of them.

The first two furnished no information of value; however, the third attendant was very defensive and extraordinary nervous at the start of his interview, which quickly changed into an interrogation. After a couple of hours, I had a voluntary, signed statement in which he admitted that he had pilfered some sleep medication from other patients and added it to the sleep aid prescribed for the airman's wife. He acknowledged that a few hours after she took the medication he entered her room without anyone's knowledge and had sexual intercourse with her. He stated

65

she neither responded to nor resisted him, as she was in a stupor.

This case was not unusual, nor did it take a great deal of investigative effort to resolve. I have told it for two reasons: Prior to the time I worked this case, nearly all of the criminal cases I was assigned had been either homosexual investigations or thefts of personal property. As previously stated, the homosexual investigations were for security purposes, and nearly all resulted in the subjects receiving discharges under other than honorable conditions. The theft cases usually involved money stolen from enlisted personnel. ONI seldom became involved in these larceny cases until there was a series of them resulting in a morale problem. When the perpetrator was identified, he was tried by a special court-martial which usually resulted in a short sentence in the brig and a bad conduct discharge. The rape case of the airman's wife was the first case I worked that was tried by a general court-martial. The defendant was convicted and received a dishonorable discharge, forfeiture of all pay and allowances, and a ten-year sentence at the Naval Prison at Portsmouth, New Hampshire. The other reason I told of this case was that it took place in Charleston in 1960, and involved a black victim and a white perpetrator. At no time was race ever mentioned, nor was it ever an issue. It made me proud.

20

Charleston was the home of the Navy Minecraft Base. Minecraft, referred to as mine sweepers, are small vessels equipped to destroy enemy mines. The captains (skippers) of these vessels were usually lieutenants, and the crews were small in number so that the skippers knew who had alcohol, gambling, girlfriend, marital, or financial difficulties.

In early 1961, several mine sweeper captains were having drinks one evening at the officers' club when they discovered that each of them had crew members who never appeared to have any money, even though they were being paid every two weeks. The captains considered the matter to be a morale problem and agreed to conduct some inquiries as to why these sailors were nearly always broke. A few nights later, they met again at the officers' club and compared notes. Their inquiries had determined that the men were the apparent victims of a usury operation, as someone was lending money to them and charging exorbitant rates of interest. The captains made the results of their inquiries known to the Minecraft Base Commander who requested ONI for an appropriate investigation.

I was selected as lead investigator, with three agents assigned to me for assistance. We interviewed the captains of the mine sweepers and from them obtained the names of the sailors who were reportedly victims in the usury operation. We interviewed these men and took signed statements from them in which they acknowledged that over various periods of time they had borrowed money from a first class petty officer named Tony Celli. He was stationed aboard a mine sweeper, but also owned and operated a tavern near the Naval Base in North Charleston. Information received from the sailors revealed a very simple operation. Celli would lend money between paydays. The loans were always in five-dollar denominations, and for each five dollars loaned, seven had to be repaid. Navy paydays were every two weeks, and the loans had to be repaid the next payday after they were made. If payday was on a Friday and a sailor borrowed $25.00 from Celli on Thursday, then the loan would be due the next day and the amount payable would be $35.00. If a sailor borrowed $5.00 from Celli the day after payday, he could go until the next payday (thirteen days) and would then have to pay $7.00. Another way of looking at the operation was that for every $100.00 Celli loaned, within two weeks he collected $140.00. Over a period of a year, and evidence was obtained that reflected that Celli had been doing this for many years, the original $100.00 would yield interest totaling $1,040.

As the other agents and I obtained statements from the mine sweeper sailors, they furnished information regarding personnel stationed aboard other ships and shore installations who had borrowed from Celli. It became obvious that this was a very large operation and the tavern, which clearly was a money-maker itself, served as a front for the usury business. We received dozens and dozens of statements from enlisted personnel throughout the Charleston area who had received loans from Celli and repaid them at the usurious rate.

Examination of Celli's personnel file reflected he was certainly not the typical twenty-year-old sailor involved in thefts or other wrongdoings that I usually investigated. He had served eighteen years in the Navy, and had fought during World War II. He was thirty-six years of age, married, and the father of three children.

Celli was the only enlisted man living in an affluent neighborhood in North Charleston. His neighbors were Naval officers, business owners, and shipyard executives. He and his wife each had large, late-model automobiles—all of this on the salary of a boatswain mate first class. No way!

For weeks we collected statements from those who had borrowed from Celli. As the number approached a hundred, we just quit. We could have gone on indefinitely. We even received information that Celli was aware of being under investigation, but nevertheless was still lending money.

We located a former bartender who had worked at Celli's tavern whom Celli had fired for allegedly failing to ring all sales on the register. Needless to say, this subject was more than pleased to tell all he knew of the usury operation. He claimed to have come to Charleston from Savannah about two years previously, and had obtained part-time employment as a house painter. A few weeks after his arrival in Charleston, he started hanging out at Celli's beer joint, and shortly thereafter started helping tend bar on weekends and paydays. He stated Celli's usury operation was not a secret, as sailors were constantly coming to the joint to obtain loans and on payday nights literally lined up to pay off. A few days later, many of the same ones would borrow again. The former bartender said that Celli trusted no one and that only he made loans and only he collected. He recalled that Celli kept his records in a looseleaf, pocket notebook, which he always kept with him. He also recalled that Celli maintained only current records of those indebted to him and how much they owed and that as soon as all debts on a page of the notebook were paid, the page was then destroyed. The former bartender came by his information from what he had observed at the beer joint and from after-hours drinking bouts with Celli in which Celli reportedly talked about his loan business.

The information regarding the looseleaf notebook always being with Celli was welcome news to us. We could search him and his possessions anytime we wanted without a search warrant, as long as he was on a military base or ship. We could also seize from him anything we considered contraband or evidence of a crime.

Celli's ship was a mine sweeper ocean (MSO), which was docked at the Minecraft Base when not conducting exercises in Charleston harbor or along the coast. His skipper had been made cognizant of the investigation and had offered his full cooperation. I could sense he disliked Celli.

I made the decision to search Celli aboard the MSO when it docked at the Minecraft Base the day before payday. I figured his notebook would contain the most information at that time and, if we seized it, Celli would really suffer the next day without any records of the outstanding loans he had made.

I chose agent Johnny Howard to conduct the search with me. The day before payday, Celli's MSO conducted local exercises, but experienced mechanical problems and was late docking at the Minecraft Base. Johnny and I went aboard and contacted the skipper. I explained to him that we wanted to search Celli's person for the notebook, and if it was not found on his person we wanted to search his locker. Of course, the skipper readily agreed and led Johnny and me to the crew's quarters where Celli was located. Johnny and I identified ourselves to Celli, and informed him that we were conducting an investigation regarding loans he apparently was making to other military personnel. I also informed Celli that under Article 31 of the Uniform Code of Military Justice, he did not have to answer any questions or make statements, and anything he did say could be used against him in a trial by court-martial. I then asked Celli if he had any records regarding such loans. Celli didn't even answer. He was about six feet tall and weighed about two hundred pounds. He had coal-black hair, a ruddy pockmarked complexion, and a thick black mustache. He could have easily passed for the villain in a B-movie. He just sneered at us.

I patted Celli down, but didn't locate the notebook. I then asked Celli to open his locker, which was secured with a combination lock. He didn't move. The skipper spoke up and said, "Celli, either open your locker or I'll send for the bolt cutters and cut the damned lock off."

Celli hesitated for a moment, but then calmly worked the combination and swung open the locker door. His locker was nearly bare, but on the top shelf was a pocket-size, looseleaf notebook. It was filled with pages listing names, with duty stations and monetary amounts beside each name. I asked Celli what the notebook was for, and again he didn't answer, but just sneered. I took the notebook and Johnny and I accompanied the skipper to his quarters. We each dated and initialed the book. Because of the mechanical difficulties experienced earlier that day, the skipper advised that the MSO would not be going on exercises the following day. It was late, and neither Johnny nor I were going back to the office that night. We also knew it was useless to attempt an interrogation with Celli. Something had to be done with the notebook, and I certainly didn't want to take it home with me. The skipper volunteered to keep it in the ship's safe until Johnny or I picked it up the following morning. He assured me that only he, the executive officer, and the engineering officer had access to the safe. He also advised he would order both officers not to open the safe until after Johnny or I had returned

70

the next morning, when he would open the safe and turn over the notebook. This was agreeable to me, so Johnny and I left the MSO with feelings of accomplishment.

The following morning I returned to the MSO, where I had coffee with the skipper. We then went to the safe, and upon opening it discovered the notebook was gone! I don't know who felt worse, the skipper or me. I was upset, and the skipper was angry, embarrassed, and humiliated. He said, "When I find out who opened this safe, I'll have his ass court-martialed."

The skipper and I went to his quarters, where I questioned him regarding the other two officers who had access to the safe. He advised that the executive officer was a lieutenant, junior grade, who was an Annapolis graduate and lived off-base with his wife and two small children. The skipper described him as a dedicated career officer who got along well with the crew, but never crossed the line of being overly friendly with them.

He described his engineering officer as an ensign commissioned less than a year earlier, right out of a college ROTC program. He said the ensign was not married and lived alone in a Charleston apartment. The skipper believed he lacked leadership qualities and was spineless when attempting to discipline some of the more rowdy crew members. He finally said in no uncertain terms, "He's a damned wimp."

I kind of tucked my tail between my legs, told the skipper I would be in touch, and returned to the office to face Tom. I knew he was going to be mad as hell.

As I explained to Tom exactly what had occurred, I could see his face turning red and his cold gray eyes seeming to sink deeper into his head. He appeared ready to explode! When I finished, Tom lit a cigarette and inhaled deeply. He didn't say anything for a few moments, and when he did he looked directly at me. I thought I was due for a good old-fashioned ass-chewing, and braced myself for it.

Tom said, "That notebook was placed in a safe aboard a warship of the United States Navy. There shouldn't be a place much more secure. It appears we have been betrayed by an officer of the United States Navy, and we are damned sure going to have his ass, and Celli's, too."

Tom then told me to find Johnny, and for the two of us to return to the MSO to pick up Celli and bring him to the office. I did as instructed without asking any questions. After returning to the office with Celli, I left him in the interrogation room with Johnny and found Tom having coffee in Dave's office.

I told him where Celli was and Tom, who by then was completely composed, said, "I'm going to talk to Celli alone, but I want you and Johnny to monitor from the sound room." The room he was referring to was located next to the interrogation room, where we could observe through a two-way mirror and listen via a hidden microphone.

When Tom entered the interrogation room he immediately dismissed Johnny, who joined me in the sound room. We both readied ourselves for what we thought would be Tom chewing on Celli like ugly on an ape. After Tom very politely identified himself and explained to Celli his rights under Article 31 of the Uniform Code of Military Justice, he nicely asked Celli if he would like to comment on his usury business. Celli promptly replied that he wouldn't answer any questions regarding usury. Tom then very nicely asked Celli if he cared to answer any questions regarding his notebook. Celli again invoked Article 31. Tom thanked him and told him to wait in the room until he could locate some transportation to return him to the Minecraft Base. He then told Celli he would have some coffee sent to the room!

Johnny and I were astounded. We had never seen Tom treat anyone as gently as he had treated Celli. Tom came over to the sound room and noted our concern. He said, "Gentlemen, there is more than one way to skin a cat. Stay out of sight for a couple of hours and then deliver Celli back to the Minecraft Base. Johnny, you stay in the car with Celli while Bob goes aboard the MSO for the ensign. When Bob gets back to the car with the ensign, Johnny, you get out with Celli and shake his hand and thank him for his cooperation. Be sure to do this in the presence of the ensign. Under no circumstances let Celli and the ensign talk to each other. Bring the ensign back here and leave him by himself in the interrogation room. I want the two of you to monitor from the sound room, but I'll talk to him alone."

Johnny and I did exactly as Tom had instructed. We were still puzzled at the kind treatment Celli had received from Tom and we were sure Celli was just as puzzled when Johnny shook

72

his hand and thanked him for his cooperation as I approached the car with the ensign.

After we left the ensign in the interrogation room, Johnny and I reported to Tom's office. He said, "You boys haven't had lunch. Grab a bite at the officers' club and be back here in about an hour."

When we returned from lunch, Tom was still at his desk doing paperwork. He said, "I guess I've let the ensign stew long enough." He went to the interrogation room and Johnny and I made our way to the sound room. Tom identified himself and informed the ensign of his rights under Article 31 of the Uniform Code of Military Justice. There were beads of sweat on the ensign's forehead, and both his hands were trembling.

For several minutes, Tom didn't say a word, when he finally broke the silence it was with a voice I had never heard before. In a tone that was not threatening but very demeaning, Tom said, "You wear the uniform of an officer of the United States Navy. You are a disgrace to that uniform. I have more respect for Celli than I do for you. He has never claimed to be an officer and a gentleman."

The ensign started to shake, dropped his head, and muttered, "I didn't think I had a choice. Celli said he would report me if I didn't give him the combination to the ship's safe. He said he wanted to get his loan book from the safe. I told him the combination and he wrote it down. I don't know whether or not he opened the safe. Since he cooperated with you, I guess he told you about me."

Without lying to the ensign, Tom said he would like to hear the story directly from him and not consider what Celli had said.

"I'm gay, and somehow Celli found out. He told me he would report me if I didn't give the combination to him. I don't know how long he has known about me. I didn't know about him lending money until last night, when the skipper told me not to open the safe as Celli's records had been seized and were in the safe. I want to say again that I didn't condone Celli's loan business and didn't even know about it until last night. I'm ashamed for what I am and for what I did."

After the ensign had been returned to the Minecraft Base, Tom met with Johnny and me. He explained that from the brief-

73

ing he had received from me regarding the three officers who had access to the safe, he believed the one most likely to conspire with Celli would be the ensign. He also figured Celli to be a "sea lawyer," who wouldn't answer any questions. Tom further explained that he went through the perfunctory interrogation of Celli, along with the delay in returning him to the Minecraft Base, so that it would have a psychological effect on the ensign. He explained that Johnny shaking Celli's hand and thanking him for his cooperation in the presence of the ensign was another psychological tactic employed to cause the ensign to believe Celli had talked. Tom looked at me and said, "I told you there was more than one way to skin a cat."

Celli received a general court-martial and was convicted on numerous counts of usury, conspiracy, and conduct prejudicial to the good order and discipline of the military service. He received a dishonorable discharge, an order to forfeit all pay and allowances, and a ten-year active prison sentence. The ensign resigned his commission and was separated from the Navy under other than honorable conditions. He was a witness against Celli at the court-martial.

I have written about the Celli case for only one reason. During the nearly five years I was a Special Agent for the Office of Naval Intelligence, I was aware that all branches of the military, as well as all government agencies, were trying to identify and weed out homosexuals. They were considered security risks, but liberals scoffed at the possibility of them being blackmailed. After the Celli case, I had firsthand knowledge that a homosexual had been blackmailed.

21

While working investigations in the Charleston area, I would often cross paths with FBI agents assigned to the Charleston resident agency. These chance meetings would usually result in us having coffee together and swapping information. Also, when these agents were in the vicinity of the Naval Base they would drop by our office, as they knew an invitation for lunch at the officers' club would be extended. I was impressed with these agents and envied the prestigious position in which they and their organization were held by other investigative agencies and the general public.

During the summer of 1961, I noticed that my contact with the FBI appeared to be more frequent, as they would call to make sure I would be at the office before they would drop by. I also noticed that in conversations with them, they appeared very interested in my background and what I thought about the FBI. It didn't take me long to figure out they were feeling me out. I had a good rapport with one of their young agents, and at my request we met for lunch. I didn't beat around the bush and told him up front that I liked ONI and especially my fellow agents in the Sixth Naval District. However, I also told him that I didn't want to spend the rest of my career working mostly backgrounds, homosexual investigations, and larceny cases. I asked about the possibility of applying with the Bureau. He responded that for several months he and other agents had discussed recruiting me for the Bureau, but had refrained from doing so for they were afraid it might jeopardize their good relationship with ONI. He went on to say that barring anything disqualifying in my background, he didn't see any reason why I wouldn't be a good candidate for a Special Agent position. I was already aware of the myth that the Bureau only accepted accountants and attorneys as applicants. I was also aware of the Bureau policy to transfer new agents to offices far from their hometowns and last places of residence. I left the meeting with my Bureau friend with mixed emotions.

For the next several months, Vicky and I discussed the possibility of my applying for the Bureau. Some days we were both for it, and a few days later we would be undecided. We still visited our folks frequently back in Chatham County, and in the fall of 1961, while on a visit home, I discussed my dilemma with Dad. He didn't hesitate to say, "The FBI is considered the best law enforcement agency in the world. If you want to be with the best, then make the move."

Upon returning to Charleston, I went to the Bureau resident agency and applied. A battery of tests soon followed, as did an interview with the Special Agent in Charge (SAC) of the Savannah Field Office. A background investigation was next, and then a complete physical examination. In December 1961, I was notified that I had been accepted by the Bureau and was to report to Washington, D.C., for new agents' training, starting February 12, 1962. The Bureau and ONI had arranged for me to continue as an ONI Special Agent until I was sworn in as a Special Agent with the FBI, so I would have no break in government service.

Vicky and I sold our home in Charleston and placed our furniture in storage. I left Vicky and our two-year-old daughter, Gloria, with our folks in Chatham County. I arrived in Washington on February 11, 1962. I checked into the Mayflower Hotel and spent a sleepless night wondering what the future held.

The next day, February 12, 1962, I reported to FBI Headquarters at 9th and Pennsylvania Avenue, NE, where my identification was verified. A short while later, twenty other young white males and I were sworn in as Special Agents of the Federal Bureau of Investigation. We were immediately transported by bus to Quantico, Virginia, where we were to spend the first four of our fourteen weeks of new agents' training. Many books and articles have been written about the FBI, and most go into detail about their very fine training program for new Special Agents. I will not attempt to duplicate the work of these authors, but I do believe the Bureau training program was in 1962, and still continues to be, the world's best for law enforcement officers.

New agents' training was much easier for me than for the other members of my class, as I was the only one who had previously served as a Federal Agent. In fact, only one other member of the class had any law enforcement experience, and that was with the New York City Police Department. Other class members came from various civilian occupations including banking, teaching, coaching, and one had been a professional wine taster. I thoroughly enjoyed being with these fine men, but none of us could ever let our hair down or confide in each other, as a rumor spread from day one was that one of us was not a new agent but a Bureau "plant." Of course, this turned out not to be the case.

During new agents' training, we had dozens of different Bureau instructors in the various subjects we studied. Most of these instructors didn't hesitate to inform us that if an agent ever embarrassed the Bureau or screwed up in any manner he could expect, depending on the severity of his transgression, a letter of censure or a letter of censure and a disciplinary transfer. Of course, a very severe case would result in his employment termination. These instructors also led us to believe the Bureau had its own Siberia for agents who had screwed up royally, but not quite enough for termination. It was the Bureau office at Butte, Montana. For fourteen weeks, several times a day, we would hear the words, "Screw up and go to Butte."

My new agents' class started with twenty-one and finished with nineteen. One new agent lasted less than a week when it was discovered that he had difficulty flexing the index finger on his left hand because of a childhood injury. He was right handed, but all agents were required to be proficient with the revolver with both hands. As soon as the discovery was made, his dream of being an FBI agent was over. The other agent was with us for about three weeks, and appeared to be getting along well. He had a good personality and was well-liked. One day he was with us, and the next he was gone. We never knew why.

A few days before my class completed training, we received sealed orders assigning us to our first Bureau offices. During training, things that were done individually were performed in alphabetical order, so I was always the third in line. After the sealed orders were handed out, the class counselor, an experienced Bureau agent who had wet-nursed us for the entire fourteen weeks, suggested that each agent stand and open his orders and announce to the rest of the class the office to which he would be reporting. His suggestion was well-accepted by the class, as we were not only interested in where we would be going ourselves, but also where our classmates would be stationed.

The first agent stood, opened his orders, and announced, "Memphis, Tennessee." All of us applauded.

The second agent stood, opened his orders, and announced with exuberance, "San Diego, California." Again, we all applauded.

Then it was my turn. I stood and eagerly opened my orders. I read them and could hardly believe what I saw. I felt nauseous and in a faltering voice, announced, "Butte, Montana." There was no applause, and the room became absolutely silent. I took my seat and suddenly became aware that the counselor was talking to me. I only understood that an Assistant Director wanted to see me in his office immediately. He was on another floor in a different part of the building. As I slowly made my way to his office, I tried to think of what I had possibly done to deserve Butte right out of new agents' training. I couldn't think of anything, but told myself that I was probably on my way to his office to receive a letter of censure to go with the assignment to Butte.

I was ushered into the Assistant Director's office by his secretary. To this day, I can't recall his name but, like yesterday, I remember him as a large, middle-aged man in a dark blue suit, white shirt, and maroon tie. He was prematurely gray and had a warm, friendly smile and a firm handshake. He came straight to the point, explaining to me that Butte had the reputation within the Bureau of being a disciplinary office. He said the Bureau wanted to change that image, and I had been selected to serve there as a first office agent. He went on to tell me the Butte Division covered Montana, Idaho, the Yellowstone and Glacier National Parks, and several Indian reservations. He also told me I could expect to be there for about two years before transferring to my second office. He congratulated me on completing new agents' training and my selection to the Butte office.

I made my way back to the classroom, and, when I entered,

the counselor had a wide grin on his face. My fellow agents applauded, and I felt damned good as I knew the counselor had obviously been involved in the selection process and had explained it to the class during my absence. I looked forward to my first assignment with enthusiasm.

22

Vicky, Gloria, and I started the long drive to Butte after a short visit to Chatham County. We had packed our car with personal effects, placed a crib mattress on the back seat, and supported and leveled it with boxes of toys and infant items that we placed on the back floorboards. This was where Gloria was to spend most of her time for the next five days. Vicky had used a road atlas and planned our entire trip. She had also recorded the route on three-by-five cards, which were placed above the driver's sun visor.

The three of us greatly enjoyed traveling across country, with me driving and Vicky navigating and entertaining Gloria. The trip was easy, except for a horrifying hail storm we encountered in Nebraska. Our car suffered slight damage, including a broken headlight. As we approached Yellowstone National Park, we were forced to spend the night in Cody, Wyoming, as roads through Yellowstone were temporarily closed because of snow, even though it was late May. The way had been cleared by the next morning, and our drive through Yellowstone was something I'll always remember. The scenery was breathtaking, and Gloria was astonished at the sight of bear, deer, elk, moose, and other animals beside the road. She especially enjoyed throwing cookies out the windows to the bears.

Later that day, we crossed the Continental Divide, and a few miles later approached the city of Butte. There were only a few scattered trees and shrubs and very little grass or other greenery. Many streets were not paved, and, as we neared downtown, we noticed each block contained several saloons. It was Saturday afternoon, and cowboys and miners lined the sidewalks. A goodly number appeared to be intoxicated.

I glanced at Vicky, and tears were running down her cheeks. She looked at me and said, "I don't like this place." I replied that we probably would be there but for a year or two.

She appeared to cheer up a little and said, "As long as the

three of us are together, I guess we can live anywhere for a short time."

We located the Butte office at the Thornton Building, and I left Vicky and Gloria in the car while I went inside and signed the register. It was late afternoon, and only a clerk was on duty. He suggested a motel near town until I could meet with the SAC on Monday. I signed out, and half an hour later checked us into the motel he had recommended.

The next day, we rode around and discovered, to our surprise, that near downtown Butte was one of the world's largest open pit copper mines. We also learned that underneath Butte were miles and miles of ore mines. It seemed as though we had gone back in time: most people were dressed in western attire, many of the saloons did not have locks on their doors; (they never closed), there was no state speed limit, and silver dollars had replaced dollar bills.

On Monday, I again signed in at the Butte office, and a few minutes later was in the office of SAC Wade Burke. He was in his late forties and was approaching his twenty-fifth year with the Bureau. He greeted me warmly, and my uneasiness quickly disappeared when he told me he had previously been SAC in Charlotte and knew my dad by reputation. I relaxed as we chatted about some mutual acquaintances and North Carolina in general. He then got down to business. He told me to rent an apartment or a house, but not to sign a lease. He said that for several weeks I would be assigned cases in and around Butte, but later, if I demonstrated I could work without close supervision, I would help out from time to time at some of the fourteen resident agencies scattered throughout Montana and Idaho. He also said some "old dogs" would be assigned to me. He explained these were very old unsolved cases that were ready to be closed. However, a final examination of the case files by a new agent might result in the discovery of investigative leads that had not been explored. The meeting was over when I was told to take a few days off to locate a place to live.

Vicky and I rented a nice duplex, but had to continue living in the motel for nearly three weeks until our furniture arrived from Charleston. In the meantime, I received my "old dogs," along with other cases requiring investigation in the Butte area.

I screened the "old dogs" diligently and came up with some leads in each of them that called for investigations in other Bureau offices. I must admit some of the leads were rather far-fetched.

I next concentrated on the local cases that had been assigned to me. I knew as a new agent I wouldn't receive any cases of importance, but I also knew that I would be carefully evaluated on how I handled the trivial ones that were assigned to me.

My first case involved the theft of an M-1 rifle from the local Army Reserve Rifle Team. They had participated in a match a few weeks earlier at a range on the outskirts of Butte, and that was when the weapon was apparently stolen. There were five or six members of the rifle team, and I interviewed each of them, including the officer in charge of the team. From him I obtained the serial number of the weapon and a detailed description of it, as the rifle had been customized for use in rifle match competition.

All members of the rifle team appeared to be very concerned over the theft of the rifle, which was apparently taken from their truck while they were having lunch. There were several other rifle teams participating in the match, and several dozen spectators were also present.

The only lead I developed from the interviews was from a nice young man who worked at a local hardware store. He was a corporal in the Army Reserve and a member of the rifle team. He told me he was a guns enthusiast, and a couple of days earlier had been talking about guns with an unidentified customer who told him about an M-1 rifle hanging over a bar in a saloon in a small town about thirty miles from Butte. I had a list of all the teams that were involved in the match, and a civilian team from that town had participated.

I arrived in the town, which consisted of six or eight buildings on either side of the one paved road that ran through it. It wasn't difficult to locate the only saloon in town. I parked directly in front of it and walked inside. It was much larger inside than I expected, with a long bar across the back of the room running nearly from wall to wall. There were ten or twelve tables scattered about the room. It was devoid of customers, except for five beer-drinking rook players seated at a table near one end of the bar. They all appeared to be in their late sixties or early seventies, and all were dressed in western garb. They didn't even look up as I walked toward the bartender, who was near the cash register at the opposite end of the bar from the rook players. As I approached him, I glanced above the bar and saw an M-1 with a customized stock on display. It was supported by a beautiful rack of deer antlers.

The bartender was about fifty years of age and nearly as round as he was tall. His friendly smile quickly faded as I identified myself. A concerned look appeared on his face as I asked to see the M-1 over the bar. He stood on a stool and retrieved it from the antlers and passed it to me, butt first. I pulled my notebook from my pocket and checked the serial number. It was the stolen weapon.

I asked the bartender about the M-1. He replied that he was the owner of the saloon, but that the rifle did not belong to him. He said that his son, who worked the bar at night and was at home asleep, had purchased the rifle a few weeks previously while attending a rifle match in Butte. I asked the bartender for the name of his son and the location of the residence where he was sleeping. He reluctantly gave me both. I then informed him the rifle had been reported as stolen and that I would have to take it with me. I wrote out a receipt on a sheet from my notebook.

I drove directly to the residence via the bartender's directions. It was a small frame home with a narrow porch across the front. There was a swing on one end. A young man with long, dirty-blond hair sat in the swing. He was shirtless, and a cigarette dangled from between his lips. A can of Schlitz beer was in his right hand. As I approached the porch, he said that his dad had called. He then asked if I was there about the rifle. I flashed my badge and verbally identified myself and told him I was indeed there about the rifle. I used an old trick to get him away from his own surroundings—I told him I needed to talk to him, but would like to do it in my car so I could monitor the radio traffic.

I sat behind the steering wheel, and he was beside me on the passenger side. After I obtained his full name, date of birth, and other identifying data, I started my interrogation. He readily confirmed he was a member of the rifle team that had competed a few weeks previously in the match at Butte. He also stated he had purchased the rifle for fifty dollars from one of the members of the Army Reserve Team from Butte. When I asked for a description of the man, he hesitated and then said he was a slim and tall white male, a PFC with dark curly hair. I knew he was not being truthful, as there was no PFC on the Army Reserve Team and the physical description did not fit any of the team members. I then went on the offensive. I explained to him that I could arrange for a lineup of the team members, and he could point out which one sold the rifle to him. He would be called upon to testify before a Federal Grand Jury and later in United States District Court. I then cautioned him that under Title 18, Section 1001, anyone giving false or misleading information during the course of an official government investigation was subject to a possible prison sentence of five years or a fine of $5,000, or both. I looked him right in the eye and asked him if he wanted to tell me the truth about the rifle. He dropped his head and nodded. He said he took the rifle on impulse when he saw it and several others unattended in a military truck. He explained that other members of his rifle team were unaware that he had taken the rifle, as he immediately put it in the trunk of his car, which was parked beside the truck. He later told his dad and others at the saloon that he had bought the rifle from someone attending the match.

I thanked the young man for being truthful with me and informed him I would make the results of my investigation known to the office of the United States Attorney. I drove back to Butte satisfied with what I had accomplished with the first Bureau case assigned to me for investigation. It was close to five o'clock when I walked into the Butte office with the M-1 over my shoulder. Most of the Butte agents were in the office preparing to leave for the day. I knew they were thinking, "Who the hell is this new agent with a damned rifle on his shoulder?" Secretaries and clerks stopped what they were doing and stared.

I walked over to my supervisor's desk, leaned the rifle against it, and briefly explained to him where and how I recovered the rifle and related the admission of the subject who had stolen it. The supervisor seemed to be a little shocked, and tried to suppress a smile. He instructed me to secure the rifle in the weapon's room, and said he would arrange for me to present the case to an Assistant United States Attorney.

The next day I got my notes in order and late that morning briefed a young Assistant United States Attorney on the entire investigation. When I had completed the briefing, he didn't ask the first question. He only said that he would not authorize prosecution. This meant that I could not obtain a warrant for the subject nor would the case be presented to a Grand Jury for an indictment.

I was a new agent. Who was I to question the wisdom of an Assistant United States Attorney? I simply muttered a thank-you and returned to the office. For the first time since I had been with the Bureau, I felt despondent.

23

My next assignment was a case of theft from interstate shipment. It didn't involve jewels or valuable art being stolen while being transported in interstate commerce, it concerned a couple of boxcars being broken into at the local railyard and the theft of some merchandise of paltry value. After a couple of days I had determined the culprits were a group of neighborhood youths. This time I agreed with the United States Attorney's Office when the case was referred to local authorities to be handled as a juvenile matter.

Other cases I worked during my first days at Butte were just as trifling as my first two assignments. Even though I had been a Federal Agent for five years, I knew I was being tested and had to prove myself all over again. The type of cases I was working would have been assigned by me a few months earlier to an inexperienced ONI agent.

After about six weeks in Butte, I participated in my first apprehension of a fugitive. A teletype was received at the Butte office that stated a Federal fugitive from back east was reportedly at the residence of an acquaintance at Bozeman, Montana. A supervisor assigned the case to an experienced agent named Roy McDaniel and selected me to accompany Roy to Bozeman. As I recall, a warrant was on file for the fugitive for the interstate transportation of a stolen motor vehicle. The teletype furnished his name and physical description and would have said if he was considered armed and dangerous. I don't recall whether or not he was so classified. I do remember it was early on a Friday morning when we received the assignment, as Vicky and I had been invited to dine that evening with the Assistant Special Agent in Charge (ASAC) and his wife at their residence. There was a resident agent at Bozeman, but for some reason he was not available to handle the assignment.

Roy and I drove the eighty-five miles to Bozeman and located the residence where the fugitive reportedly was staying.

It was in an upper-middle class neighborhood. There were no vehicles in the driveway and there didn't appear to be anyone at home, as the drapes were pulled and the grass needed cutting. Roy went to the front door and I scampered around the house to the back door. Ringing of the front and back doorbells and loud and repeated knocks on the doors brought no response. Since there appeared to be no one home, we decided to contact the local police to determine where the homeowner might be employed. As we were getting in the car, I glanced back at the house and noticed the drapes slightly part in the front room and I caught a glimpse of someone quickly peeking out. I told Roy what I had seen and then, without being told, returned to my position at the back door. Roy, who was already in the car, backed it out of the driveway and across the street into the driveway of a neighbor's house. He then made his way to the neighbor's front door all the while keeping an eye on the front of the suspect's residence. Roy identified himself to the housewife who came to the door and from her learned that the lady who lived across the street was a nurse and was employed at a local hospital. Roy told the housewife to call the nurse's place of employment and inform her that the FBI was at her home and she was needed there immediately. Roy returned to his position at the front door of the residence and in about fifteen minutes the nurse arrived. Roy explained to her why we were there. She acknowledged knowing the fugitive and claimed he had not been to her residence and certainly was not there at that time. Roy asked for permission to search and it was readily granted. Roy and the nurse entered through the front door and Roy immediately let me in through the back.

It was a one-story frame home with an attic and a partial basement. We carefully searched the main living area without success, and then completed a fruitless search of the attic. Roy and I then cautiously descended the steps into the basement. Neither of us had our weapons drawn but each had his suit coat unbuttoned for easy access to our revolvers. A hasty inspection of the basement revealed only a laundry room and another area, which had been made into a small bedroom. There was only one place to hide, and that was under the bed. We lifted the bedspread and looked under. There, lying in a fetal position, trying to make himself as small as possible, was our fugitive. We got him out, searched him, and found him to be unarmed. He was handcuffed and transported to the local jail to await return to the jurisdiction where he had been indicted.

Roy and I drove back to Butte feeling like we had done a good day's work and believing we had put feathers in our caps. I picked up Vicky and arrived at the ASAC's residence about twenty minutes late. I explained to him about the fugitive being apprehended in Bozeman, but instead of getting a pat on the back, I got an ass-chewing for being late to his dinner party.

Years later, when I told Big Glen the stories of the M-1 rifle, my first fugitive apprehension, and the ass-chewing I received, he said he wouldn't have received the ass-chewing. When I asked why, he replied, "When that government lawyer wouldn't prosecute the rifle case, I would have told him where he could shove that M-1. I would have been fired and wouldn't have been around to go to a damned dinner party."

24

The next few weeks were hectic. I made a trip with three other agents to Mountain Home Air Force Base, located about fifty miles south of Boise, Idaho. We were dispatched there to investigate the civil rights complaints of a couple of black airmen. The complaints were found to be without merit.

I returned to Butte for a few days before being sent to Missoula, Montana, for a week. I filled in for the resident agent who was on vacation. I was back in Butte for a week and was then sent to Coeur d'Alene, Idaho, which was a two-man resident agency. Coeur d'Alene is in the northern part of the state, about thirty-five miles east of Spokane, Washington. In 1962, it had a population of about 14,000. My assignment was for two weeks, and I was to fill in for a very popular agent who had been there for many years, but had recently been transferred to another Bureau office. He had been well-liked in the community and well-respected by local law enforcement officers.

I arrived in town late at night after a nearly 300-mile drive from Butte. I checked into a small, downtown hotel, and the next morning located the resident agency in the Post Office building. I found the remaining resident agent, Bob Kirkland, at his desk. He was a twelve-year Bureau veteran who was of medium height, slightly heavyset, and had dark hair, which was beginning to recede. When I introduced myself, a warm and friendly smile welcomed me, and I knew it was sincere. After bringing Bob up-to-date on happenings around the Butte office, he handed me a folder containing a neat stack of files that needed immediate attention before they became delinquent. There were leads to be checked involving a mixture of routine cases. I reviewed the contents of the folder and asked a few questions, but before I could leave the office, Bob extended an invitation for dinner that evening at his home. I eagerly accepted.

I found Bob's wife, Lillian, to be a splendid cook and a gracious hostess. She taught English at North Idaho Junior College, and she and Bob were the proud parents of a cute little girl, Kathy, who was a few years older than Gloria. I don't recall where Lillian was from, but I do recall Bob being from Ohio and an attorney. If they had been from Charleston, I would have described Lillian as a Southern Belle and Bob as a true Southern gentlemen.

My two weeks' assignment at Coeur d'Alene was most enjoyable. The weather was cool even though it was late August, and the scenery magnificent. Bob was a delight to be around, and we quickly became friends. We worked separately, but radio contact enabled us to meet frequently for lunch.

Upon returning to Butte, I told Vicky about the captivating city of Coeur d'Alene, but could not find adequate words to recount the splendor of the area. I also told her about Bob and Lillian Kirkland, and how I wished she could know them. I considered Coeur d'Alene the garden spot of the Butte Division.

I had been back in Butte for less than two weeks when I was called into the office of SAC Burke. He asked me how I liked my assignment at Coeur d'Alene, and I replied that it was my most enjoyable time with the Bureau. He smiled and handed me a sealed envelope. It was a Bureau letter, dated September 11, 1962, transferring me from the Butte office to the Coeur d'Alene resident agency. I was astounded. During new agents' training we had been told agents were not assigned to resident agencies while still in their first office. I was ecstatic when the SAC instructed me to make arrangements promptly for the move to Coeur d'Alene.

I nearly ran from the SAC's office to my desk to call Vicky. When she answered, I immediately said, "We've been transferred!"

There was no response for several seconds, and then a weak, "To where?"

I couldn't control my enthusiasm when I replied, "To that beautiful little city of Coeur d'Alene."

I detected jubilation in Vicky's voice as she responded with, "Thank goodness." Vicky had not been content in Butte, but had held up like a trooper. She didn't like the miners, the dirt streets, or the saloons, nor did she enjoy the long days and nights while I had been away. She knew that in a two-man resident agency I would more or less be my own boss and that overnight travel would be very limited.

A few days later, we arrived in Coeur d'Alene and again found it necessary to live in a motel for a month as rental housing was scarce. What we finally rented was well worth the wait. It was a nice three-bedroom home with a garage and a full basement.

After my return to Coeur d'Alene, Bob apprised me as to how the territory covered by the resident agency had been divided between him and the agent whom I was replacing. He advised that Coeur d'Alene was in Kootenai County, and they both worked cases there and both worked cases in Benawak County to the south of Coeur d'Alene. Bob advised that he worked Bonner and Boundary counties to the north and the other agent worked Shashone County to the east. Bob explained that Boundary County bordered British Columbia, and therefore he maintained liaison with the Royal Canadian Mounted Police. He further explained that if any case needed the attention of two agents or was considered dangerous, then they worked it together regardless of where it was located.

Continuing his briefing of the territory, Bob advised there was a small town in Shashone County with a population of less than 3,000 people. It had two houses of prostitution, each with a madam and from six to eight girls at any one time. He said that a girl would work for awhile and then move on only to be replaced by a girl arriving from another city. Bob stated that when a new girl arrived at either house, the madam would immediately send her to the local police department where she paid a small fee to be photographed and fingerprinted. The prints were submitted to the Bureau and an extra photograph was made and later delivered to the FBI agent working the territory. Bob advised the agent would then open a White Slave Traffic Act (WSTA) case to determine if anyone had caused her to travel interstate for immoral purposes. In other words, did a pimp transport her or cause her to be transported across state lines to the house of prostitution?

Continuing, Bob explained that upon learning from the police department that a new girl had arrived in town, the agent would proceed to the house of prostitution and interview her for background data and to attempt to determine what means of transportation she used to arrive in town, with whom, and, if a common carrier was used, who paid for it. Leads would then be sent to the appropriate Bureau offices to check out her story.

I asked Bob if prostitution was legal in Idaho, and he laughed and replied that it was not. He said the two houses had existed since before the turn of the century, when mining was at a peak and the population of the town and surrounding area was predominately male. He said that the current clientele were mostly local miners and regular customers from Coeur d'Alene and Spokane. Bob was of the opinion that local authorities believed prostitution to be an economic necessity for the community, and just ignored the fact it violated state law.

Bob asked me how I felt about working WSTA cases, interviewing prostitutes, and having to go in and out of houses of prostitution. I grinned and replied that it would be a welcome change. A look of concern crossed his face. I then told him about the numerous homosexual investigations I had worked with ONI and how WSTA cases would be something different.

Vicky and I were happy. She and Lillian became instant friends, and she also made friends with other housewives in the neighborhood. I took to my work like a duck to water, and stayed busy, but was home almost every night. The Chief of Detectives of the Coeur d'Alene Police Department, Dick Beam, lived a few houses down the street from us, and he and I became friends. Nearly every weekday, around 9:30 A.M., the Chief of Police, Dick, Bob, a Deputy United States Marshal, other local officers, and I would have coffee at the Tepee Room across the street from City Hall. A lot of information was exchanged at those meetings.

I had been in Coeur d'Alene for about a month when I had my first unassisted apprehension. It was a cool, damp morning and I had just left the Tepee Room and was en route to interview a prostitute whom I didn't have time to talk to the day before. I was about three miles east of town when I noticed a hitchhiker ahead. I slowed as I approached him. He appeared to be in his early twenties and was dressed in jeans and a parka. I looked him over very carefully as I passed. What was familiar about him? Then it dawned on me. I saw what I had looked at for nearly five years. He was wearing what appeared to be black shoes issued to Navy enlisted men. I braked to a stop and backed up. He opened the back door and placed a small overnight bag on the floor. He then opened the front door on the passenger side and sat down. A glance at his shoes confirmed my suspicions. A startled look appeared on his face as he saw the Bureau radio and a second radio on the frequency of the Idaho State Police. I used the element of surprise as I quickly flashed my badge and asked how long he had been AWOL.

Without hesitation, he blurted out, "About two months."

Military personnel who were Absent Without Official Leave (AWOL) in excess of thirty days were declared deserters and their cases were then within Bureau jurisdiction. I placed him under arrest, searched and cuffed him, and returned to Coeur d'Alene. I turned him over to a uniformed officer at the Coeur d'Alene Police Department for processing. I didn't want to be bothered with the paperwork, and I also knew the military paid small monetary rewards to local officers who apprehended deserters. I also figured this move would help cement my good relationship with the police department.

For the next several weeks I worked routine cases and helped Bob on a few of his cases including the burglary of a United States Forest Service office. We also received a call on a cold November morning from the Butte office informing us that a military deserter was to receive a money order later that day at the local Western Union office. We staked out the office with me inside and Bob in his Bureau car parked near the front entrance. Our wait was no more than an hour when the subject came in and, using his true name, asked the clerk if a money order had arrived for him. I stepped behind the subject, between him and the door, and gently tapped him on the shoulder. As he turned I flashed my badge and spoke those magic letters, "FBI." I had another apprehension.

25

From the time I arrived in Coeur d'Alene, in September, until mid-November, I had been in and out of the two houses of prostitution several times each week. I was not there for recreational purposes, but to interview new hookers after they arrived in town. Each of the houses had small sitting rooms for the madams, which they also used as offices. I was allowed to use the rooms for interview purposes. Several times, girls came in to be interviewed scantily clad, and I would send them back to their rooms to get fully dressed. They didn't seem to mind, and would usually respond with friendly smiles.

It soon became apparent to me that the girls had been previously interviewed as they anticipated most of my questions and had acceptable answers readily available. For example, when I would ask how they arrived in town they would say by bus, and frequently without me asking, would volunteer that they had purchased their own tickets. I never interviewed one who could produce her ticket stub. Most times when their fingerprint records came back from the Bureau, they would reveal several arrests for prostitution in various states and under several names. It was obvious the girls were well aware of the elements necessary for violation of the WSTA statute. Their pimps may have driven them to town in their pink convertibles, but you could bet the ranch they would say they came by Greyhound.

I reviewed old files, talked to Bob and some of the older agents at the Butte office, and learned that the game between the Bureau and the hookers of the two houses had gone on for years. Girls would arrive at the houses and shortly thereafter be interviewed. WSTA cases would be opened and leads sent to other Bureau offices for their stories to be checked out. No evidence would be developed to substantiate WSTA violations, and cases were then closed. I felt as though the Bureau was treading water. I was also frustrated because I knew prostitution was a violation of Idaho law and local officials were blatantly ignoring that fact. I didn't like the situation I was in, and made up my mind to do something if and when I had the chance.

Sometime around early December 1962, my opportunity came. I went by the police department and learned a new hooker had checked into one of the houses. A look at her photograph and I knew she was different from the dozens of others I had seen. She didn't have the hard eyes and early facial wrinkles common to most prostitutes. Her physical description information reflected her to be free of tattoos. Except for the identification board held in front of her, the photograph could have passed for one from a high school yearbook. Her name was listed as Jeanette Leigh Holloway, and her age as twenty-two.

I went to the house where she worked and was admitted by the madam. I told her I was there to interview Jeanette. She made her office available to me and excused herself. A few minutes later, a very beautiful young girl entered the room and walked slowly and gracefully toward me.

I stood as she extended her right hand and said, "I am Jeanette Holloway, and I understand you are from the FBI." I was taken aback as I shook her hand, since I had never before touched a hooker, nor had one ever extended her hand for me to shake.

I told her that I was indeed from the FBI as I displayed my credentials to her. She glanced briefly at them as I looked her over. She was of medium height with a figure many starlets would have envied. She had sandy hair in a pageboy cut, a soft olive complexion, and deep blue eyes with long, natural lashes. I knew this girl was different, as she looked back at me with a sincere smile that displayed sparkling white teeth perfectly spaced and obviously the result of teenage braces. As they would say back in Chatham County, she came from good raisin'. Many thoughts raced through my head, but the one that I still recall is that somewhere there were probably parents wondering if their beautiful daughter was dead or alive. I was going to get the truth from this young lady, no matter how long it took.

Her initial interview went like most of the others I had conducted. She claimed to have spent the past six months in Seattle working as a bar girl and turning a few tricks. She said she had heard about the good money that could be made at the houses in Idaho, and had bought her own bus ticket to town. She claimed to have been born and raised in California, but would not identify her hometown or furnish any family information. I thanked her for her cooperation, gave her a friendly smile, and left.

I took an extra-long time for lunch at a local restaurant and then went to the other house and interviewed a new girl who had checked in there. It was mid-afternoon and nearly three hours had passed since I left Jeanette. I returned to the house where she worked and informed the madam I needed to see Jeanette again, as there were a couple of questions I had forgotten to ask her.

Jeanette appeared very well-composed when she came into the madam's office, but I could detect the slightest trace of nervousness in her voice as we exchanged greetings. I pulled out my credentials and held them very close to her face.

I said, "When I talked to you this morning, I showed you these credentials and verbally identified myself as a Special Agent of the Federal Bureau of Investigation. Now I want you to look at these credentials, which identify me as a Federal Agent. I want you to know that I am willing to forget the interview we had earlier provided the information you furnish me now is truthful. Furnishing false information to a Federal Agent could result in punishment of up to five years in prison. I have been a Federal Agent going on six years, and have interviewed my share of thieves, hookers, homosexuals, and other scum. I know people and have made my living up to this point getting them to tell me the truth. You may be a hooker now, but you weren't raised to be one. You come from a good family, and the only thing I want you to do is to tell me what you were taught to tell from infancy—that is the truth."

I had gotten pretty wound up, so I went ahead and played my trump cards. "It took me only a few telephone calls to determine the California Bureau of Vital Statistics has no record of the birth of a Jeanette Leigh Holloway, and there is no such bar or address as you gave for Seattle. If you tell me the truth, I think we can be friends, and the misleading information (never use the word lie) you furnished this morning will be forgotten."

Jeanette dropped her head slightly and I could see her eyes

tear up. She forced a little smile and said, "My name is Jeanette Leigh Pickett. My parents live in San Diego, California. My father is a corporate attorney and is deeply involved in civic and charitable activities. I am eighteen years old. I was due to graduate from high school this past June. In late May, a group from my class had a party at the country club where my parents are members. I have been oversexed since puberty. I had too much to drink at the party and got on the bar and danced. I disrobed until I was completely nude. My parents later found out what I had done and confronted me. We had a big fight, and I ran away from home. I went to Portland, Oregon, where I got a job as a bar girl. It didn't take long for the bar owners to convince me to prostitute myself for them. They kept me in room, board, clothing, a little spending money, and plenty of customers. They also kept most of my earnings. A couple of months ago I heard from another girl who worked at the bar about the two houses here in town. I held back some of my tips for a few weeks and then skipped out. I was truthful when I told you I arrived in town alone by bus."

I obtained from Jeanette the names of the two bar owners in Portland and the address of the bar. She was reluctant to furnish this information, as she was afraid they would send someone to bring her back to Portland. I had to assure her that she would be treated as an informant and that her identity and location would be protected. It took awhile, but I finally won her confidence. She opened up and told how she had been only one of a stable of half a dozen girls who worked out of the bar. I learned from Jeanette all the information she could recall regarding the Portland operation, including personal and identifying data regarding the girls who worked there. I furnished Jeanette my office and home telephone numbers and instructed her to call if she remembered additional information that might be of value.

The next day, I sent off leads to check out Jeanette's story with the San Diego and Portland offices. Within a couple of weeks I had heard from both. Jeanette's identity and other personal data as furnished by her were discreetly confirmed by the San Diego office. The Portland office advised they were well aware of the bar where Jeanette had worked and were cognizant of the owners being members of a local syndicate, which they had under investigation. I hoped Jeanette's information would be of value to them.

About a week after receiving the leads back from San Diego and Portland, I was awakened during the middle of the night by a telephone call at my residence. It was Jeanette, and she said she needed someone to talk to. From the sound of her voice I could detect she had been drinking; however, she assured me that no one could overhear her. She talked about all the hypocrites in town, including some public officials who frequented the houses of prostitution. She also named a few of the officials who didn't have to pay. This really angered her as she complained bitterly of having to pay a fee to be photographed and fingerprinted in order to work in an illegal whorehouse. It was obvious she not only had been drinking, but was, as they said in Chatham County, drunk as a skunk. She talked on for nearly an hour, but I finally got rid of her after promising to drop by and see her in a day or so. I didn't get back to sleep immediately, as Vicky was by then wide awake. It took at least another hour to convince her that the call was strictly business and from a drunken prostitute.

The next morning I decided on a course of action that I knew could result in me being very unpopular in northern Idaho. I drove through lightly falling snow to the house where Jeanette was located. I told the madam that some things in Jeanette's interview didn't check out, and I needed to talk to her again. A few minutes later, she came into the room dressed in tight jeans and a man's light blue dress shirt. She apparently had no hangover as she greeted me pleasantly and with a devilish grin. We exchanged small talk for a few minutes before I said, "Jeanette, I've been thinking about what you said last night. I agree with you that things here are rotten to the core. I think something can be done about it, but I'll need your help. How would you feel about appearing before a Federal Grand Jury in Boise, Idaho, and testifying about how things are here in town?"

She had many questions about the Grand Jury, such as how it functioned, who would be there, who would know of her being there, how would she get there, et cetera. I attempted to answer her questions as best I could, but all the while kept telling her I actually didn't know if the matter would be considered by the Grand Jury and, if so, if her appearance would be required.

Jeanette appeared deep in thought for a brief moment and then looked me directly in eye and said, "If you want me to testify, I will."

The Bureau had recently been given jurisdiction in enforcing a new law enacted by Congress involving Interstate Transportation in Aid of Racketeering (ITAR), and I opened one of the first Bureau cases under this classification. All the information I had developed regarding the operation of the two houses of prostitution and how they were sanctioned by the town, plus the information regarding Jeanette, was furnished to the United States Attorney in Boise. I felt he acted prematurely when he immediately had subpoenas issued for Jeanette, the two madams, the Chief of Police, the Town Treasurer, some other town officials, and myself. We were all to appear the next month before the Federal Grand Jury in Boise. I believed he was attempting to ascertain if organized crime was involved in the operation of the two houses.

Shortly after the subpoenas were served, I was awakened during the early morning hours by a telephone call at my residence. I became instantly awake when the caller identified himself as being on staff at a hospital in Spokane, Washington. He advised Jeanette had been seriously injured when she fell or was pushed from an automobile. He further stated she was unconscious, having suffered a severe head injury. He also advised her purse had been located nearby and it contained my name and telephone number. He said she was about to go to surgery and wanted to know if I was a relative. I told the caller I was not related to her and only knew her casually. He didn't press the matter and apologized for awakening me.

I was upset and couldn't get back to sleep. Vicky, being the good Bureau wife, got up and made coffee. She listened as I tried to figure out what the hell Jeanette was doing in Spokane and who the hell had thrown her out of a damned car. I quickly eliminated a mob connection, as they would have executed her before throwing her out of a car. Would she live? This and many other questions were on my mind as I nibbled over an early-morning breakfast.

99

I arrived at the office an hour earlier than usual and started calling the Spokane resident agency. Finally, an agent answered shortly before 8:00 A.M. I briefed him regarding Jeanette, her Portland and Idaho activities, and how she was being groomed to become an informant. He advised he would immediately start making inquiries. It was late afternoon when he called back. He stated Jeanette had successful surgery for a small blood clot on the brain, was doing very well, and was not expected to be hospitalized very long. He said his investigation disclosed that Jeanette was given a ride by one of her customers to Spokane, who dropped her off at a local bar before going home to his wife. She began drinking with some local thugs and went for a ride with them. There was a disagreement over money and sex, and she either jumped or was pushed from the car. The agent advised there appeared to be no Federal violation involved and local authorities were conducting their own investigation. I thanked the agent for his prompt and able assistance and offered to return the favor should he need anything in my territory.

This story needs a good ending, but unfortunately it didn't turn out that way. Jeanette was released from the hospital after a couple of weeks and immediately returned to work as a prostitute at the same house wearing an auburn-colored wig. A few weeks later, she testified as a witness before the Federal Grand Jury in Boise. I also testified. The Chief of Police, Town Treasurer, some other local officials, and the two madams also appeared before the Grand Jury. I recall that I testified about how the houses operated, the girls had to check in with the police department, and had to pay fees to be photographed and fingerprinted. I also testified that the existence of the two houses was well-known to prostitutes in the western United States, and that they traveled interstate to work in the houses. I don't know what the other witnesses testified to, if anything, as Grand Jury proceedings are secret and some witnesses may have taken the Fifth Amendment. I do know that not a damned thing resulted from the Grand Jury investigation. The houses kept on operating. Jeanette returned to work for awhile longer and then one day was gone. I felt as though I had failed her, and to this day wonder what happened to her.

26

Dirty snow still lay unmelted along the sidewalks, even though it was mid-March and a touch of spring was in the air. Bob and I had missed our regular morning meeting at the Tepee Room, as we both had reports to dictate. I finished dictating first and drove over to the police department to check a name through their files. While there I stepped into the office of my friend, Dick Beam, Chief of Detectives. I explained to him why Bob and I had missed the morning coffee meeting. He kidded me about the Bureau having so damned much paperwork to do that we didn't have time to enjoy life. I kidded him back by saying he was probably upset because he must have been stuck with the coffee tab that morning. I told Dick I was on my way to Wallace, Idaho, to check out a lead on a fugitive who reportedly wintered there but had apparently moved on. Before I could leave, Dick told me about a couple of unknown subjects who were last known to be operating in the southern part of the state. He advised that they were suspected of passing stolen payroll checks taken in safe robberies. He knew the Bureau would be interested if the checks went out of state to a Federal Reserve Bank before making their way back to the drawee banks in Idaho. Dick also described the color, make, and model of the automobile they were suspected of using along with the number of the stolen license tag believed to be on the vehicle. I pulled out a small notebook, which I always carried, and recorded the vehicle description and tag number.

I drove to Wallace enjoying the bright sunshine and the warm day. It was Friday, and Vicky and I intended to drive over the next day with Gloria to do some shopping in Spokane. I stopped at the Wallace Post Office and received instructions on how to get to the rural address where the fugitive had possibly spent the winter. While at the post office, I learned no mail had been delivered to the address for several years and that they had no record of the fugitive by his true name or any of his known aliases.

I drove on out to the location, which was a few miles west of town. It was an old boarded-up frame dwelling which obviously had not been occupied for a number of years. Another false lead. However, before heading back to town, I thought I would give it the old extra effort. There was a small general store nearby, and I stopped near the front doors as there were no other vehicles around. I didn't have a photograph of the fugitive, just his name, aliases, and physical description. I entered the building, which must have dated back to the previous century. The odor of oil and leather permeated my nostrils as I made my way across the room. The only person around was a small man who appeared to be in his seventies. He was dressed in cowboy garb, including a large western hat. I assumed he was the proprietor. He looked me over as I approached. I pulled my credentials from my pocket and displayed them to him as I explained I was with the FBI and was seeking information regarding a Federal fugitive who may recently have been in the area. The old gentleman studied my credentials, which contained my photograph, for an unusually long time.

Finally, he looked at me and said, "Nope, never seen him before in my life. He's a mean looking sum bitch. I sure as hell hope you catch him." What could I say? I thanked him for his interest and walked back to my car chuckling all the way. I could hardly wait to tell Bob, Lillian, and Vicky what had happened.

Years later, when I told this story to Big Glen, he grinned as he spat tobacco juice and said, "Maybe you should have told the old fellow to call you if he ever saw the mean-looking sum bitch."

I decided to check the fugitive through the files of the police department and sheriff's department in Wallace. It was shortly after noon, and I thought maybe I could have lunch with Richard Mall, who was Chief of Police. There was a small restaurant in Wallace that served an absolutely delicious roast beef sandwich. As I drove along Pine Street, I noticed an automobile parked parallel to the curb with a white male sitting behind the steering wheel. The vehicle matched the description of the one furnished to me earlier that day by Dick Beam. I drove on down the street for a couple of blocks and turned around. As I slowly approached from the rear, I noted the number of the license tag and knew without looking it was the same as the one I had recorded in my notebook. My heart skipped a beat or two as I drove past the vehicle and pulled into a gasoline station half a block away. I parked so that I could see the suspect's vehicle and the occupant. I then noticed the second subject. He was pacing up and down the sidewalk about fifty yards behind the automobile. He appeared to be extremely nervous or hyper and walked hurriedly back to the vehicle and conversed briefly with the driver through the passenger's window. He then returned to his original sidewalk location behind the automobile. Several times he looked into a large window of a store or office. I couldn't make out what type business it was from my vantage point. Finally, he went inside. I figured the subjects were either in town casing a place for a safe robbery or were trying to pass stolen payroll checks.

I made the decision to leave my car and casually walk past the suspect's vehicle and see if I could glance in the window of the building to see what the subject was doing inside. As I approached the car, a jolt of adrenaline went through my body. The motor of the automobile was running, and the driver sure as hell didn't need the heater on such a nice day. It meant one thing to me, and that was a quick getaway! I didn't even glance at the driver as I hastened my pace. The sidewalks on both sides of the street were devoid of pedestrians. A few yards from the building I noted a sign on the window reflecting it to be the office of Anderson Oil Company. What in hell would the suspect be doing in there? As I got even with the large window, which bordered the sidewalk, I turned my head slightly to the left and looked inside. There was no question as to what the subject was doing. He was squatting in front of a safe with his back to me. Desk and file drawers were open and obviously had been rifled as papers and debris littered the floor. I was about to dash inside but stopped abruptly when I saw a middle-aged lady lying on her back on the floor near the counter. Her dress was in disarray and her eyes were closed. She was not moving. I didn't know if she was dead or alive. In a split-second I made my decision. If she was alive and I went inside, she could be hurt or killed in a gun battle or taken hostage. If I waited outside, I could make my move when the subject exited the building. I stood with my back to the wall

103

directly beside the door, but on the opposite side from the wait-ing car. I was carrying the .38 caliber Colt revolver Dad had given to me nearly six years earlier. I had fired it hundreds of times on the range, but never had occasion to draw it for its intended pur-pose. I only had to wait a few seconds before the subject came out the door, turned to his right, and started toward the waiting car. He didn't even glance in my direction.

He only got a step or two beyond the window when I over-took him from the rear and loudly uttered those magic words, "Halt, FBI."

The subject stopped dead in his tracks. In his left hand he held a brown paper bag, which I ordered him to drop. He did so without hesitation. My heart was pounding, and I could feel the blood rushing through my body. I ordered the subject to face the brick wall and lean against it with his hands and his feet spread. This is known as assuming the position. The subject knew the drill very well. What now? I didn't have handcuffs with me and didn't like being exposed for any action his partner might take. Apparently, the subject sensed I was in a dilemma. He turned quickly and faced me. He was slightly shorter than me but much more muscular with the body and build of a middleweight. He had black wavy hair and deepset dark eyes behind a ruddy com-plexion. As the old gentleman said a half hour earlier, he was a mean-looking sum bitch.

His lips barely parted, and with a sneer he said, "You ain't FBI."

I drew my badge from the left front pocket of my trousers in what must have been record time. I flashed it and at the same time cocked the hammer of my pistol and said, "This badge says I am, and you take one more step and I'll damn sure kill you." He immediately assumed his position against the wall.

I saw movement to my right and a quick glance revealed it to be a uniformed Wallace policeman whom I knew. I quickly told him the subject against the wall had just pulled a robbery, and that his partner was waiting down the street. As the policeman cuffed the subject, the county sheriff screeched to a stop in his cruiser. Fortunately, he came from the opposite direction from the waiting getaway car. Before the sheriff could get out, I jumped in beside him and said, "There's a robbery in progress.

The getaway car and driver are just down the street."

The sheriff screeched off and at my instructions pulled beside the suspect vehicle. I had been fortunate, as a delivery truck had parked behind the getaway car, blocking the driver's view to his rear. I bailed out of the sheriff's cruiser and, with my pistol in the face of the getaway driver, ordered him to turn off the motor and slowly place both hands on the steering wheel. He complied with my instructions to the letter. By that time, sheriff's deputies and local policemen were everywhere. The suspect driver was searched and handcuffed by local officers as I walked back to the oil company office. The local rescue squad was just arriving, and I waited outside with Chief Mall. He told me a lady in a store across the street had seen me holding a man at gunpoint and thought I was robbing him. She had called the police station and the first officer to my assistance was nearby and heard the radio broadcast.

In a few moments a member of the rescue squad emerged from the oil company office and said the lady would be okay. She had been knocked unconscious. It was subsequently determined the blow came from a sock filled with soap and was in the paper bag which I had the subject to drop. Currency from the office was also in the bag.

It was over! My hands shook as I lit a cigarette. Who were these two thugs? The one I had apprehended leaving the office was Gino Scusselle, age thirty-five. The driver was Robert Wellman Nelson, age forty-five. Both were Federal parolees from the Federal prison at McNeil Island, Washington. Scusselle had been convicted of bank robbery and Nelson of mail fraud. The paroles of both subjects were revoked, and they were returned to prison to complete very lengthy sentences.

The actions I took that warm March day many years ago did not go unnoticed. The story was featured on the evening news of a Spokane television station. The AP and UPI also picked up the story, and it appeared in newspapers throughout the country. A few weeks later, I received a personal letter of commendation from Director Hoover, along with a check for an incentive award. I still have the letter, which is framed and hanging on my den wall. I can see it across the room as I write this story.

Many times I have been asked how I felt during those hectic moments in Wallace, Idaho. It is difficult to describe, but somewhat similar to the feelings I had in high school waiting for and returning the opening kickoff of a football game. Was I nervous? I think extremely stimulated would be a better description. Adrenaline was pumping through my body as it never had before. I was very concerned as to the condition of the lady lying on the floor. I knew one thing for sure, and that was I had rather have been where I was at that moment than any other place on earth. I did what I had been trained to do.

When I got home that evening, Vicky had already heard the story on the radio. I nevertheless had to tell her about it in detail. She then asked more questions than a Philadelphia lawyer.

After I finally settled down, I thought how close I had come to killing a man who was just a few feet from me. I carefully unloaded my Colt revolver and cocked the hammer. I then very gently applied pressure to the trigger. I was astonished at the minimum amount needed before the hammer fell. Gino Scusselle was a very, very lucky man.

Years later, when I told Big Glen of this incident, he said, "If that Italian bank robber had taken one more small step, it would have been one giant step for mankind."

FBI Agent Gets His Man at the Door

WALLACE, Idaho (AP) — A Federal Bureau of Investigation agent, shadowing two men, frustrated a daylight robbery of an oil company in downtown Wallace Friday, Shoshone County sheriff's deputies said.

Charged with robbery and held under $10,000 bond each were Teino Scuselle and Robert W. Nelson, recently employed at the Bunker Hill Co. at Kellogg.

Deputies said Robert Emerson, FBI agent in charge of the Coeur d'Alene office, was following the pair on another matter when he saw a clerk in the office of the Anderson Oil Co., sprawled on the floor and Scusselle hurrying for the door.

He took Scusselle into custody as he left the office and picked up Nelson in a car a block away from the scene, deputies said.

Mrs. Bertha Wood, clerk at the oil company office, said she had just put the day's receipts in the safe when a man entered, knocked her to the floor with a soap-filled sock. He grabbed her purse and rifled several office drawers before fleeing — right into the arms of the man standing outside, Mrs. Wood said.

AP story about the author's daring capture of two robbery suspects.

UNITED STATES DEPARTMENT OF JUSTICE

FEDERAL BUREAU OF INVESTIGATION

WASHINGTON 25, D.C.

April 23, 1963

PERSONAL

Mr. Robert D. Emerson
Federal Bureau of Investigation
Butte, Montana

Dear Mr. Emerson:

It gives me considerable pleasure to commend you
and to advise that I have approved an incentive award for you in
the amount of $150.00 in recognition of your superior perform-
ance in apprehending Robert Wellman Nelson and Gino Scusselle
immediately after they had collaborated in an armed robbery.
Enclosed is a check for $123.00 which represents this award
less withholding tax.

You certainly were most alert in recognizing the
automobile license number which had been furnished you as that
on the car being used by Nelson and Scusselle who also were
possible suspects in an Interstate Transportation of Stolen Property case. Your prompt, aggressive and courageous actions
after observing these two men acting in a suspicious manner were
exemplary. I do not want the occasion to pass without expressing
my appreciation for the splendid job you did in this instance.

Sincerely yours,

J. Edgar Hoover

Enclosure

*April 23, 1963 letter from FBI Director J. Edgar Hoover to
the author.*

27

The first week of May 1963 brought a visit from Mom and Dad. Vicky, Gloria, and I met them at the airport in Spokane. I knew Dad had flown before and had even taken a few flying lessons just prior to World War II. I also knew Mom had never been near an airplane. We didn't know what to expect. Vicky and I were both relieved to see her smiling face as she and Dad disembarked from the plane. On the drive to Coeur d'Alene, Dad told us how once they got airborne, Mom requested his window seat so she could better see outside.

I had taken ten days annual leave to be with my parents and to take them on an automobile tour of Montana and Idaho. It was to be topped off with a visit to Yellowstone National Park. Dad had brought a movie camera with him, and we used it frequently. Vicky filmed Dad and me throwing snowballs at each other in a canyon near Kellogg, Idaho.

Before starting our trip to Yellowstone, I wanted my parents to rest for a couple of days so we did some local sight-seeing. Dad accompanied me to meet the local sheriff and chief of police. It appeared they enjoyed meeting him, as they had many questions about southern law enforcement.

When we started the long drive to Yellowstone, I chose to go by way of Missoula, Montana, and on down to Butte. As we neared Missoula, we saw the smoke jumpers of the United States Forest Service conducting practice at their headquarters. After passing through Missoula, Dad became very impressed with the vastness of the territory and the long distances between towns. He would watch for the small homemade signs, which appeared occasionally, designating narrow unpaved trails indicating the Bar X or some other ranch was ten, fifteen, or even twenty miles down the trail. He was fascinated by not seeing any fences beside the road and cattle grazing unattended on open ranges, which seemed to extend forever.

I'll always remember when a large flock of sheep blocked the road as they crossed. There were hundreds of them, worked only by an old sheepherder and one sheepdog. Soon sheep were all around our car. Dad was enchanted with the work of the sheepdog. Gloria was beside herself and insisted on getting out of the car to touch a lamb. The old sheepherder didn't even acknowledge our presence as he carefully guided the flock to safety.

We spent a day in Butte, and while there Dad and I visited the Butte office, where he met SAC Burke. They had a long chat about law enforcement in North Carolina compared to that of the Great Northwest. They also discovered they had many mutual friends in North Carolina. We completed our stay in Butte with a visit to the large open-pit copper mine, and then it was on to Yellowstone. Mom and Dad loved every minute of the two days we were there, as did Gloria, Vicky, and I. Our next stop was Virginia City, Montana. It is a small town preserved just as it was before the turn of the century. What caught Dad's eye was a two-story wooden hotel with a two-story outhouse attached to it. I'm not an architect, so I don't know how it worked, but it darned sure was there.

For several days we leisurely made our way back toward Coeur d'Alene, following the Bitterroot Mountains along the Montana–Idaho border. It was an interesting and exciting trip for all of us. A couple of days later, Vicky, Gloria, and I bade farewell to Mom and Dad as they boarded their flight at Spokane. It had been a wonderful ten days.

28

When I returned to work, there was a letter waiting for me from the Bureau. It was transferring me to the resident agency at Grand Forks, North Dakota, which was in the Minneapolis Division. I received the letter with mixed emotions, as I was anxious to report to my second office, and yet Vicky and I enjoyed Coeur d'Alene and had made several close friends there. A day or so later, I received a second letter from the Bureau, dated May 17, 1963. It rescinded the transfer to Grand Forks with an explanation that Bureau policy prohibited a transfer from a resident agency in one Division to a resident agency in another Division. An agent had to be at the Division office for at least six months before being sent to a resident agency. This second letter transferred me to the Minneapolis office on or after the date of receipt. Apparently, the Butte office was unaware of the six-month rule, or elected to ignore it, as I was at Butte for just over three months before being transferred to Coeur d'Alene. A day after receiving the transfer letter to Minneapolis, I received a call from the Butte ASAC, who instructed me to remain in Coeur d'Alene to assist Bob in training my replacement and to make arrangements to leave for Minneapolis immediately after the Fourth of July. Within a week, my replacement, Al Gibson, arrived in Coeur d'Alene. For the next several weeks, I worked run-of-the-mill cases and familiarized Al with my territory.

It was late on a Friday afternoon during mid-June, and Bob and I were still at the office. Al had left for the day. Bob answered the telephone as I kept on dictating. When he hung up, I stopped and gave him my attention as I sensed something was up. He said the call concerned a possible Information Order (IO) fugitive. Most people refer to IO's as wanted posters. Continuing, Bob said the caller was a United States Forest Service employee stationed at a remote camp several miles southeast of St. Maries, Idaho. He had driven to St. Maries to deliver mail to the post office, and while there noticed the IO's on the bulletin board.

111

Bob advised the caller firmly believed one of the IO's was identical to a temporary Forest Service firefighter at the camp. The caller identified the IO as Jack Dempsey Green. Bob instructed the caller to wait at the police department in St. Maries, and we would meet him there as quickly as possible. It was not unusual to receive information from citizens who believed they had seen IO fugitives, and their interest and help were always appreciated. Unfortunately, nearly all of their sightings turned out not to be IO subjects, but rather people who resembled them. Agents always promptly responded to all reported sightings, as they could lead to the capture of badly wanted and dangerous criminals. IO subjects were like the Who's Who of criminal society.

Bob and I located the IO in our files and hurried to Bob's automobile. He drove as I read aloud to him all the information contained in the IO. Jack Dempsey Green had aliases of Charles Raymond Boden, Charles R. Boulton, Jack Henry Green, Jack Carl Lane, Carl J. Lucker, John Henry Luckert, Bill Martin, Dennis Shavers, Robert Jack Starr and others. Green was a white male born August 23, 1929, at Lyman, Mississippi. He was five-six and weighed from 140 to 150 pounds. He had brown eyes and brown, receding hair. The IO reflected a prior conviction for armed robbery and escape. It also stated a Federal warrant was issued November 7, 1962, at Denver, Colorado, charging Green with unlawful flight to avoid prosecution for armed robbery. The IO contained a photograph of Green and a copy of his inked fingerprint impressions. It also indicated he should be considered dangerous.

We covered the sixty-five miles to St. Maries in what must have been record time. As we entered the police station, we spotted the Forest Service employee and identified ourselves to him. He introduced himself as Paul Tannen, and said he was second in command of a group of about one hundred firefighters who were at a camp in a remote area about fifteen miles from St. Maries. We displayed the IO of Jack Dempsey Green to him, and he said the photograph appeared to be identical to that of a temporary firefighter who was sent to the camp a few days earlier. Mr. Tannen studied the IO and said the person he suspected was not employed under the name Jack Dempsey Green. He told us

INTERSTATE FLIGHT - ARMED ROBBERY
WANTED BY FBI
JACK DEMPSEY GREEN

I. O.
No. 3682
6-4-63

FBI No. 335,287 A

ALIASES: Charles Raymond Boden, Charles R. Boulton, Jack Henry Green, Jack Carl Lane, Carl J. Lucker, Jack Henry Luckert, Bill Martin, Dennis Shavers, Robert Jack Starr and others

11 S 30 Wt 14   Ref: 22 22 30
  I   3 W   3 19 19

Photographs taken 1962

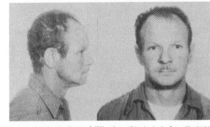

DESCRIPTION
AGE: 33, born August 23, 1929, Lyman, Mississippi
HEIGHT: 5'6"   COMPLEXION: medium
WEIGHT: 140 to 150 pounds   RACE: white
BUILD: medium   NATIONALITY: American
HAIR: brown, receding   OCCUPATIONS: laborer, ranch
EYES: brown   worker, smelterman, truck driver
SCARS AND MARKS: scar above left eye, scar center of forehead, scar right eyebrow, several pitted scars on forehead, cut scar left elbow, faint burn scar right elbow, small scar right wrist

CRIMINAL RECORD
Green has been convicted of robbery and escape.

CAUTION
GREEN IS BEING SOUGHT IN CONNECTION WITH A ROBBERY IN WHICH A .38 CALIBER SNUB-NOSED REVOLVER WAS USED. CONSIDER DANGEROUS.

A Federal warrant was issued on November 7, 1962, at Denver, Colorado, charging Green with unlawful interstate flight to avoid prosecution for armed robbery (Title 18, U. S. Code, Section 1073).

IF YOU HAVE INFORMATION CONCERNING THIS PERSON, PLEASE CONTACT YOUR LOCAL FBI OFFICE. PHONE NUMBER LISTED BELOW. OTHER OFFICES LISTED ON BACK.

Identification Order No. 3682
June 4, 1963

Director
Federal Bureau of Investigation
Washington 25, D. C.

Apprehended June 1963 by FBI Special Agents, Robert J. Kirkland and Robert D. Emerson, near St. Maries, Idaho.

the name the suspect was using, but I don't recall what it was except it was not one of Green's known aliases. Mr. Tannen readily agreed to lead us to the camp, and said he didn't think Bob's Bureau automobile would have any difficulty traversing the trail. It was dark when we followed the Forest Service pick-up out of St. Maries, and the drive to the camp took as long as the drive from Coeur d'Alene. As agreed, Mr. Tannen stopped his pickup a few hundred yards from the camp, and we left the Bureau automobile beside the trail and rode into the camp with Mr. Tannen. To our surprise, there were no permanent structures in the camp, as it was an interim facility with the office, mess hall, and all living accommodations being tents. Bob and I knew we would stick out like sore thumbs if seen in our business suits, so

113

we waited in the pickup while Mr. Tannen went to the office. He returned in just a couple of minutes, and said the suspect was in a tent at the far end of the camp. Bob and I were unobserved as we followed Mr. Tannen in the darkness to the camp office, which we found well-illuminated by Coleman lanterns. We met the camp's Chief Forest Service officer, Doug Hunt, who cordially received us. He studied the IO and agreed with Mr. Tannen that the photo appeared identical to that of the temporary firefighter who had recently joined them.

As Mr. Hunt, Bob, and I discussed how best to check out the suspect, Mr. Tannen went to the mess hall and returned with Spam sandwiches and coffee. Bob and I were famished, as neither of us had eaten anything since lunch. After wolfing down the sandwiches, we sipped on the coffee as we settled on a plan. Mr. Tannen would go to the suspect's tent and inform him that he and several other firefighters were being transferred to another camp the next morning, therefore he was needed at the office so some paperwork could be completed.

When Mr. Tannen left on his mission, Bob and I took our positions on each side of the single entrance to the tent. In a few minutes, Mr. Tannen returned, followed by the suspect. When the suspect entered the tent, Bob and I blocked the only escape route he might have. Bob announced to him that we were FBI agents, and I told him to keep his hands where we could see them.

Bob displayed the IO to the suspect who said, "It may look like me but it ain't." Bob asked for some identification, and the suspect said he didn't have any, as his wallet and other personal effects had been stolen.

I wish I could take credit for what took place next, but it was all Bob's idea. He had noticed a small folding desk in the tent with an inkpad on it. He asked Mr. Hunt for a plain sheet of bond paper, and I knew immediately what was to take place. Bob folded the paper, placed it over the edge of the desk, and held it in place with tape. Without asking, Bob grasped the right hand of the suspect, and quickly rolled his thumb and index finger on the inkpad, and then rolled the same two fingers on the bond paper. The suspect didn't say a word as Bob compared the newly acquired inked impressions with the same two fingers on the IO.

Bob then handed the bond paper and IO to me while he watched the suspect. It didn't take an expert to immediately know the prints were identical. I looked at Bob and nodded. Bob told the suspect he was under arrest. He mildly resisted as we handcuffed him. He was not armed. On the trip to jail in Coeur d'Alene, Jack Dempsey Green acknowledged his true identity.

Some Bureau agents have spent an entire career without participating in the apprehension of an IO fugitive. My first office had proven to be an interesting and exciting fourteen months. I looked forward to Minneapolis.

29

A day or so after the Fourth of July, 1963, Vicky and I placed our furniture in storage for the third time in eighteen months. We packed our car and bade farewell to our many friends, the Kirklands, and to my replacement, Al Gibson. We started the long drive to Minneapolis. We arrived in Butte late the first day and spent the night in a hotel across the street from the Butte office. The next morning, I signed out of the Butte Division after brief good-byes with the ASAC and the new SAC (Burke had retired).

The second night was spent in Miles City, Montana, and the third somewhere in South Dakota. We arrived in Minneapolis after dark on the fourth day and checked into a very nice hotel in the heart of the city. The next morning, I reported to the Minneapolis office and shortly thereafter met with the SAC. He was aware of my cancelled transfer to the Grand Forks resident agency. He advised I would be assigned to the Minneapolis office and should locate an apartment in the area. He said I would be there very little, as he wanted me to travel to various resident agencies in the Dakotas and Minnesota for the next six months helping out as needed. He advised that after meeting the six-month requirement of being assigned to the Division office, I would be transferred to Grand Forks. This didn't make sense to me. I had already been a resident agent for ten months, and was now expected to travel from one resident agency to another over three states for six months while my family maintained a residence in Minneapolis. I felt as though my family and I were being penalized just so the six-month assignment rule could be fulfilled. What could I say? I would be gone for weeks at a time, leaving Vicky and Gloria in a large city where they didn't know anyone. After being told to take my time in locating an apartment, I left the SAC's office in a daze. I went back to the hotel and checked us out, as it was too expensive. Vicky and I found a nice motel on the outskirts of Minneapolis. It was to be our home for the next six days as we explored the city of Minneapolis looking for a suitable apartment. We even crossed the river and looked in the St. Paul area. Several times we thought we had located an acceptable place, only to learn that children were not allowed. Each day Vicky and I became more discouraged, knowing that when we found an apartment and our furniture arrived, I would be gone.

I didn't think I could leave Vicky and Gloria to fend for themselves in a metropolitan area like Minneapolis. It would be mid-January before I would be eligible for transfer to Grand Forks. How would Vicky drive on snow and ice in a Minnesota winter? Who would look after Gloria if Vicky became ill while I was several hundred miles away at some remote resident agency? These and many other questions worried me. After a fruitless week of apartment searching, Vicky and I were exhausted, disappointed, and depressed. I had lots of annual leave accumulated, so we decided to take three weeks vacation and drive home. We wanted to think about our situation and discuss it with Dad.

As we entered North Carolina, across the Great Smoky Mountains, an incident occurred that profoundly affected Vicky and me. We had been telling Gloria about her grandfather Moore's farm and the various animals she would see. We also told her how she could fish in his pond. Her response was: "If I catch a fish, we can take it back to the motel and cook it."

I looked at Vicky and saw tears in her eyes. I knew at that moment I wasn't going back to Minneapolis and spend six months on the road away from Vicky and Gloria, just so I could be a resident agent in, of all places, Grand Forks, North Dakota. I loved the FBI, but I loved my family more.

After our arrival in Chatham County, we tried to relax while visiting our folks. I could tell Dad knew something as wrong, but he didn't pry. He knew our trip home was premature, as he and Mom had visited us in Idaho just two months earlier.

On the third night at Christian Hill, Dad, Mom, Vicky, and I were sitting in the big rockers on the large front porch. A welcome coolness was in the air, and lightning in the distance was followed by the deep rumble of thunder. Gloria was sleeping soundly after a hard day of play. Dad was smoking a pipe for a change and the sweet aroma from the Prince Albert seemed unusually pleasant.

117

It was dark, and I couldn't read expressions as I related the plight that Vicky, Gloria, and I faced. After I had my say, with Vicky occasionally joining in, I was startled to hear Mom immediately respond, "Robert, I don't want you to leave Gloria and Vicky in Minneapolis, and I don't want the three of you in faraway North Dakota. I want you closer home." Mom was from the old school and usually did not actively participate when serious situations arose. In this case, I could tell from her voice that she was adamant in her opinion.

Dad put another match to his pipe, took a few puffs, and asked, "What do you want to do?"

I thought for a moment and replied, "If I remain with the FBI, I can expect to be in my second office for about five years. This would mean five years at Grand Forks, and after that, another transfer. If I'm lucky, it would be to somewhere in the South; if not, to a large office, such as Chicago or New York. I want more than anything to remain in law enforcement and intend to do so; however, Vicky and I love North Carolina, and we want to raise our family here."

Dad immediately had a possible solution to our problem. He said, "You and I will go to Raleigh tomorrow and see Walter Anderson." I knew Mr. Anderson to be Director of the North Carolina State Bureau of Investigation (SBI).

The following morning, July 22, 1963, Dad and I left Christian Hill early and stopped at the Sheriff's Office in Pittsboro. Shortly after 8:00 A.M., Dad placed a telephone call to Mr. Anderson, whom he had known for several years. An hour later, we were in Mr. Anderson's office at SBI Headquarters. He was a giant of a man who stood about six feet four inches and weighed in excess of two hundred and fifty pounds. He had spent his entire career in law enforcement, having previously served as Chief of Police in both Winston-Salem and Charlotte. He was also a lay minister in the Methodist church. Mr. Anderson listened attentively as I explained my situation to him. I finished by telling him I wanted to remain in law enforcement and wanted to do so in North Carolina.

Mr. Anderson knew I was well aware of the mission of the SBI and only briefly mentioned their main responsibility was to assist local officers. He stated he only had twenty-eight Special Agents assigned throughout the entire state; however, he advised the legislature had just authorized two additional Special Agent positions. He stated one position had already been filled, but if I elected to resign from the FBI, he would start me as Special Agent (Grade II) if I would agree to serve as resident agent at Marion, North Carolina for two years. He said he would then transfer me back to Raleigh or even Siler City, if I desired. Mr. Anderson informed me Marion was the county seat of McDowell County, and was located about thirty-five miles east of Asheville.

I could hardly believe what I had just heard. I was being offered an opportunity to do what I loved doing in my home state. Of course I would have to give up six years of government service and take a substantial reduction in salary, but I wouldn't be in Grand Forks, North Dakota. Vicky and I could visit our folks, and Gloria could grow up in the Old North State visiting her grandparents regularly. I didn't hesitate, and did a good job of controlling my emotions, as I informed Mr. Anderson I would be proud to become a Special Agent of the SBI. We shook hands, and he stated I should report to his office on August 1, 1963, to be sworn in. He advised a week of training and indoctrination would follow, during which time I could continue to live with my parents. The following day, July 23, 1963, I telephoned the SAC in Minneapolis and tendered my verbal resignation from the FBI. On July 27, I submitted it in writing to Mr. Hoover.

Years later, when I told Big Glen about my resignation from the FBI, he responded with, "You shouldn't have rented houses and apartments. You should have bought a Winnebago and when they said move, just cranked up the damned thing."

30

Vicky was happy over my decision to join the SBI and could hardly wait to see the town of Marion. A couple of days after my meeting with Mr. Anderson, Vicky, Gloria, and I drove to Marion and found it to be a typical small North Carolina town with a population of about 3,500. We rented a three-bedroom brick home in a very nice neighborhood. I then called the movers in Coeur d'Alene and gave them instructions to deliver our furniture to our Marion address on or about August 13.

On Thursday morning, August 1, 1963, one of Dad's deputies dropped me off at SBI Headquarters. Mr. Anderson had previously informed me that I would be issued a vehicle on the day I was sworn in. I reported to Mr. Anderson's office, and a few minutes later we walked across the street to the state capital and entered the office of the Honorable Thad Eure, North Carolina Secretary of State. As Mr. Eure administered the oath of office to me, the hair on the back of my neck stood up and a cold chill ran down my spine. I didn't have this feeling when I was sworn in as a Special Agent with ONI or the FBI. I felt as though I had come home, and the six years of federal service had only been preparation for me to face what lay ahead.

I returned with Mr. Anderson to SBI Headquarters, where I was issued a badge, credentials, and the keys to a new 1963 Chevrolet sedan. The next few days were busy, as I was given a crash course on SBI policies and procedures, North Carolina criminal law, crime scene searches, fingerprinting, photography, and numerous other subjects. I was issued a dictaphone, camera, binoculars, fingerprint material, boxes of dental plaster, and stainless steel adjustable frames for pouring casts. I also received numerous boxes, glass and plastic containers, and envelopes, all of various sizes, for use in collecting, identifying, and preserving physical evidence. All of the material issued to me would barely fit into the trunk of my car. The only item I declined was a .38 caliber revolver with a two-inch barrel. The SBI at that time had no restrictions on agents carrying their own personal weapons. I still had the .38 caliber Colt that Dad had given to me six years earlier, and I had purchased a .357 caliber Smith & Wesson Combat Magnum while with the FBI. It was considered by most FBI firearms experts to be the finest handgun in the world at that time. When loaded with the proper ammunition, a bullet from it would penetrate the block of an automobile. I had also acquired a handmade wooden console, which was secured beside me on the front seat of my vehicle. The top of the console was slotted to accommodate a clipboard that held a legal pad. Inside the console, I kept the .357 Magnum, a three-cell flashlight, extra batteries, handcuffs, a blackjack, extra ammunition, a small magnifying glass, a list of all SBI agents with their duty stations, telephone numbers, and radio call numbers.

On Monday, August 12, 1963, Vicky and Gloria followed in our personal automobile as I drove the new Chevrolet to Marion. We stayed a couple of nights in a local motel until our furniture arrived. As it turned out, we had made a splendid selection of the house we had rented, as it had a finished basement, which became my office. Field agents at that time were not furnished office space and worked out of their homes. After a few days we were settled in, and most material issued to me in Raleigh was stored in my office. This made room in the trunk of my car for a large metal box, which contained my camera, binoculars, fingerprint supplies, evidence containers, ultraviolet powder, and pencils (used for secretly marking money or other material), an ultraviolet light and dental plaster for making casts. I also carried in the trunk a sleeping bag and several boxes of military c-rations. A person can get very cold and hungry on a long stakeout. Another item that I had acquired was a military surplus .30 caliber carbine equipped with a selector, which allowed it to be fired either semi-automatic or fully-automatic. It had a folding shoulder stock and a pistol grip. I had an ample supply of ammunition for it and several 30-round magazines. This weapon was kept in a military pouch made of canvas and was stored in the trunk of my car along with a pair of coveralls to wear when processing crime scenes, boots, a pair of army surplus canvas field trousers, an army field jacket, gloves, and a woolen army blanket. Under the front seat of my car for ready use was a .12 gauge shotgun whose double barrels had been cut to a length of eighteen inches.

31

The territory assigned to me consisted of McDowell, Avery, Mitchell and Yancey counties. They are four of North Carolina's most mountainous counties, and are bordered to the north by Tennessee and dissected by the beautiful Blue Ridge Parkway. Mount Mitchell is the highest point in the Eastern United States, and is located in McDowell County. The territory had never had an SBI resident agent assigned to it, and what little assistance local authorities had received came from a resident agent in Asheville.

During the first week in my new territory, I visited the sheriffs and chiefs of police in the four counties and furnished them my telephone number and radio call number (993). I was well-received by them; however, I was shocked by the lack of training and professionalism of law enforcement personnel in the four counties. The only thoroughly trained officers I discovered were the North Carolina State Troopers assigned to the territory and a Department of Motor Vehicles License and Theft Officer at Marion.

While I visited one of the counties, I met the sheriff and his one deputy. The sheriff was in his mid-forties and was only about five feet five inches in height and weighed about 180 pounds. He wore a black derby, a white shirt with a black string tie, and black trousers with red pinstripes. The trousers were tucked into black motorcycle boots. Around his waist was a gunbelt and hanging from it was a holstered revolver with at least a six-inch barrel, which extended to the right knee. He was a true mountaineer and in his limited conversation used the words you-uns and we-uns. He also referred to all male persons, regardless of age, as "son." He and his family were provided living quarters on the first floor of the county building, which housed the county jail on the second floor. He served not only as sheriff, but also as jailer.

On the day I met him, the sheriff took me on a tour of the

county. As we returned to town, I noticed several men sitting on the roof of the jail. I asked about them and the sheriff replied, "Son, they are prisoners. When it gets hot in the jail, they take the bars out of the window and climb up to the roof to catch a breeze. They ain't going nowhere."

The first Friday we were in Marion, I took Vicky and Gloria out to dinner at a local restaurant. Outside the restaurant was a live bear on display in a cage. Gloria was fascinated with the bear and was thrilled to hear there were many more not caged in the nearby mountains. After we returned home, I decided to drive to the McDowell Sheriff's Department, as I assumed things would be rather lively there on a Friday night, and I might meet some more local officers. I parked near the side entrance to the courthouse and was about to enter the building when the door flew open and I was nearly run over by a husky young man fleeing from two state troopers who were in hot pursuit. I followed for a short distance, until I saw the subject jump off a wall behind the courthouse and land on the roof of an automobile parked below. I ran to my car and drove down the street behind the courthouse. The troopers had detoured to the steps and were still after the subject, but at least fifty yards behind and losing ground. I didn't have any idea why the subject was being chased, but figured it to be pretty serious to cave in the top of a car in an attempt to escape. I saw the young man run behind the A&P store and knew the chase was all but over. Earlier in the week, I had been with Vicky to the A&P and noticed it was a free-standing building with a small mountain directly behind it. A high brick retaining wall circled the store and most of the parking area. I pulled my car to the opposite side of the building from where I last saw the subject and turned off my lights. I got my flashlight, drew my pistol, and eased to the front of my car. Within a few seconds, I heard heavy breathing as the subject rounded the corner of the building and headed directly toward me.

When he was about ten yards away, I turned on my flashlight and shined it directly in his eyes. I said, "SBI, halt where you are." He stopped dead in his tracks, and I ordered him to lie face down. I had him spread-eagled when the two exhausted troopers arrived.

The subject was not public enemy number one, but a local

thug who was wanted on several misdemeanor charges. By injecting myself into the chase and apprehending the subject, word spread quickly that I was one of them. I was welcomed into the local law enforcement fraternity.

32

After my visits to the local sheriff and police departments, I was swamped with calls for assistance. Most of the requests during the first month involved cases of burglaries, larcenies, and assaults. I worked the first thirteen days after I arrived at Marion before I finally had a chance to take a day off. It doesn't seem possible now, but looking back at my old records, which have yellowed with age, for the next several years I averaged working in excess of eighty hours a week. Leaving home at 8:00 A.M. and getting back at midnight was common, as were all night stakeouts.

It didn't take me but a short while to learn that when a department requested my assistance, it actually meant the case was turned over to me. A chief of police or a sheriff could then tell the local news media and the victim that the case had been referred to the SBI. This took them off the hook. However, I quickly learned that when I solved a case it immediately became a "we case," as the victim and news media were then told, "We" have charged so and so with the crime after "our" investigation disclosed. . . . The handling of cases in this manner really didn't bother me, as when I arrived on the scene I could work on the investigation as I saw fit. I was not interested in seeing my name in the newspaper, and the SBI Director knew how the cases had been resolved.

During my first month in the mountains, I was extremely fortunate in solving the cases that were referred to me. I discovered that most times local officers were pretty sure as to the person or persons who had perpetrated the crimes, but didn't know how to proceed to obtain evidence resulting in their arrests and convictions. They were completely inexperienced in collecting and preserving evidence and were unfamiliar as to how the SBI laboratory could assist them. These mountain lawmen were decades behind in all aspects of law enforcement. The one thing that hurt them most was their inability to interview and interrogate. They just didn't know how to sit down with a suspect and obtain the truth. Word soon spread that I had the ability to "make concrete talk." This prompted more and more requests for assistance.

33

September 12, 1963, started for me at 8:00 A.M. as a routine Thursday. I was working on a four-year-old homicide case, which I inherited with the territory. Shortly before 3:00 P.M., I received a radio call from the Asheville Highway Patrol Station requesting a telephone number where I could be contacted. I was in the vicinity of Marion, so I gave my office number with an estimated time of arrival (ETA) of ten minutes. The telephone rang as I walked into my office. It was Jack Vance, Sheriff of Avery County.

"Son, Roy Lee Beaver has been shot dead and his house burned down. I need help." The sheriff was more than a little excited and referred to Roy Lee Beaver as though he was a personal acquaintance of mine.

I didn't know Roy Lee Beaver from page eight in the telephone book and asked, "Who the hell is Roy Lee Beaver?" The sheriff replied that he was a seventy-four-year-old retired army sergeant who lived near Elk Park. I told the sheriff I would leave immediately and meet him at his office in Newland.

I went up the stairs from my office two at a time, and as I dashed through the kitchen I told Vicky I was on my way to a murder in Avery County. The tires squealed on the Chevrolet as I spun out of the driveway. I drove north on Highway 221 as fast as I could safely negotiate the tricky asphalt road. In less than an hour I walked into the Avery County Sheriff's Office. Sheriff Vance was waiting for me and, without me asking, related the following: Around noon on that date, an elderly female neighbor of Roy Lee Beaver saw smoke coming from his house and alerted construction workers who were working on a nearby bridge. They ran to the Beaver house and discovered that the front door was locked. They forced the door open, and two workers crawled under the smoke and located Mr. Beaver on the floor of the living room. They pulled him outside and discovered he was dead apparently as the result of several gunshot wounds. He (Sheriff

Vance) was summoned to the scene, as was Carl Osborne, the Avery County Coroner. Efforts to extinguish the fire were unsuccessful, and the residence was completely destroyed. Mr. Beaver had lived alone at his residence as his wife and grown children lived nearby in Johnson City, Tennessee. Mr. Beaver was very well-liked in the community and had no known enemies.

Sheriff Vance had been in office for less than a year and had no previous law enforcement experience. He didn't know the basics of how an investigation should be conducted; however, he knew every square inch of Avery County and nearly all of the county's 12,000 inhabitants. He also desperately wanted the person or persons responsible for this horrible crime quickly identified and charged.

Sheriff Vance rode with me to the crime scene, which was 1.5 miles from Elk Park on the Elk River Road. The Tennessee state line was just a couple of miles away. The smoldering ruins of the Beaver home were located about one hundred yards from the road. There was no driveway to it, and the only access was by a footbridge, which crossed a narrow stream. Approximately 200 men, women, and children were standing around in small groups. They spoke in low voices usually reserved for funeral homes and churches. The children stared wide-eyed at what had been Mr. Beaver's home. Most of the men wore gallused overalls and felt hats. The women were mostly attired in long dresses, some with aprons and some with bonnets. I was reminded of a scene from the movie *The Grapes of Wrath*. At my suggestion, Sheriff Vance cleared the spectators away from the scene. They crossed over the footbridge and stood along the road.

Within a few minutes, Deputy Sheriff J.C. Isley came from the woods behind where the house had stood. He and several volunteers had conducted an extensive search of the area. Isley advised that about fifty yards into the woods they had discovered the following items, which he displayed: (1) A size 7 straw hat with the brim pinned to the crown on both sides by safety pins; (2) a size 7 1/8 brown felt hat; (3) one pair of brown woolen gloves with red lining; (4) one pair of brown woolen gloves with no lining; (5) one .32 caliber cartridge; (6) five .32 caliber cartridge cases; (7) one .32-20 caliber cartridge; (8) two .32-20 caliber car-

129

tridge cases. Isley also displayed one .32 caliber cartridge case that he had located in the debris of the burned dwelling. I received it, and all other items recovered by Isley, from him and each was properly marked for identification for subsequent submission to the SBI laboratory.

Sheriff Vance and I held another brief meeting. He stated bloodhounds from a prison camp in a neighboring county were on their way to the scene. We decided he would wait for their arrival and direct the search. The hats and gloves were left with Sheriff Vance, hopefully to give the dogs a scent.

I proceeded to the funeral home in Newland, where the body had been taken. Coroner Osborne was there when I arrived, and stated he had already made arrangements for the body to be transported to Morganton, North Carolina, for an autopsy after it was examined by me. Before examining the body, I inventoried the personal effects of Mr. Beaver. From his wallet, I located an identification card reflecting him to be a white male, seventy-four years of age, five feet ten inches in height, 210 pounds, with gray hair and blue eyes. A ten dollar bill was in the secret currency compartment of his wallet and a quarter in the change compartment. Other items of his personal effects consisted of a set of false teeth, eight keys attached to a string, one pocketknife, one handkerchief, three sticks of gum, one Elgin pocketwatch, shoes, socks, trousers, shorts, an undershirt, and a plaid sportshirt. The undershirt and sportshirt each had what appeared to be two bullet holes in them. While inspecting Mr. Beaver's clothing, I discovered a spent bullet in a fold in the sportshirt. It was retained for evidentiary purposes.

Examination of Mr. Beaver's body disclosed four apparent bullet wounds. One entered behind the left ear and exited just in front of the right ear. Another entered near the top of the victim's head with no exit wound noted. Two apparent bullet wounds were in the chest area with no exit wounds. I made photographs of the body with closeups of the wounds.

After leaving the funeral home, I returned to the scene and located Sheriff Vance. He said the bloodhounds had failed to strike a trail and had been returned to the prison camp.

Sheriff Vance pointed out a lady whom he said was the victim's wife. She appeared to be about sixty years of age and was stylishly dressed and well-groomed. It was obvious she didn't fit in with those around her. She was very composed and readily agreed to be interviewed. She stated she lived in Johnson City, Tennessee, but was not legally separated from her husband. She didn't go into detail, and simply said she preferred to live in Johnson City, and her husband preferred to live alone. She stated her husband had no enemies to her knowledge, and was not known to have large sums of money. Mrs. Beaver recalled that her husband had a rifle and a pistol, but she didn't know what kind, nor could she describe them. She terminated the interview with, "Everyone liked Roy Lee, and Roy Lee liked everyone."

Sheriff Vance and I continued interviewing people, including those who had pulled Mr. Beaver from the burning house. We also talked to the neighbor who first noticed the smoke coming from his home. We learned that shortly before noon, she saw Mr. Beaver walk down Elk River Road from the direction of Elk Park and across the footbridge leading to his residence. About fifteen minutes later, she saw smoke coming from his home. Prior to the fire, she had not seen a vehicle parked in the area, nor had she seen anyone around the Beaver home or walking along Elk River Road. She did advise that someone could have approached the Beaver house from the woods behind it without being seen by her.

Another source interviewed was a distant cousin of Roy Lee Beaver who lived in Elk Park. He advised that Mr. Beaver owned two firearms: a .32 caliber Smith & Wesson revolver and a .32-20 Winchester lever-action rifle. He stated he was very familiar with both guns, as Mr. Beaver would leave them with him if he was away from home overnight. He was afraid someone might steal them. The cousin said Mr. Beaver didn't suspect anyone, and just wanted to be on the safe side. He knew of no one who disliked the victim or why anyone would want to kill him.

Sheriff Vance and I interviewed neighbors and other sources until shortly after 10:00 P.M. Neither of us had stopped for dinner, and I was working on my third pack of cigarettes. We were both dead tired. I started for Marion after promising to meet Sheriff Vance at 8:00 A.M. the next day. As I drove, I could think of nothing but the horrible crime that had taken place. Had I done everything right? Had I missed anything? What should be done tomorrow? These and many other questions kept popping into my mind. At 11:30 P.M. I pulled into my driveway. Vicky was still up and hurriedly warmed a late dinner for me. I could only nibble at it, as I told her of the day's events. I slept fretfully. The smoldering remains of Mr. Beaver's home, the exit wound near his right ear, these and other thoughts of Mr. Beaver stayed with me throughout the night. I could hardly wait to get back to Avery County.

I was up before six and, after a shave, shower, and light breakfast, I again headed north on Highway 221. This time I drove the speed limit and concentrated on all that had taken place the previous day.

By the time I arrived at Newland, I had reached a couple of conclusions that I wanted to present to Sheriff Vance and Deputy Isley. When I walked into the Sheriff's Office, Isley handed me a cup of steaming coffee. Several courthouse officials and employees were standing around sipping coffee and talking in low tones. Their offices were not scheduled to open for nearly an hour. I told Sheriff Vance I wanted to talk to him and Isley in private. The three of us went into the Sheriff's small private office, not much larger than a walk-in closet. The Sheriff took a seat behind a wooden desk that bore scars and cigarette burns. Isley took a seat straddling a straight-back chair and faced backwards. I lit a cigarette and continued to stand. I asked the sheriff if anything had developed since last night.

He replied, "Son, not a damned thing." I told the Sheriff that I had a theory and would like his and Isley's thoughts after they heard it.

He said, "Let's hear it. Me and J.C. will tell you what we think."

I said, "It appears to me that at least two people were responsible for Mr. Beaver's death. They came through the woods from behind his house and entered the house while he was gone. They located his guns and waited for him to return. When he did they shot him. They apparently didn't even remove his wallet from his trousers, which means robbery was not the motive, or else fear of what they had done kept them from searching the body. Two guns were taken, two pairs of gloves and two hats. Now what the hell kind of robbery is that? To me it indicates two people were involved. Now, who would safety-pin the brim of a straw hat to the crown, shaping it similar to a cowboy hat? It was probably done while the subjects were waiting for Mr. Beaver to come home, and it was not done by an adult. Sheriff, I think Mr. Beaver was killed by juveniles who got scared after he was shot. They then set the house on fire in an effort to hide their crime."

I didn't think my theory would be received as it was. Sheriff Vance bolted out of his chair and nearly shouted, "Howard Horton and Danny Rome!" As calmly as I could, I asked who they were.

Sheriff Vance said, "Horton is fifteen years old and Rome is twelve. Me and J.C. have been after them boys for two weeks. They are wild and live mostly in the woods. Ain't been to school this year. We think they stole and forged some checks taken in a break-in, and stole a car over in Tennessee which they abandoned near Elk Park. They are mean as hell and ain't going to play by nobody's rules."

Sheriff Vance, Deputy Isley, and I agreed that our efforts should be concentrated on locating the two boys. The sheriff and I drove to the residence of Danny Rome, located about a mile and a half from where Roy Lee Beaver had lived. We spoke with his father, who said he hadn't seen Danny in several days. We left word with Mr. Rome that we wanted to talk to Danny, and he should bring him to the Sheriff's Office as soon as possible.

As we started to leave, Mr. Rome said, "I guess it's about Roy Lee's death."

Sheriff Vance replied, "That and a few other things."

Sheriff Vance and I drove to the home of Howard Horton, which was about a mile from the Beaver place. We talked to Mr. Horton, who told us he didn't know where his son was and had not seen him for nearly a week. We advised Mr. Horton to notify the Sheriff's Office when he had contact with his son. Mr. Horton also guessed the reason involved Mr. Beaver's death.

Shortly after noon on September 13, Danny Rome, accompanied by his father, presented himself at the Avery County Sheriff's Office. He said his father had told him of Mr. Beaver's death, and he might be suspected of having something to do with it. He stated he didn't know anything about Mr. Beaver's death, and didn't like being a suspect. He readily agreed to be interviewed.

I had expected something different than a nice-looking boy of twelve who stood five feet six inches and weighed 115 pounds. He had bright blue eyes, blond hair, and a fair complexion. He was nicely dressed and well groomed. He had obviously gotten "slicked up" to come in. For the next hour, he was questioned by Sheriff Vance and me during which time he furnished the following information:

He and Howard Horton had been running together for about two weeks. They had broken into several vacant houses in the Elk Park community. They had also broken into Mr. Bixby's home near Elk Park when he was not at home. They had taken some of his checks and forged his name to them. They knew they were being sought by the Sheriff, and therefore lived mostly in the woods. Most of their food was furnished to them by Howard's younger brother, Ronnie, age eleven.

He knew Roy Lee Beaver, and visited him about a week ago along with Howard and Ronnie, and their sister, Jenny Horton. They watched television with Mr. Beaver for about an hour. That was the only time he had ever been in Mr. Beaver's home.

He and Howard stayed at the Horton home on Wednesday night, September 11. They got up at about 6:00 A.M. on the twelfth, and the two of them walked to the home of Howard's sister, Ruby Clinton. They arrived there about mid-morning and stayed until about 2:30 P.M. The two of them left and walked back to the Horton home. He remained there until about 10:00 A.M. the next day when he left and walked to his home. When he got there, his father told him about Mr. Beaver's death. He didn't want to be suspected of having anything to do with it, so he agreed to come with his father to the Sheriff's Office.

During the course of Danny Rome's interview, Sheriff Vance questioned him about a car stolen in Tennessee and abandoned near Elk Park. He vehemently denied any knowledge of the vehicle.

In view of Rome's age, Sheriff Vance and I were careful not to frighten or intimidate him in any manner. We also limited our interview to a period of one hour.

After the interview of Danny Rome, it was decided that

Sheriff Vance would check out Rome's story with Ruby Clinton while I went over to Johnson City, in Tennessee. Information had been received that a subject was in jail there who might be a suspect in the Beaver case. I drove to Johnson City and interviewed the man in question. He had an alibi for the previous morning, and local authorities and I determined he could not have been at Elk Park when the Beaver murder occurred.

I drove back to Newland and en route stopped for gasoline, a Coke, and a cold sandwich wrapped in cellophane. It was the first thing I had eaten since breakfast. I arrived at the sheriff's Office at about 6:00 P.M., and found Sheriff Vance anxiously awaiting my return. I told him of the Johnson City lead petering out, and disappointment crept across his rugged face.

Sheriff Vance then shocked me by saying that on the way to see Ruby Clinton he had stopped by the Horton residence, and that Howard was there. He had taken him into custody and already interviewed him. He advised Howard's story was identical to that of Danny Rome's, except that Howard admitted that he and Danny had stolen the automobile in Tennessee and left it near Elk Park. Sheriff Vance also said Horton had decided to quit running, as he was afraid of being suspected in the death of Mr. Beaver. The Sheriff advised he had taken Howard Horton and Danny Rome before the Avery County Clerk of Court who had jurisdiction in juvenile cases, and that they had had separate hearings. Both boys were found to be delinquents, and Horton was sentenced to the Stonewall Jackson Training School at Concord, North Carolina. Rome was placed on probation and released into custody of his father.

Sheriff Vance, Deputy Isley, and I sat in the Sheriff's Office and talked, smoked, and drank coffee. Sheriff Vance and I had interviewed Danny Rome, and he had denied any knowledge of Mr. Beaver's death. I had not been interested in the stolen automobile, and had only listened while Sheriff Vance questioned Danny about it. He had also denied any knowledge of the car. I had detected nothing to indicate he had lied, and yet, he had skillfully done so. I thought Danny Rome needed to be re-interviewed, and the Sheriff agreed. He sent Deputy Isley to bring him in.

When Deputy Isley arrived at the Sheriff's Office with

Danny Rome, his personality was completely different from the boy we talked to earlier that day. He was defensive, hostile and arrogant. When told of Horton's admission regarding the stolen automobile, he grew more hostile before he finally admitted to his participation in the theft of the car.

He became even more angry when questioned again about Mr. Beaver's death and said, "I told you before I don't know nothing about it. Ain't nothing changed. I still don't." His interview was again terminated prematurely because of his age.

It was nearing 9:00 P.M., and all of our leads had been explored without success. I sat in the Sheriff's Office wondering what to do next. I asked Sheriff Vance where Horton was located. He replied that he didn't have a lockup for juveniles, and since he didn't have any female prisoners, he was holding him in the segregated cell reserved for them. He also advised that Deputy Isley was to transport him the next day to the training school at Concord. I told Sheriff Vance that I would like to talk to Horton alone. I explained that if Horton had lied to him earlier, it would be more difficult to get him to admit the truth in the presence of the person to whom he had lied. Sheriff Vance nodded his understanding, got up from his chair, and took a cell key from a ring on the wall. He handed the key to me, and I handed him my revolver.

Horton was sitting on one of two bunks in the cell. He started to stand as I unlocked the door, but I motioned for him to remain seated. A basic rule of interrogation is, if possible, to keep the subject being interrogated below the eye level of the interrogator. I therefore remained standing as I displayed to him my badge, which was attached to my leather credential case. I verbally identified myself to him by name and as a Special Agent of the North Carolina State Bureau of Investigation. I reached out to shake hands and in return received one that was cold and clammy. I started by obtaining personal and physical descriptive data from Horton. I obtained his date of birth and ascertained him to be five feet seven inches in height and weighed 130 pounds. He had blond hair, blue eyes, and a two-inch scar on his right temple. He had only completed the sixth grade.

I eased into the heart of my interrogation without any display of emotion. I told Horton of the many people I had talked to who had spoken of Mr. Beaver being a nice, Christian gentlemen who had no enemies. Of how he had honorably served his country and retired from military service hoping to live out his life in peace and how he had been shot to death in his own home, and his house burned in an effort to cover up the cowardly act. I told Horton how I had examined Mr. Beaver at the funeral home and photographed his wounds. I told him of the discovery of the two hats, two pairs of gloves and the cartridge and cartridge cases in the woods behind Mr. Beaver's home. I figured Horton would not be aware that latent fingerprints could not be obtained from the gloves or hats, nor would he know that the cartridge and cartridge cases would apparently be of no value for fingerprint purposes as they had been handled by the volunteers who found them. I believed all Horton knew about fingerprints, and other scientific investigative aids, was what he had seen on television. I informed Horton that all evidence gathered in this case would be submitted to the SBI Laboratory in Raleigh, including his fingerprints, which I was going to obtain. I also informed him that if hairs were discovered in the hats which were not those of Mr. Beaver, they could be compared with his hair.

Horton lost his voice and began to shake. I knew my search for Mr. Beaver's killer(s) was over. I looked at Horton and, as gently as possible, asked, "Are you sorry you shot Mr. Beaver?"

He looked me directly in the eyes and, in a barely audible voice, replied, "Yes." His expression didn't change. He related the following story, which he later reiterated in the presence of Sheriff Vance:

On the night of September 11, he and his brother, Ronnie, age eleven, and Danny Rome were in the woods behind Roy Lee Beaver's home. He thought of the idea to rob Mr. Beaver. He tried to get Ronnie to go to the house and knock on the door. When Mr. Beaver came to the door, he (Howard) was going to hit him in the head with a stick and then take his money. Ronnie was afraid to go along with the plan, so the idea was dropped.

He and Danny Rome spent the night of September 11 at the Horton home. They figured out a plan to kill and rob Mr. Beaver. They knew his habit of walking to Elk Park each morning, and they also knew he had some guns. They believed he had some money. The plan was for them to walk through the woods and

137

hide behind Mr. Beaver's house until he left for Elk Park. They would then break into his house, get his guns, and wait for him to come home. When he did, they would shoot and rob him.

He and Danny left Horton's home at about 8:00 A.M. on September 12. They walked through the woods and hid behind Mr. Beaver's house. They waited until they saw him leave and start walking toward Elk Park. He and Danny then went to the rear of the house, where they broke out a window to gain entry. They found a lever-action rifle and a pistol in a cabinet. Both guns were already loaded. He took the rifle and Danny got the pistol. They also got some extra ammunition for both guns. They then went back into the woods and fired both weapons to make sure they worked. He and Danny returned to Mr. Beaver's house and waited for him to come home. When Mr. Beaver came home, he entered the front door and started walking across the living room toward the kitchen, where they waited. When he was about ten feet away, they both shot him several times. Mr. Beaver fell to the floor and didn't move. They could see that one bullet had gone through his head. He and Danny were too scared to touch Mr. Beaver, so they didn't rob him. They decided to hide their crime by burning the house, with Mr. Beaver in it. They piled some papers in the dining area and set them on fire. They left the house, taking with them the two guns, extra ammunition, and two hats and two pairs of gloves they had found in the house. They went into the woods, and a short distance from the house they threw away the hats and gloves and unloaded the guns. They walked several miles through the woods to the "Old Nat Gwynn Place," where they reloaded the guns and hid them. They then walked to his sister's house.

After Horton's admission, Sheriff Vance again dispatched Deputy Isley to bring in Danny Rome. He arrived at 11:30 P.M., and I immediately started his interview. This was the same twelve-year-old who had twice before successfully lied to me. For six years, I had been interviewing people from all walks of life and interrogating car thieves, pimps, whores, bank robbers, murders, rapists, and others who chose to live outside the law. I must say that until that time I had never interviewed a harder case than Danny Rome. He was cold and cunning and very intelligent. He apparently had no feelings of guilt or remorse. As

I started his interview, he interrupted me and said, "Mister, I done told you twice that I don't know nothing about how Old Man Beaver died. I know that's what you are going to ask me about, 'cause you ain't up here in Avery County for nothing else."

I looked at Danny Rome and said, "Son, you don't have to tell me anything. Howard has already told me how the two of you planned to kill and rob Mr. Beaver. How the two of you waited behind his house for him to leave, and after he did y'all broke out a window to get in his house. Y'all found his rifle and pistol, and went back into the woods and shot them to make sure they worked. The two of you went back inside Mr. Beaver's house and waited for him. When he came home, you shot him with the pistol, and Howard shot him with the rifle. You both were too scared to rob him, so y'all set the house on fire to hide the crime. Y'all left with the guns, two hats, two pairs of gloves, and extra ammunition. In the woods behind the house, the guns were unloaded and the gloves and hats thrown away. You and Howard walked to the 'Old Nat Gwynn Place,' where the guns were hidden. Howard is going to show us where they are tomorrow morning. Son, I think from what I have said you know we now know the details of Mr. Beaver's death. Howard is sorry for what took place, as he has told the truth. Apparently, you aren't sorry. As things now stand, if I am asked in court, I'll have to say you were not truthful, and you showed no feelings of sorrow for what you did."

Danny Rome looked at me, and if looks could kill, I would have been dead. He didn't say anything for a couple of minutes, during which time I thought he must be trying to decide what was best for him. Something I said must have convinced him to tell the truth. Showing absolutely no emotion, he furnished essentially the same information as Howard Horton. He also agreed to show us the location of the weapons.

I left Avery County and headed home. It was 1:30 A.M. when I walked into the house. Vicky was asleep on the couch, but quickly awakened. As she warmed my dinner, I told her of all that had occurred that day. I was famished, tired, excited, and pleased with myself. I ate heartily as Vicky kept asking questions about the case. She was horrified that boys ages fifteen and twelve could commit such a horrible deed and neither show any remorse. She couldn't understand it and neither could I. Getting a child to confess was a problem I never thought I would encounter.

The next morning I left home at 7:30 A.M. and returned to Avery County. I went directly to the jail where I found Sheriff Vance waiting. After hearing Danny Rome's confession the night before, he had somehow made room in the jail for him, and had kept him separated from Horton. I told the Sheriff I thought it would be best to continue to keep the two boys separated, and allow each one to point out the location of the hidden guns. He readily concurred. The two North Carolina Troopers assigned to Avery County, Lloyd Letterman and Robert Bowman, were both at the jail and volunteered their services. The Sheriff and I left the jail first with Horton in the cruiser operated by Bowman. Five minutes later, Deputy Isley followed with Rome in a cruiser operated by Letterman. I requested Horton to direct us to where the guns were located. Without any prompting, he directed us to a hill near the "Old Nat Gwynn Place." We walked up the crest of the hill, when Horton stopped.

He pointed to a brush pile and said, "The rifle is under it." He then pointed to a stump and said, "Danny put the pistol in that stump."

We stood back several hundred feet and waited. In a few minutes, Letterman and Isley arrived on the scene, accompanied by Danny Rome. Danny wouldn't look at me but responded to Isley's questions as to where the guns were: "The rifle is in that brush pile and the pistol is in the stump." Sheriff Vance walked over to the brush pile and pulled the rifle from under it. I recovered the pistol from the stump.

The remainder of the day was spent wrapping up loose ends of the case. Contact was made with the District Attorney, and we learned that because of Rome's age he could only be tried as a juvenile on a charge of delinquency. Horton could be handled as an adult. I finished the day with a trip to Morganton to obtain the results of Mr. Beaver's autopsy. It was 7:00 P.M., Saturday, September 14, when I arrived home. In the last three days, I had worked a total of thirty-five and one-half hours. I was physically tired and mentally drained. The investigative portion of

140

the case was complete, but I still had to dictate a detailed investigative report, transport the physical evidence to the Raleigh laboratory and attend the trials.

I got to sleep in on Sunday the 15th, but later in the day was called out to a burglary in McDowell County. On Monday the 16th, I was back in Newland to attend Juvenile Court for Danny Rome held before Dean B. Elton, Clerk of Avery County Court. Rome, who was represented by an attorney, pleaded guilty to being a delinquent. He acknowledged his participation in the murder of Roy Lee Beaver and the burning of his home. He was sentenced to the Stonewall Jackson Training School until such time as the Superintendent of that institution deemed it appropriate for him to be released.

In a separate hearing before Mr. Elton, Howard Horton was bound over without privilege of bond to the next term of Avery County Superior Court. There was no facility for his incarceration in Avery County, and arrangements were made to keep him in the McDowell County Jail. Since I was returning to Marion, Sheriff Vance asked me to deliver Horton to the McDowell Jail. I agreed to do so. Out of sight from Horton, I removed my revolver from the holster on my right hip and put it in the left pocket of my suit coat. I handcuffed Horton's hands behind him and had him to sit on the passenger side of the front seat. I buckled the lap seatbelt around him. I knew his position was uncomfortable, but I also knew Horton would like nothing better than to be free again in those Avery County mountains. I delivered Horton to the McDowell County Jail without incident. From Newland to Marion, neither of us said a word, but I could feel the hatred he had for me. I knew he deeply regretted having ever spoken to me.

On December 9, 1963, Howard Horton appeared in Avery County Superior Court before the Honorable J. Will Pless, Judge of Superior Court. He was represented by attorney Ray Braswell. He entered pleas of guilty to charges of murder in the first degree and the unlawful burning of a dwelling house. I was the only witness to testify for the State. With the courtroom packed with spectators, and snow slowly falling outside, I told in complete detail how Horton and Danny Rome had killed Mr.

Beaver and burned his home. At the completion of my testimony there was utter silence for a few moments in the courtroom. In closing arguments by the defense, Mr. Braswell told of the conditions under which Horton had grown up and brought up other extenuating circumstances on his behalf. At the completion of the trial, Judge Pless sentenced Horton to life in prison for the murder and ten years for the arson. The sentences were to run concurrently. I could detect looks of hostility directed at me by Horton and members of his family.

One would think this would end the murder case of Roy Lee Beaver. Not so! On August 8, 1966, Howard Horton was an inmate at a prison camp located at Lillington in eastern North Carolina. On that date, Horton wrote a letter to Mr. Braswell in which he claimed he had taken $6,427.00 from Mr. Beaver's home and had hidden it. His letter indicated it would be useless to try to tell where the money was hidden, but if he was returned to Avery County he would show "the law" where it was located. He stated he wanted the money turned over to Mr. Beaver's family. A copy of the letter was sent to the SBI Director, but I don't recall if it came from Mr. Braswell or the Prison Department.

I was stationed at the Raleigh Office when the Director received his copy of the letter. He sent for me, and, as I made myself comfortable in one of the large chairs in front of his desk, he handed the copy to me. I read it rather quickly and then read it again very slowly. When I finished, I very candidly told the Director I didn't believe a word of it. I also informed him I thought it may be a well-conceived plan for an escape. I said that Horton had never shown he was remorseful over killing Mr. Beaver, and I was well aware of his ability to live off the land in mountainous Avery County. I said I was also aware of the tradition of mountain folks to stick together and look after their kin, no matter what they had done. I continued by saying if Horton's relatives knew he was being returned to Avery County, and if they knew the location of where he was going to lead the officers accompanying him, it was possible the officers could be ambushed so Horton could escape. The Director looked at me with concern in his eyes. After a moment of thought he said, "Handle it carefully, but check it out. I don't want anyone hurt."

Everette Norton was a new agent undergoing training at

Raleigh before being assigned to the field. A great deal of his training was under my supervision. I told him I needed to interview a prisoner at the Lillington Camp, and on August 14, 1966, we made the forty-five minute drive. On the way, I briefed Norton on the details of the case and of my suspicions of Horton fabricating the story of the stolen money.

When Horton walked into the interview room at the Lillington Camp, I could tell by the expression of scorn on his face that he immediately recognized me. I could almost see the venom in his eyes. This time we didn't shake hands. It was going on nearly three years since I had last seen Horton, and he had changed. He appeared to be nearly six feet tall and had added at least thirty pounds of what appeared to be solid muscle.

He was not a boy anymore, but a man hardened by prison life. In a voice that spewed animosity, Horton asked, "You here about the money?"

I replied, "Yes, if there is any money. And if there is, I'd like for you to tell me where."

Horton said there was no way he could give directions to where the money was hidden, but quickly volunteered to show me where it was. I asked why Danny Rome couldn't show me. Horton responded that during the night after he and Danny killed Mr. Beaver, he slipped away and hid the money while Danny slept. He also said the money should be well-preserved, as he put it in a plastic jar before hiding it under a rock.

I told Horton I would see what I could do. Agent Norton and I drove back to Raleigh, where arrangements were made with the North Carolina Prison Department to have Horton immediately transferred to Central Prison in Raleigh. The next day I went to Central Prison and met with the warden, Sam Garrison. I explained the entire case to him and he immediately said, "It appears to me to be an attempt to escape." However, we both were of the opinion that we had no choice but to provide Horton the opportunity to produce the money. We settled on a plan to let things calm down for a couple of weeks, and the day before I was to transport Horton to Avery County, I was to call Warden Garrison. He would assign one of his best men, Sergeant William Dove, to escort Horton on the trip. We also decided the best time to leave would be about 4:00 A.M., which would make our arrival time at Newland around 8:00 A.M. Warden Garrison advised Horton would not know anything about the trip until awakened for it.

Agent J. B. Boone had replaced me at Marion when I was transferred to Raleigh. After my meeting with Warden Garrison, I contacted Boone by telephone and explained the situation to him. We agreed every effort should be made to keep secret Horton's return to Avery County. Boone said that if I notified him the day before I was to leave Raleigh with Horton, he would contact Sheriff Vance and Troopers Bowman and Letterman. He would have them standing by at the Sheriff's Office waiting for our arrival. He would also be there and would not brief anyone on what it was about until shortly before 8:00 A.M.

I selected agent W.F. Crocker of the Raleigh Office to make the trip with me. On September 27, I placed telephone calls to Warden Garrison and Agent Boone. The following morning, at precisely 4:00 A.M., Agent Crocker and I arrived at Central Prison. Sergeant Dove was waiting with Horton who was secured by a restraining belt. This was a thick belt made of leather which fastened not in front but in the small of the back. There was an iron ring attached to the front of the belt through which handcuffs had been placed which were secured to Horton's wrists. The year before, the Chevy had been replaced by a new Ford, and we made excellent time as we sped across the mountains of western North Carolina. Crocker, Sergeant Dove and I chatted about sports, Vietnam and other topics. Horton remained silent.

Upon our arrival at the Sheriff's Office in Newland, I found Sheriff Vance, Deputy Isley, Troopers Bowman and Letterman, and Agent Boone waiting for us. I didn't waste any time as I turned to Horton and said, "Okay, you wanted to show us the money, now do it." He directed us to the same area where the weapons had been recovered nearly three years earlier. The brush pile where the rifle was hidden was still there, as was the stump where the pistol was found. Horton wandered around for about half an hour with Sergeant Dove right on his heels.

Horton kicked over a few rocks and finally turned to me and said, "We might as well go, I don't know where it is." It was a long trip back to Raleigh.

At my request, Agent Boone had located and interviewed Danny Rome, who had been released from Juvenile Training School earlier that year. Boone reported Danny said no money was taken from Mr. Beaver or his house, and if Horton said there was, he was lying. Boone further advised Danny was under the supervision of the Avery County Welfare Department and was doing well in school and playing football as a ninth grader.

There was one last thing I wanted to do to put this case to rest. On the way from Avery County back to Central Prison, I asked Horton if he would take a polygraph (lie detector) examination as to whether or not money was taken from Mr. Beaver or his home. He volunteered to do so. On October 7, 1966, Horton was administered a polygraph test at SBI Headquarters. In the opinion of the examiner, Horton was not truthful when he said money was taken.

You would think this would put an end to this bizarre case. Not so again! On May 5, 1970, a subpoena was served on me to appear in Avery County Superior Court on behalf of the state. Horton had filed a petition seeking a new trial under the Post Conviction Statute. He claimed that I had violated his constitutional rights in my original interview with him on September 13, 1963. He said his statement was made under duress, and threats and promises were made to him. I didn't have to make the long trip back to Avery County as I furnished an affidavit to the court regarding Horton's interview, and his request for a new trial was denied.

Over the years, I have thought of this case quite often. I am firmly convinced that if proper precautions had not have been taken, efforts would have been made to free Horton when he was returned to Avery County. I believe bloodshed was probably avoided. Until I started this book, I had never checked to see how long Horton remained in prison. I have learned he was paroled March 6, 1978.

Years later, when I told Big Glen about the murder of Roy Lee Beaver, he shook his head, flicked ashes from a Tampa Nugget cigar, and said, "That Horton boy was a bad-un, but I ain't never seen nor heard tell of a twelve-year-old child who had committed burglary, larceny, forgery, automobile theft, arson, and murder."

145

34

It was a beautiful autumn morning when I left home on Wednesday, October 2, 1963. I drove north on Highway 226. Leaf color was near its peak as I crossed the Blue Ridge Parkway. The scenery was breathtaking, but I was not on a sight-seeing trip, as were the tourists creeping along the parkway. I was en route to the tiny village of Bakersville, seat of Mitchell County, to see Sheriff Sam Guy. He had requested assistance in an arson case. I stopped at the Sheriff's Office and learned the sheriff was at his nearby residence. I located him there and, over cups of coffee in his kitchen, he filled me in on the details of the case.

A vacant tenant house owned by D. Y. Adcock was completely destroyed by fire on the night of September 7, 1963. The house was located in a very remote section of the county off Pigeon Roost Road in the Tipton Hill community. The frame house was very old and in disrepair. It had no running water or electricity. Mr. Adcock, a successful dairy farmer, was an outspoken community activist and was not well liked by many of his neighbors. He was convinced his tenant house had been deliberately burned, but there was no evidence at the scene to indicate arson. Two possible suspects named by Adcock were eliminated, as their locations and activities had been accounted for on the night in question. However, Adcock still believed arson was the cause of the fire.

I received directions from Sheriff Guy to Mr. Adcock's dairy farm and located it without difficulty. I found Mr. Adcock at the barn and received a welcome greeting from him. He was not what I expected. He was a tall, slim man who appeared to be in his mid-forties. He was well spoken and obviously well educated. As I recall, he had some teaching experience in the local school system. Mr. Adcock furnished the following information:

About 8:00 A.M. on September 8, he discovered his vacant tenant house had been destroyed by fire. He made the discovery while in the area checking on his cows. The fire was still smoldering with small flames coming from the larger sills. He looked around the area but found no tire tracks, footprints, or containers that may have held inflammables. He notified Sheriff Guy who came to the scene, and his search for evidence was also negative. Sheriff Guy checked on a couple of men with whom he previously had disagreements. They were discarded as suspects as both were apparently not in Mitchell County on the night of September 7.

Several days after the fire, Homer Ferrell told him on that Saturday night he observed a bright glow in the area of the tenant house. He said he was at his residence about a mile away when he saw the glow, and it was about 10:00 P.M. Ferrell also told him that he had heard that Jack Hawkins wanted to get even with him. Mr. Adcock explained that about six months earlier he had reported to State Wildlife officers that he had observed Jack Hawkins with a deer that he had killed out of season. The officers conducted an investigation, which resulted in Hawkins being convicted of the deer incident. Mr. Adcock also advised Ferrell told him that on the night of the fire Jack Hawkins was at the home of his cousin, Benny Hawkins, who lives within a mile of the burned house. He also reported Jack Hawkins worked at a sawmill in Tennessee but came to his parents' home in Mitchell County on weekends.

After interviewing Mr. Adcock, I returned to Bakersville and met with Sheriff Guy. I informed him of what I had learned from Mr. Adcock and suggested that an appropriate time to continue the investigation would be on a Saturday morning when Jack Hawkins was home for the weekend. We agreed to meet at the sheriff's office at 9:00 A.M. on Saturday, October 12.

I arrived at the Sheriff's Office on the 12th a few minutes after 9:00 A.M. I was met by Deputy Sheriff James Ellis, who advised that the sheriff was out in the county searching for liquor, and that he was to assist me, as the sheriff would not be available. I drove as Deputy Ellis directed me and, after a lengthy search, we finally located Homer Ferrell at a farm where he was employed. Deputy Ellis knew him fairly well and told me he was a shy, religious man who didn't condone anyone violating the laws of God or man. He introduced me to Ferrell who was about fifty years of age and of medium height and build. He was dressed in jeans, a blue denim shirt and a baseball cap with an emblem on the front. He was wearing rubber boots that came nearly to his knees. I asked him to tell us what he knew about the fire and Jack Hawkins. He didn't hesitate to tell us of Jack Hawkins's threats to get even with Mr. Adcock and of him spending the night of September 7th at the house of his cousin, Benny Hawkins. He also reported he had heard Jack Hawkins say he had proof of where he was when Mr. Adcock's tenant house burned.

Deputy Ellis and I located Benny Hawkins at the residence of his parents in the Relief Community of Mitchell County. He was a surly nineteen-year-old with a sallow complexion highlighted with a severe case of acne. He claimed that on the night of September 7th he and Jack Hawkins double-dated with Nancy Key and Joyce Price. He dated Joyce, and Jack dated Nancy. He and Jack picked up the girls at their homes around 6:00 P.M. He claimed they drove in his 1954 Mercury to Bakersville and rode around. They returned the girls to their homes between 9:30 and 9:45 P.M. He and Jack then drove to his home, arriving there about 10:00 P.M. They both went immediately to bed. He denied any knowledge of the cause of the fire. Benny Hawkins's interview had taken place in my Chevy. As soon as it was completed, I told him to remain in the car with Deputy Ellis. I went inside the house and interviewed his parents. They recalled on the night Mr. Adcock's tenant house burned, Benny and his cousin, Jack Hawkins, were courting. They did not know what time the boys came home, as they went to bed around 9:00 P.M. and were asleep within a few minutes.

Deputy Ellis and I left Benny Hawkins at his residence and started looking for Jack Hawkins. I wanted to get to him before Benny did. We didn't even think about lunch. Jack was not at his home and his mother didn't know where he was. We finally located him at about 2:00 P.M. at a field in the Pigeon Roost community where a baseball game was in progress. He voluntarily agreed to be interviewed and again it was conducted in the Chevy. Jack was a handsome young man of eighteen with neatly trimmed black hair and blue eyes. He was five feet, ten inches in height and a muscular 180 pounds. I drove a short distance away from the ball field where there were no distractions. Jack

148

was beside me on the front seat and Deputy Ellis was on the back seat. As usual, I started the interview with simple questions such as his date of birth, address, occupation, et cetera. He was extremely nervous in answering these questions and stuttered slightly from time to time. He was too nervous, so I immediately went on the offensive. I looked directly at Jack and in a friendly voice said, "Jack, I am not even going to give you a chance to fib to me. A little earlier today we talked to Benny and he told us what he said was the truth. A question I failed to ask Benny is one I'll now ask you. If people had been living in that old abandoned house, would you have burned it?"

I could feel Deputy Ellis squirm on the back seat. Jack dropped his head and replied, "No, sir." I then asked if the girls were present when the house was set on fire, and Jack replied with the answer I wanted to hear: "No, just me and Benny." In response to further questioning, he furnished the following information:

After dropping the girls at their homes, he and Benny arrived at Benny's home about 9:45 P.M. D.Y. Adcock had reported him for killing a deer out of season, and he wanted to get even with him. He knew of Mr. Adcock's vacant tenant house located about a mile from Benny's home. He wanted to burn it, and Benny agreed to go along with him. They walked to the house and both struck matches to leaves and other debris they placed in the house. After the fire was well started, they walked back to Benny's house and went to bed.

Immediately after Jack Hawkins was interviewed, he was placed under arrest, searched and handcuffed. With Jack in our custody, Deputy Ellis and I returned to the home of Benny Hawkins. He was not there so we waited. Late that afternoon he arrived in his old Mercury. He was arrested, searched and handcuffed to Jack.

Bakersville was nearly ten miles away over a twisting blacktop through some of North Carolina's most mountainous terrain. It was approaching dusk when we started the journey. We had gone only a couple of miles when I noticed in my rearview mirror three or four vehicles behind me with their headlights on. I thought it strange but didn't become concerned until a few miles further down the road the line of vehicles behind me had grown

149

to eight or ten. I noticed Deputy Ellis glancing over his shoulder and twisting and turning in his seat. None of the vehicles behind us attempted to pass and each maintained a constant speed. The number of vehicles following us continued to grow as we approached Bakersville until it must have looked like a funeral procession with me being the lead vehicle, and you know what that is. I knew it was a volatile situation and was concerned over what would happen when we got to the Sheriff's Office. Deputy Ellis was not saying a word nor were the Hawkins boys. I stopped my car directly across the street from the Sheriff's Office, and as Deputy Ellis and I were getting the two subjects out, I noticed vehicles parking around us. There must have been at least twenty cars and pickups. Some had only one occupant and others five or six including women and children. We hustled the Hawkins boys through the crowd into the Sheriff's Office.

Once inside the Sheriff's Office, I again interviewed Benny Hawkins but not in the presence of Jack Hawkins. He again denied participation in the burning of the tenant house. I had Jack Hawkins brought into the room, and at my request he reiterated his confession in Benny's presence. Benny didn't say a word while Jack was in the room, which is exactly what I wanted. If Benny had denied Jack's statement was true in Jack's presence, it could not have been used against him. After Jack was taken from the room, Benny turned to me and in a voice filled with hatred said, "Jack is a liar. I didn't burn nothing with him." I didn't respond, but thought to myself that his denial was just a wee bit too late.

Fortunately, the jail was connected to the Sheriff's Office, so Deputy Ellis and I didn't have to go outside with the Hawkins boys. Prior to them being placed in separate cells, I fingerprinted them at a table within the jail but outside the cell area. When this was finished, Deputy Ellis locked them up with a few empty cells between them. I remained at the table completing information on the fingerprint cards while Deputy Ellis returned to the Sheriff's Office. The two boys couldn't see me and apparently thought I had left with Deputy Ellis.

After a couple of minutes, I heard Benny say to Jack, "Why did you let them pick it out of you? Why did you admit it? They

couldn't have proved it." Jack answered, but I couldn't understand what he said.

Upon returning to the Sheriff's Office, I was surprised to
find Nancy Key and Joyce Price waiting to see me. I knew they
were not there of their own volition, but were probably sent by
the families and/or friends of the Hawkins boys. Deputy Ellis
had gone to the residence of Justice of the Peace M.B. Russell to
obtain warrants charging both boys with the felonious burning
of a dwelling house. State Trooper D.G. Power was at the Sheriff's Office. I requested him to sit in with me as a witness, as I
didn't want to interview the girls alone.

Nancy Key, a nice looking girl of eighteen, was interviewed
first. She stated that Benny and Jack Hawkins picked her up at
her residence at about 6:30 P.M. on September 7th. She had a
date with Jack. Joe, her fourteen-year-old brother, decided to accompany them. They drove to Joyce's house and picked her up,
as she had a date with Benny. They drove over to Burnsville in
Yancey County and went to the Riverside drive-in movie. They
remained at the movie until about 10:00 P.M. and then drove back
to Mitchell County. Joyce was returned to her home and then
she and Joe were dropped off at their home. It was shortly after
11:00 P.M. when Benny and Jack left to go to Benny's home where
they were to spend the night. She claimed to know nothing about
the fire at Mr. Adcock's tenant house and said on that Saturday
night his name was not mentioned.

Joyce Price was a tall girl of eighteen with auburn hair,
green eyes and a sad face. She said that on September 7th Nancy
and Joe Key were already at her home when Benny and Jack
Hawkins arrived there about 8:00 P.M. She had a date with
Benny and Nancy had a date with Jack. She stated Joe accompanied them and they all rode in Benny's car to Burnsville,
where they rode around for awhile. She said they didn't go to a
movie and the five of them returned to Joe and Nancy's home between 11:00 and 11:30 P.M. About ten minutes later, Benny and
Jack left to go to Benny's home where they were to spend the
night. She spent the night at Nancy's home.

The interviews with the two girls disclosed glaring discrep-
ancies in their stories, and also revealed Joe Key was with them

151

and the Hawkins boys on the night of September 7th. When asked where Joe could be located, Joyce said he was waiting right outside the front door of the Sheriff's Office.

When I opened the front door, I was shocked by the crowd outside. There were about one hundred people milling about, and all appeared to be in an angry mood. Several derogatory remarks were yelled at me. The crowd was so hostile it reminded me of a lynch mob in a Western movie. The big difference was their hostility was not directed toward those held in custody, but toward the one responsible for them being in custody. And that was me! I was a stranger, and they didn't trust me. I was meddling in affairs that were none of my business. I was an outsider.

When Deputy Ellis and I had earlier escorted the Hawkins boys from my car to the Sheriff's Office, I noticed the crowd had parted and let us through without difficulty. I sensed the crowd was more hostile now, and I believed they would become a mob if an effort was made to interview a fourteen-year-old behind the closed doors of the Sheriff's Office. I made a decision that was a calculated risk on my part. I said to Trooper Power, "Let's talk to him in my car where the crowd can see he is not being mistreated."

I told Joe to follow us, and as Power and I led the way the crowd parted. Power got in back and Joe sat beside me on the front seat. The crowd seemed stunned and stayed at a respectable distance. At first, Joe told of being present on the double date, which he claimed ended between 11:00 and 11:30 P.M. at Joyce's house. However, when confronted with the information obtained from Jack Hawkins, he changed his story. He stated the double date ended at the Key residence between 9:00 and 9:30 P.M. with Benny and Jack leaving, and advised that the next day Benny returned and said to him, Nancy, and Joyce that if they were ever asked about that Saturday night to say they went to the drive-in at Burnsville and got back between 11:00 and 11:30 P.M. Joe's statement was the first corroborating evidence I had to substantiate the admission of Jack Hawkins. Until then I had only a naked confession, no physical evidence, and three people (Nancy, Joyce, and Benny) saying the confession was not true. I was determined to obtain more evidence.

I knew the crowd was confused over Joe being interviewed

152

right out in the open. They could see the interview being conducted, but couldn't hear anything as they remained several yards away, and thanks to the cool mountain air, we had the car windows closed. When Joe's interview was completed, I asked him to locate his sister and have her to come to the car. The next move I made was strictly for the crowd. When Joe got out of the car, I leaned over and knocked on the window on the passenger side of the car to get his attention. He turned around, and I rolled the window down and extended my hand.

We shook hands as I said, "Maybe next time you go on a double date, you'll have a girl." This simple statement had the effect I hoped for, as Joe grinned from ear to ear. I suspected most of those in the crowd thought interviews or interrogations consisted of deceit, rubber hoses, and other brutal tactics. They didn't know what to think when they saw us shake hands and Joe grinning.

Nancy Key was reinterviewed in my car in the presence of Trooper Power. When confronted with the information obtained from Joe, she acknowledged she had not been truthful in her first interview and was trying to protect Jack and Benny. She then furnished essentially the same information as had been supplied by her brother.

At my request, Nancy located Joyce Price and escorted her to my car. She retracted her original statement and furnished information consistent with that of Nancy and Joe Key.

I returned to the Sheriff's Office and conferred with Deputy Ellis. We agreed a Justice of the Peace should be summoned to the courthouse, and the Hawkins boys could appear before him and either waive or demand a preliminary hearing. This is a judicial proceeding in felony cases to determine if there is sufficient evidence to bind the accused over for a trial. If probable cause is found, bail is set in non-capital cases. Deputy Ellis made a telephone call to Mr. Russell, who advised he would be at the courthouse at 8:30 P.M. The crowd outside now numbered well over one hundred. It was Saturday night, and many of the men folks had consumed more than a smidgen of moonshine. They had gotten louder and were on the verge of turning into a mob. It was a very dangerous situation, and Trooper Powder, Deputy Ellis, and I knew it. Efforts by Deputy Ellis to locate the Sheriff

153

by telephone and radio were unsuccessful. Bakersville had no police department, and to make matters worse, Trooper Power had to leave to investigate a serious accident near Spruce Pine. At my suggestion, Deputy Ellis stepped outside and announced to the crowd that the Hawkins boys would appear before Mr. Russell in the courtroom at 8:30 P.M. An immediate silence engulfed the abnormally cool evening. A slight breeze stirred autumn leaves, which danced lightly in the street as though too nervous to stay put. It made for an eerie feeling.

Mr. Russell arrived at the Sheriff's Office at about 8:20 P.M. He was a small man who appeared to be in his early seventies. He had big eyes as nearly as large as the lens in his wire-rimmed glasses. He was completely bald and deep worry furrows crossed his brow. He was wearing an ancient blue suit, a frayed white shirt, a black string tie, white socks and brown brogans. Trooper Power had told me before he left that he doubted Mr. Russell had ever held a preliminary hearing. I introduced myself to him and told him that I had conducted the investigation resulting in the charges against the Hawkins boys and believed I would be the only witness necessary.

I knew things were bad, but didn't know how bad until Mr. Russell asked, "Necessary for what?"

I then explained to him why the boys were to appear before him, what a preliminary hearing was for, and how it should be conducted. If either boy wanted a preliminary hearing, then he should set a date for it.

When I finished, he said, "Let's go to court."

The spectator section of the courtroom was almost filled. What I noticed immediately was that the crowd had quieted considerably, but I expected it was only temporary. The courtroom was not well illuminated, and shadows played along the walls. Deputy Ellis escorted Jack Hawkins into the courtroom and marched him directly in front of Mr. Russell, who sat on the bench as though he ruled over all those assembled before him.

He said, "Jack Hawkins, you are charged with burning D.Y. Adcock's tenant house. You are here to tell me if you want a preliminary hearing. It's a hearing to see if the State has enough evidence to bind you over to court and, if so, to set bail. Do you want a hearing or not?"

154

Jack Hawkins looked up and nearly shouted, "Mr. Russell, I'm guilty and I don't want no hearing. I burnt it." I was startled, and so was the crowd.

Mr. Russell looked down and said in his mountain drawl, "Jack, I didn't ask you how you plead. I only asked if you wanted a hearing. Bail is set at $1,000.00."

Deputy Ellis led Jack from the courtroom as a murmur went through the crowd. So far, so good. He returned with Benny Hawkins. Mr. Russell looked down at him and explained why he was there. He then explained what a preliminary hearing was and how it could be requested or waived. Mr. Russell also explained that a preliminary hearing would determine if bail should be set and, if so, how much. Benny barely allowed Mr. Russell to finish when he said in a contemptuous voice, "I ain't done nothing, and I want one of them hearings, and I want it now."

Mr. Russell replied in a firm voice, "Very well. Mr. Emerson of the SBI, take the stand." I took my seat in the witness box, and Mr. Russell looked over at me and said, "Tell me what you know about this matter."

I proceeded to attempt to tell what the investigation had determined. However, as unbelievable as it seems, I was repeatedly interrupted by questions shouted from the spectators. Mr. Russell made no effort to stop these questions, so I just answered them the best I could. Some of the questions I recall were: "What's the *FBI* got to do with this? What are you doing up here, anyway? Why did you drive Jack away from the ball ground to talk to him?" These and other questions were not asked politely, but rather in menacing and contemptuous tones.

During my testimony, I informed Mr. Russell what I had learned from Joyce Price and Joe and Nancy Key. When I finished testifying, several spectators stood up and demanded that Mr. Russell allow the girls to testify. He said, "Let's hear them."

Nancy was first, followed by Joyce. Both girls testified that on the night of September 7th, they attended a drive-in movie at Burnsville with Jack and Benny Hawkins and Nancy's little brother. That they returned to Nancy's home between 11:00 and 11:30 P.M. Under questioning by Mr. Russell, both girls acknowledged they had admitted to me their dates ended between

9:00 and 9:30 P.M. with Jack and Benny saying they were leaving to burn Mr. Adcock's tenant house. However, they both said I scared them into making the admissions.

Mr. Russell had me fooled. I thought he was gutless and would cave in to the demands of the crowd, but Jack Hawkins's appearance before him had made an impression. Mr. Russell looked out over the hostile crowd in the courtroom and, in a steady and firm voice, said, "When Jack Hawkins stood before me a short while ago, he was not frightened into saying he was guilty. It's a fact Mr. Adcock's tenant house burned. Jack Hawkins said he was guilty of it. Mr. Emerson also testified Jack said Benny helped burn it. That's enough for probable cause. Bail is set at $1,000.00 for Benny Hawkins."

I followed Deputy Ellis as he escorted Benny Hawkins back to jail. I stopped at the Sheriff's Office and waited for Ellis to return. When he did, he informed me the next term of Mitchell County Superior Court would be in April 1964.

I opened the door to exit the Sheriff's Office and saw that most of the crowd was still there. They were more subdued, but there was still tension in the air, and they were between me and my car. I could either retreat and seek sanctuary in the Sheriff's Office, or attempt to make my way through an inflamed horde of mountain people. I had never taken a step backward when faced with endangerment, and didn't intend to do so. I lit a cigarette as casually as I could, inhaled deeply, and started on a direct path toward my car. As I made my way forward, the crowd slowly parted. There was complete silence, with no catcalls, no cursing, and no spitting. I looked from side to side and remembered catching the eye of an elderly mountain man with a full beard, and long dirty hair hanging from under the traditional brown felt hat. A pipe with a long straight stem protruded from the corner of his mouth. When our eyes met his expression didn't change, but I detected the slightest nod of his head. I instantly knew what it meant. As far as he was concerned, I had passed muster.

As I approached my car, I didn't notice any damage to it. I unlocked the door and started the engine. I picked up the radio mike and spoke into it. "Asheville, 993 is 10-8 (in service)." I drove slowly out of Bakersville and headed toward Spruce Pine.

A few miles from town I contacted Trooper Power by radio. He had quickly finished his investigation of the accident and was worried about the situation at Bakersville. He was en route back there, but turned around when I contacted him. We arranged to meet at a cafe on the outskirts of town. I hadn't eaten since breakfast and it was past 10:00 P.M. Power and I talked as I drank a milkshake and ate two cheeseburgers. What he told me made me feel very fortunate. He said Bakersville was the only county seat of the one hundred North Carolina counties that did not have a resident State Trooper. He advised that efforts to station troopers there had been unsuccessful, as their state and personal vehicles were vandalized, as were their houses. He advised the situation there earlier in the evening was very explosive, and I was lucky to have avoided injury, or even worse.

It was 11:30 P.M. when I pulled into my driveway at Marion and told Asheville radio I would be 10-7 (out of service) at my residence. Vicky was still up, and opened the front door for me. It had been another routine fifteen-hour day. I must have looked awful, but she smiled and said, "Another hard day at the office?"

I responded with a weak smile and replied, "Yes, a damned hard day."

In the April 1964 term of Mitchell County Superior Court, I testified before the Grand Jury and true bills of indictment were returned charging both Hawkins boys with the felonious burning of a dwelling house. Shortly after their arrests back in October bail was posted for both, and they had been free since then. Their cases were continued until the September 1964 term of court so Jack Hawkins could undergo examination at the state mental hospital in Raleigh. He was examined and found competent to stand trial. The cases against the Hawkins boys were called for trial in the September 1964 term of court and both failed to appear. A capias (order for arrest) was issued for each. In the April 1965 term of court both boys were present for court and were represented by counsel. They both were allowed to enter pleas of guilty to the misdemeanor of Injury to Personal Property. Each received a two-year sentence, suspended for five years, and each was fined $650. Call it what you want, but I call it mountain justice.

Years later when I told Big Glen about this case he said, "If all them cars and pickups had been following me through the mountains, I don't believe I would have stopped at Bakersville. I would have kept on going to Spruce Pine, and then across the parkway to Marion. I would have seen how far the bastards would have followed me."

35

The winter of 1963–64 passed swiftly, as I was busy working an assortment of cases including murders, armed robberies, rapes, burglaries, arsons, larcenies, safe robberies, and various other offenses. I had a great deal of success in solving these crimes, and attribute most of it to hard work, and, from time to time, a little luck. Speaking of luck, I remember receiving a telephone call early one morning from Dad. This was unusual, as he and Mom usually called on Sunday nights. At first I was concerned, as I thought something bad might have happened. I was quickly relieved, as I detected a rare note of humor in his voice as he inquired about Vicky and Gloria. When told they were doing well, he changed the subject immediately and asked very casually if I had had a burglary the previous day at a residence near Old Fort in McDowell County. I replied that if there had been one I was unaware of it, and my assistance had not been requested. In a voice imitating disgust, he said, "Yesterday morning a home near the railroad tracks at Old Fort was broken into and a .38 caliber revolver, suitcase, food, clothing, and a few other items were taken. Two AWOL sailors are responsible, and I have them in jail."

I felt embarrassed. Here was my father calling from nearly 200 miles away telling me he had two subjects in custody who had burglarized a residence in the county where I was stationed, and I was not even aware of it. I didn't know what to say, but finally asked why he had them in jail in Chatham County. He explained that the two subjects had unsuccessfully attempted an armed robbery in Chatham County the previous night, and shortly thereafter had been arrested by him and a deputy. He had interrogated the pair and learned the gun they used was stolen earlier that day from a home they burglarized near Old Fort. In addition to the gun, they also admitted taking the other items he had mentioned. I told Dad I would check with the McDowell Sheriff's Department and determine if they had a report of the burglary. Dad furnished me the names, ages, and other identification data regarding both subjects. He also told me it wouldn't be necessary to rush warrants to Chatham County, as neither of the subjects would be able to make the high bail that would be set for them for attempted armed robbery.

Later that morning, I went by the McDowell Sheriff's Office and learned they had a report of a home broken into the previous day near Old Fort. A .38 caliber pistol, suitcase, food, clothing, and several other items were taken. They had no suspects. I informed Sheriff F. D. Glenn of the telephone call I had received. He was elated as it gave him a great deal of pleasure to pick up the telephone and inform the homeowner that two subjects had burglarized his residence and that both were in custody and his property recovered.

Several days later, I had to make a trip to the laboratory in Raleigh regarding evidence in another case. I had warrants for the two subjects with me and stopped by the jail in Pittsboro to interview them and serve the warrants. Afterwards, I went to lunch with Dad and a couple of his deputies. I received good-natured ribbing from them about how difficult it was to keep crime under control in Chatham County without also having to do my work. I thought about Grand Forks, North Dakota, and how fortunate I was to be back in North Carolina.

36

Another case that occurred during that winter involved a suspect who was arrested by the Spruce Pine police late at night near the scene of a jewelry store break-in. Spruce Pine didn't have a permanent jail, so persons arrested were confined to a temporary lockup until they could be transported to the county jail in Bakersville. The temporary facility was unattended, and the cell door was secured by a large padlock. Unbeknownst to the officers, the suspect they had arrested and placed in their holding cell had a lengthy criminal record and a history of several escapes from the North Carolina Prison Department. Sure enough, the next morning the padlock and the suspect were both missing. A search of Spruce Pine and the surrounding area failed to locate the suspect. Several days later, my assistance was requested. Nearly three weeks passed before a tip was received that the suspect was shacked up in Burke County with Hilda Pratt, who was originally from Spruce Pine. The informant furnished the exact location of the house where they reportedly were living. It was about fifty miles away near the community of Icard at the end of a rural paved road. Burke County joined my territory but was in the area covered by SBI Agent Charlie Whitman.

I contacted Charlie by telephone and apprised him of the situation. Charlie said to give him a day or two and he would be back in touch. He called me at home early the next day. He had located the house where Hilda Pratt was living. Charlie and I were both well aware that the ideal time to conduct a raid to effect an apprehension is just before dawn. Most people are in a deep sleep at that time and are less likely to be aware of approaching danger. When they do awaken, they are not as alert as they normally would be and are not suitably attired to quickly flee. They are also less inclined to resist arrest when in their birthday suits or skivies. Charlie and I decided to meet the following morning at 5:30 A.M. at Icard. He said two Burke deputies would be with him, and I advised that two Spruce Pine police-men would accompany me.

The following morning we met as agreed. It took us only a few minutes to plan the raid. Charlie, a Burke deputy, and a Spruce Pine policeman would be in Charlie's car. I would follow on his bumper with a Burke deputy and a Spruce Pine police-man in my car. We would drive the last quarter mile with our lights off and pull quietly into the yard. All six of us would exit from the cars simultaneously, making sure no car doors were slammed. Both of our vehicles had been fixed so that the dome lights wouldn't come on when the doors opened. Charlie and a deputy would immediately dash to the back door and a Spruce Pine policeman would cover each side of the house. I would go to the front door accompanied by the other deputy.

We drove to the residence as planned and stopped quietly in the yard. Everyone hurried to their assigned positions. I knocked loudly on the front door with my flashlight. A light came on in-side the house, and I thought I could hear voices. I rapped on the door again and a faint female voice from inside asked, "Who's there?"

I replied, "State Bureau of Investigation. Open the door."

I heard the door unlock, and then it was slowly opened by a fairly attractive, but sleepy-eyed female in her late twenties. She had on a long Mickey Mouse sweatshirt, and if she wore any-thing else I wasn't aware of it.

I asked if she was Hilda Pratt, and she nodded and said, "But I ain't done nothing." I told her we had warrants for the suspect and asked if he was there. She didn't verbally respond, but motioned with her head toward a room in back of her. The door to the room was closed, and I carefully stood to the side as I turned the knob and pushed it open.

The lamp on the nightstand was on, and sitting in the mid-dle of the bed Indian-style with his legs crossed was the suspect. He was smoking a cigarette and was "naked as a jaybird." He looked at the deputy and me and said, "Come in, gentlemen."

The arrest warrants were read to the suspect, and I told him to get dressed. The other officers, with the exception of Charlie, came in out of the cold. After the suspect had put on his trousers, I noticed him pick up a small leather key case from the nightstand. He was about to put it in the front pocket of his trousers when I reached out and relieved him of it. I unzipped the case and there in my hands was a beautiful lock-pick set. In fact, it was the only set I had seen since I was with ONI.

I didn't need an explanation as to how the suspect had escaped from the lockup at Spruce Pine. I was holding the answer in my hands. The suspect looked at me and said, "What are those things?"

I replied, "About five to ten years."

I turned to Hilda and asked if the 1955 Ford parked outside belonged to her. She pointed at the suspect and said that it was his. At about that time, Charlie came into the room and said, "The hell it is. I just checked by radio and it was stolen in Asheville."

As I handcuffed the suspect, I told him that in addition to the warrants just served on him from Mitchell County, it appeared he would be charged with possession of burglary tools (lock-picking devices) in Burke County and automobile larceny in Asheville. I thought that would do it, until a Burke deputy said there was food in the kitchen taken from the break-in of a nearby school cafeteria. I just shook my head. Accompanied by the Spruce Pine officers, I transported the suspect to the Mitchell County jail in Bakersville.

I was fascinated by the lock-pick set and spent many hours practicing with it on a padlock I had at home. I learned to open it within a few seconds. At my earliest opportunity, I returned to Burke County and took the lock-pick set and my padlock with me. I briefed the District Attorney on the details of the case and included the suspect's criminal history and past escapes. I then pulled from my briefcase the lock-pick set and the padlock. It took me about five seconds to get the padlock to pop open. The District Attorney raised his eyebrows and grinned sheepishly as he said, "Charge the sum bitch with possession of burglary tools." I went straight to the magistrate's office and swore out a warrant.

While the suspect was sitting in the Mitchell County jail waiting to be tried on the two cases in that county, deputies from Burke County arrived and returned him to their county to face a misdemeanor charge of breaking into the school cafeteria. He was convicted and received an active sentence of eighteen months. He was turned over to the North Carolina Prison Department, but Burke County authorities failed to notify prison officials that he had felony cases pending. He was therefore sent to a misdemeanor camp and, needless to say, escaped the first day he was there. In 1966, he was apprehended in Louisiana but extradited to Arkansas to serve a short sentence for a crime committed in that state. In December 1967, he was returned to North Carolina. At that time I was stationed at Raleigh. I was subpoenaed to appear in Burke County Superior Court regarding the burglary tool indictment. I returned to Burke County and had the lock-pick set with me as evidence. The District Attorney remembered the case well, and he still had in his case file a copy of my investigative report that I had sent to him. He knew I had driven a long distance and was anxious to get back to Raleigh. He called the case for trial shortly after I arrived, and a jury was quickly selected. I completed my testimony on direct examination and was then subject to cross-examination. The attorney for the defense rose slowly from his seat. He walked over to the witness stand, looked around at the jury with a sly grin, reached in his coat pocket, and pulled out a padlock. He handed it to me and said only two words: "Open this."

I waited for the District Attorney to object, but nothing was forthcoming. He only smiled at me and nodded. He must have remembered well my demonstration to him nearly four years earlier, and thought I could open anything secured with a lock. He certainly didn't know that all the practice I had had with the lock picks had been four years earlier, and was limited to my padlock. I looked at the unfamiliar lock and began to sweat. I held it low in the witness box so the jury wouldn't see my hands shake. I could feel perspiration on my forehead. I inserted a rake and tension bar into the lock and gently applied pressure as I raked over the tumblers. The courtroom silence was suddenly broken by a metallic "click" as the lock's hasp popped open. I was momentarily stunned, but extremely pleased with myself, as it had taken no more than fifteen seconds to perform the feat. I held the lock up so the jury would have a good look. The defense attorney looked at me in awe, but said nothing. The judge was grinning like a mule eating briars. He looked at the defense attorney and asked if there would be any more demonstrations or questions. The attorney just shook his head.

The defense attorney and the District Attorney were good friends, and as I returned to my seat, I heard the District Attorney lean over close to his friend and say, "Billy, how did you like them apples?"

The jury was out for only a few minutes and came back with a guilty verdict. The suspect was sentenced to not less than three nor more than five years. He still had to serve the eighteen months for the cafeteria break-in and also faced felony charges in Mitchell County and Asheville plus an escape charge from the Prison Department. My testimony wouldn't be needed at those trials.

Years later, when I told Big Glen about this case, he spit a stream of Red Man and said, "When that sum bitch is dead, the Devil had better watch him or he'll pick the locks on the gates of hell to get out."

37

During that winter of 1963–64, I was involved in a case that I'll relate the facts of but for obvious reasons won't disclose the names of the people involved or the counties.

There were many summer homes scattered throughout my four-county territory. They were owned by the wealthy, beautifully constructed and elaborately furnished. During the winter months, these homes were unoccupied and easily burglarized. Sometimes several weeks or even a few months might pass before a burglary would be discovered. This was not the case for a summer home owned by a furniture company executive. He had made friends with a nearby superintendent of a game preserve who checked on his home daily during the winter months. When the home was burglarized, and the local sheriff requested my assistance, the case was fresh. The merchandise stolen consisted of expensive china, crystal, silverware, antiques, and pottery.

A crime scene search revealed fabric marks indicating the perpetrator(s) wore gloves. Several days passed before a break came. Two deputy sheriffs from a county a considerable distance away came to the area and sought the assistance of the local sheriff's department. They had warrants for two subjects who were discovered inside a country store they had broken into in their county. The two subjects, who were brothers-in-law, had gotten away but had left behind in the store a loaded shotgun and their vehicle parked nearby. One or both may have been wounded by gunfire from the deputies. It was believed the two subjects had relatives in the county where the summer home had been burglarized. The local sheriff referred the visiting officers to one of his deputies, and the three of them spent the day without developing any leads regarding the two fugitives. The two deputies left that night thinking that their trip had been in vain. The following day, the deputy who had worked with them received information from an informant that the two fugitives were responsible for the summer home burglary I was working.

The informant also stated that the residence they shared in the county from which they fled had a hidden room in the attic that was filled with stolen property. The deputy telephoned the sheriff of the county where the subjects had lived and furnished to him the information regarding the hidden room. A few hours later, the sheriff called back and stated that he and his deputies had located the room and it contained merchandise from numerous burglaries, including the case I was working.

The following day I drove to the county where the two subjects had lived. The sheriff proudly displayed the recovered property to me. It consisted of not only the merchandise from the summer home, but also included cases of cigarettes, radios, knives, guns, wallets, clothing, shoes, et cetera; however, there was still a problem. The two subjects were not in custody and were believed to be armed and considered extremely dangerous. I learned from the sheriff that one of the subjects was married and his wife had just moved in with her parents. He gave directions to their residence.

She was short, fat, and a homely twenty-seven years of age. She was not very cooperative, as she would answer some questions but didn't volunteer any information. She vehemently denied knowing the whereabouts of her husband or brother; however, under intense questioning she finally disclosed the name of her husband's father and identified the county where she believed he lived. It was in my territory but not the county where the summer home had been entered. The next day, I returned to the county where my case had originated and obtained felony warrants for the two subjects. I briefed the sheriff on what had been accomplished, and informed him I was going over to the next county to contact the local sheriff there in an attempt to locate the father of one of the subjects. The sheriff said he would ride along with me.

We arrived at the office of the neighboring sheriff shortly after lunch. He was pleased to see us, and listened attentively as I explained the case to him. I finished by furnishing him with the name given to me as that of the father of one of the fugitives. The local sheriff shook his head, and said he wasn't familiar with the name, but to give him a few minutes. He left the office and returned about ten minutes later and said a man by that name

167

lived alone in a cabin in an isolated part of the county. I suggested we discreetly locate the cabin while it was daylight and return before dawn the following morning and arrest the subjects if they were there. The local sheriff agreed, and as we got up to leave, the sheriff who had accompanied me on the trip and whose case I was working, said, "I know a number of people here in the courthouse. I think I'll stay and visit with them while you fellows are gone."

The local sheriff and I got into his car, and before he started the engine, he looked at me and said, "What the hell?" I shrugged my shoulders. Within an hour we had located a walking trail off an unpaved road. The sheriff said his information was that the cabin was about a mile up the trail. We didn't go any further for fear of being seen. We returned to the Sheriff's Office and found the other sheriff waiting for us.

The local sheriff and I decided to raid the cabin the next morning. He said he and three of his deputies would be available. I said I would meet him at his office at 5:00 A.M. The sheriff whom I was assisting said, "I'll send a couple of my men over."

The following morning at 5:00 A.M. I arrived at the Sheriff's Office. The local sheriff, three of his deputies, and two deputies from the county I was assisting were there. We took three cars and by 5:30 A.M. parked where the trail came out of the mountains. We still had a mile to walk. Everyone was heavily armed. I took out my carbine with the folding stock and inserted a thirty-round magazine. I stuck another 30-round magazine in my pocket. I was wearing an unusual coat, which I had purchased in Idaho. It was similar to a parka, but extended below the knees. It had slits inside the side pockets that allowed the wearer to have access to his trouser pockets without unzipping the coat. I took the coat off and placed the sling to the carbine over my right shoulder. I flipped the fire selector switch to full automatic and put my coat back on. The carbine couldn't be seen unless the coat was unzipped and only then if I raised the barrel up to a firing position.

We walked nearly straight up for about thirty minutes over some of the most mountainous terrain I had encountered. We stopped about 200 yards from the cabin, which we could see clearly in the moonlight. The smell of smoke from a wood fire lingered in the air. The cabin was dark. Our climb was over as the cabin was now on a level plain with us. The seven of us huddled together and the deputies listened as the sheriff and I made final plans for the raid. We agreed there was probably a hound dog or two near the cabin, and to try to ease up to it undetected wouldn't be practical. We settled on a plan to walk quickly and quietly as possible toward the cabin and as soon as a dog barked or there was any other sign of us being detected, run the remaining distance. We wanted two deputies to cover the back door, and since there were no side doors, one deputy to each side of the house would be sufficient in the event escape was attempted out a window. The sheriff and I were to go in the front door. This was the most dangerous assignment, as entering an unfamiliar house where two fugitive felons might be waiting wasn't the way many people liked to start their day. There was one extra deputy, so I looked at the five of them and quietly asked, "Who wants to go in the front with the sheriff and me?"

There was a moment of silence before a deputy who had been sent over from the other county by his sheriff stepped forward. He knew very little about this case, but looked me square in the eye and said "By damn I'll go in with you."

We started walking quickly toward the cabin and were within a hundred yards of it before dogs started barking. We started running, and before I knew it I was rapping on the door with my flashlight in my left hand. My right hand embraced the pistol grip of my carbine. My coat was unzipped. A very dim light came on, and I suddenly realized there was no electricity in the cabin. A husky masculine voice from inside asked, "Who the hell is there?"

I replied, "Sheriff's Department and State Bureau of Investigation. Open the door." It opened quickly, and a bearded man in his fifties, wearing long johns stood barefoot in the doorway holding a lamp. The local sheriff had pinned his badge to his coat and quickly illuminated it with his flashlight. The sheriff asked the man for his name, and when he answered, I told him we had arrest warrants for two subjects, whom I identified by name. He said they were there and pointed to a room off to the side. The door was closed. The deputy took the lamp from the man and placed it on a table near the closed door. I turned the doorknob and eased the door open, holding my flashlight in my left hand away from my body. I went in, followed by the sheriff and deputy. The two subjects were both in the only bed in the room. They were awake, but offered no resistance. I'm sure the first thing they saw that morning was the barrel of my carbine extending out of the front of my coat. It was difficult getting up for early morning raids, but it was a hell of a lot better than coming home bloody.

The two subjects were returned to the county, where they had burglarized the summer home. Later that day, I interviewed both subjects, and they not only admitted the summer home burglary but nine others involving homes and stores in several counties. A few months later, both subjects pleaded guilty to the felonies of breaking and entering and larceny involving the summer home. One subject received a sentence of five to seven years for breaking and entering, and four to six years for larceny. The other subject received six to ten years for breaking and entering and five to seven years for larceny. They still had to face similar charges in other counties.

During the time I was stationed in western North Carolina, I found nearly all the sheriffs I came to know to be honest and hard-working public servants. The one who had requested my assistance in the case just related was an exception. I found him to be strictly a cheap local politician whose honesty was later determined to be very much in doubt. In fact, after the arrests of the two subjects in this case, the next edition of the local newspaper carried a story of how he had gone to the neighboring county and obtained the assistance of that sheriff and "laid a scheme" resulting in the arrests of the two subjects. Strange how I wasn't mentioned in the article.

Years later, when Big Glen and I were stuffing ourselves at a pig picking, I told him about this case. His comment was, "I'd left that crazy sheriff visiting in the courthouse, and he could have hitch-hiked home. But I won't throw off on his deputy who went in the cabin with you."

38

Madison County was not in my territory, but rather bordered Yancey County, which was. In 1964 it had a population of only 18,000. Marshall, the county seat located about twenty-five miles north of Asheville, had less than 1,000 inhabitants. The county's largest town, Mars Hill, had a population of approximately 1,500. It was, and still is, the home of Mars Hill College. I don't know why, but many North Carolinians refer to the county as Bloody Madison. I came to know this mountainous area well, as it is where I spent most of the summer of 1964. At that time Madison, McDowell, Mitchell, and Yancey counties made up the Thirty-fourth Senatorial District of North Carolina, from which one senator was elected to the state legislature. Winning the Democratic primary was tantamount to being elected, as the district had few Republicans. The Democratic primary on May 30 was won by Dano Potter of Madison County by 400 votes over Clyde Nowell of McDowell County. Nowell contested the election, as he carried McDowell, Mitchell, and Yancey counties. He claimed more votes were counted in Madison County than were legally cast.

The State Board of Elections requested assistance from the SBI regarding the allegations. The Director selected four agents from the SBI Western District to assist in the probe. I was one of the four.

I found Madison County to be unique in that most of the county was composed of hillbillies right out of *Lil'Abner*, but Mars Hill was a quaint village with a college environment. It seemed out of place in Bloody Madison. There was no question as to who ran the county. It was absolutely controlled by Sheriff Y. E. Potter and his brother, Dano Potter, who was School Board Chairman and a prominent dairyman. The Potters, and members of their clan, ran all county operations. People wanting roads, jobs, welfare, or anything associated with county government or politics had to go through the sheriff or Dano. The Potters had their own kingdom, but Dano was ambitious and wanted to expand it. He wanted to be Senator Dano Potter of the Thirty-fourth District, and his cronies wanted it for him.

Mars Hill was a laid-back Mayberryesque community, but much more sophisticated because of the college influence. The vast majority of its citizens were opposed to the Potters and the political power they wielded. When the other three agents and I arrived in the county to assist in the investigation of the alleged voting irregularities, the people of Mars Hill sincerely welcomed us and offered their full cooperation. In the smaller communities and rural areas, it was a different story. We were looked upon as an invading enemy who was there to disrupt a political machine they had come to accept and rely on as a normal part of life.

Our mission was to act as an investigative arm of the State Board of Elections, as they held hearings in the county regarding the contested election. It didn't take but a few days to ascertain that in several precincts there were more votes cast for Dano than registered Democratic voters in the precincts. Registration books were padded with people who didn't exist and pages had disappeared from the books in some precincts. The signatures of some precinct judges were forged on election results, which were sent to the County Board of Elections. The names of many persons who had moved out of the county, or were deceased, were checked off and recorded as having voted.

All my life I had heard of votes being bought, and I had often wondered how the buyer could be sure the person voted as desired. In Bloody Madison I found out. A vote buyer for a candidate would be one of the first in line when the polls opened. He would enter the polling place and receive a paper ballot. He would go into the booth and remove from his pocket a blank sheet of paper folded to fit into the slot of a ballot box. He would conceal the official unmarked ballot on his person and exit the booth, dropping the blank sheet of paper in the box. He would go outside with the official ballot and mark it as he desired. When a deal was reached with a vote seller, the buyer would give him the marked ballot with instructions to drop it in the box and return with an unmarked ballot for which he would receive the going price. It was usually a dollar. The buyer would then fill out the unmarked ballot as he wanted, and the process would be repeated throughout the day. A simple but effective way to buy an election.

Hearings by the State Board of Elections confirmed Mr. Nowell's charges of vote fraud in Madison County, which resulted in him being declared the winner of the Democratic primary. He was later successful in the general election and became the senator from the Thirty-fourth District. I considered the long, hot summer of 1964 to be only a partial success. The investigation resulted in a fraudulent primary election being reversed, but there were no indictments. Those who had perpetrated the fraud were not indicted, even though to me there seemed to be sufficient evidence. But realistically, I doubt a jury could have been found in Madison County that would have convicted them.

Years later, when I told Big Glen about this case, he grinned rather slyly and said, "I'll bet in Bloody Madison they registered folks at night by flashlight in graveyards."

39

I was glad to get back to work in my own territory after working Madison County. There was an old case pending in Avery County that needed to be resolved. It had originated in September 1962, with a request to the Director from the North Carolina Board of Medical Examiners for an investigation. That agency had received information from the Avery County Health Director that a naturopath, calling himself Dr. Lee Nu Wong, was constructing a small clinic in the county. He reportedly claimed to treat all diseases as well as perform minor surgery and deliver babies. Since naturopaths were not recognized by the state of North Carolina, a case was opened regarding Wong allegedly practicing medicine without being licensed.

The case was assigned to Agent W.C. Wall, who was one of the SBI's drug agents stationed in nearby Burke County. Wall located the residence of Wong just off Highway 105 near the Watauga County line. A concrete block and sheet metal building was under construction nearby.

On November 26, 1962, an informant introduced Wall to Wong as a used car salesman. Wong, an Asian of Chinese descent, gave Wall a tour of the building. He advised that the first floor would be used as a laboratory and for storage, and the second floor would be his clinic, consisting of a waiting room, examining room, and living quarters. Wong advised he was going to treat all diseases and illnesses by using herbal medicine, which he would produce in his laboratory. Wall's inquiries revealed Wong intended to practice medicine, but apparently was not doing so at that time. Wall left the case in open status, and it was reassigned to me on October 11, 1963, as Avery County was in my territory, and Wall had been transferred to Charlotte.

On November 17, 1963, I contacted Trooper Robert Bowman, who had been of assistance in the Roy Lee Beaver murder case. Bowman advised he was familiar with Wong, and further stated that construction of the clinic appeared to be completed.

He promised to be alert for traffic at the clinic and to record license plate numbers of vehicles observed there. Bowman said Wong did not own a vehicle and hitch-hiked wherever he went.

On February 24, 1964, Bowman advised there had been no activity at the clinic and apparently Wong was not in the area. He said the winter had been extremely harsh, which may have prompted Wong to temporarily close. Bowman advised he would continue to check the clinic and would contact me when activity resumed there.

On May 28, 1964, I was in Avery County on another investigation and passed a large sign beside Highway 105. I glanced at it and braked to a stop. I could hardly believe what I had seen. The sign read: *Welcome—Avery County Mountain Clinic—Dr. Lee Nu Wong—Licensed Naturopathic Physician.* I unlocked the trunk of my car and took out my camera. Photographs were made of the sign and clinic behind it.

Because of the Madison County investigation, I didn't have an opportunity to follow up on the Wong case until July 22, 1964, when I contacted one of my Avery County informants. He advised that he had known Wong for about three years and on one occasion had gone to him with a crick in his neck. He said Wong massaged his neck and then "snapped it." He claimed the crick instantly felt much better and within a few days was gone. The informant claimed Wong didn't charge him anything since it was his first visit as a patient. The informant further advised Wong claimed to be a doctor and apparently had many patients at Indian reservations. He also said Wong claimed to be from Hawaii. The informant furnished the name of one of Wong's regular patients from nearby Banner Elk, but stated if he was contacted Wong would be notified.

On August 28, 1964, I contacted Dr. Mary Mitchell at her office in Newland. She was the Director of the Avery County Health Department and the original complainant in this matter. She was still very much interested in the case, as she believed Wong was treating people who should be receiving proper medical attention from competent physicians; however, she didn't have the names of any of his patients. She gave a card to me that she said was one of many Wong was passing out at various places in order to solicit business. The front of the card read:

"Dr. Lee Nu Wong, Importer-Exporter, Highway Route 105, Box 100, Banner Elk, North Carolina." The other side of the card read: "Statewide Licensed Naturopathic Physician gives herbal medicine for your ailments: Leukemia, arthritis, pleurisy, bursitis, tonsillitis, acne, skin blemishes, phlebitis, rheumatism, cramps, scurvy, varicose veins, multiple sclerosis, cardiac myositis, emphysema, ulcers, etc. Treatments: Physio-Therapy, Electro-Therapy, Spine and Joint Manipulations, Massage, Nutrition, Minerals. Iris-Diagnosis."

I studied the card, and the longer I looked at it the more angry I became. This charlatan was apparently treating poor, ignorant mountain folks and Indians and depriving them of proper medical attention. I sincerely apologized to Dr. Mitchell for the investigation dragging on and assured her it wouldn't take much longer. The only thing was I didn't know how I would do it.

I walked out to my car and sat for a good twenty minutes thinking about how to nail the bastard. Finally, I settled on a plan. The case needed to be brought to a conclusion, and I intended to do just that. I took off my sportcoat and tie and placed them neatly in the trunk along with my credentials, badge, holster, and revolver. I put my personal checkbook in my right rear trouser pocket. I had on a short-sleeve dress shirt, which I unbuttoned at the collar.

I drove out of Newland to Highway 105 and headed toward Watauga County. Just before I reached the county line, I turned into the drive of the Avery Mountain Clinic. I walked slowly to the front door, where I followed the directions of a sign that said to knock loudly. The door was quickly opened by a short, fat oriental man with greasy, straight black hair hanging over his ears. He had thick eyebrows, which were partially obscured by horn-rimmed glasses. A Fu Man Chu mustache accentuated a bucktoothed smile. He was wearing sandals without socks, dark trousers, and a white lab coat that was filthy. Several buttons were missing from it. For some reason, he reminded me of a hog. I asked if he was Dr. Wong, and he replied that he was, and in very good English asked if I was sick. I replied that I was nervous and had difficulty sleeping and sometimes skin peeled from the palms of my hands. Wong invited me inside, and I stepped into a small foyer with a concrete floor. I followed him up a short flight of unfinished wooden stairs to what was apparently a small waiting room, which had only two straight-backed chairs. From there we entered what was obviously his office. It was furnished with a small metal desk with a folding metal chair behind it. A stool was beside the desk and an examining table was between the stool and the wall. Wong sat behind his desk and indicated I should sit on the stool. There was a stack of papers on his desk, and even though I was reading upside down I could easily make out on the top sheet the words "Avery Mountain Clinic" and "Iris-Graph." I could also make out that two large eyeballs were printed on the paper. As Wong asked for personal data, such as full name, date of birth, address, et cetera, I answered correctly except for occupation. I said I was a taxi driver, as I hoped it would account for the two-way radio in my car if it was observed. Wong filled in spaces at the top of the paper with my answers, and as he did so I got a better look at the two eyeballs. One was designated "Left Iris" and the other "Right Iris." Both had slots around them corresponding to the hours of a clock. The slots were labeled "heart," "lungs," "throat," "lower back," "upper back," "neck," et cetera.

From his breast pocket, Wong removed a penlight and came over to where I was sitting. Had he approached with a needle, I would have had a remarkable recovery, as there is just so much I would have done for the State of North Carolina. For the next forty-five minutes he stood over me while I looked up into his ugly face. He smelled of body odor, and his breath reeked of garlic. I was miserable, but things were going as I had hoped. As my eyes were being examined, Wong would stop often and make notations on his "Iris-Graph." I asked about the chart he was marking on, and Wong said it was his invention, which he called an "Iris-Graph." He claimed the eyes revealed many things about a person's health.

After the eye examination, Wong asked me to strip from the waist up. I reluctantly did so, but said to myself, "This is as damn far as I am going." Wong felt my back, chest, and stomach. He listened to my heart with a stethoscope and took my blood pressure and pulse. He made more marks on his "Iris-Graph." Wong then had me lie on the examining table and proceeded to manipulate my spine and neck for about five minutes. He then told me to put my shirt back on and have a seat on the stool. I did so, with what I thought was a very worried and concerned expression. Wong looked at me and, in what appeared to be a very caring voice, said his examination had disclosed several things. I looked down at the floor and muttered, "Tell me, doctor."

He said, "You have a leaking heart, an infected solar plexus, numerous excessive calcium deposits, a liver infection, a severe infection on the right side of the chest, arthritis, rheumatism, tension, and rubbish in the blood stream. Your pulse is eighty-four and your blood pressure is twenty points too high." Wong advised me to stay away from all other doctors and to throw away any medicines I had, including aspirin, which caused eleven different diseases. He also told me to quit smoking, as it caused sixty illnesses. He left the room and returned a few minutes later with medicine that he said he had made. It consisted of seven boxes of pills, three bottles of liquids, one bottle containing a powder, and one can of powder. Directions of when and how much to take were already labeled on each container. Wong said I should return for a follow-up visit in a month. He advised the charge for my first examination was seven dollars and the charge for the medicine was sixty dollars. I told Wong I couldn't afford to pay that much, and he asked how much could I pay. I replied that twelve dollars was all I could afford. Wong didn't appear to be disappointed, and said, with his buck-toothed smile, that I could pay the balance on my next visit. I pulled out my checkbook and wrote a check on my personal account for twelve dollars, payable to Dr. Lee Nu Wong. As I handed my check to him, I expressed an interest in the "Iris-Graph" invention. He beamed with pride as I said I would like to show one to some of my taxi driver friends who had ailments, and recommend they visit him as patients. I told him one was suffering with leukemia. Wong said that was not a problem, as he had cured several patients who had had leukemia. Wong handed me an "Iris-Graph" and told me to show it to my friends. He escorted me to the front door, and as I walked out I said to him with all sincerity, "I'll see you in a few weeks." As I drove away from the clinic, I said to myself, "You greasy fake, your days are numbered."

On September 2, 1964, I delivered the "medicine" received from Wong to the SBI Laboratory in Raleigh. It was checked, with negative results regarding narcotics, amphetamines and barbiturates.

On September 15, 1964, I received from my bank in Marion the check I had given to Wong. It was endorsed, "For Deposit Only—Dr. Lee Nu Wong." I retained it for evidentiary purposes.

On October 20, 1964, I testified before the Avery County Grand Jury. A true bill of indictment was returned against Lee Nu Wong charging him with engaging in the practice of medicine without first having obtained a license to do so in the manner provided by law. A warrant was issued for his arrest, and a $1000 cash bond was set.

On November 4, 1964, I met with Agent Charlie Whitman at Newland. We discussed the case and decided it would be best if Charlie, accompanied by Deputy Sheriff Isley, arrested Wong at his clinic and interviewed him at the Sheriff's Office. We thought it would be advantageous for me to wait until the trial and then make my appearance.

I waited in the office of the Clerk of Court when Charlie and Isley came into the Sheriff's Office with Wong. Grinning from ear to ear, Charlie came in the Clerk's office alone. He said, "Wong wants to see that camouflage agent from Marion who came to him as a patient."

I knew what had happened. Someone on the Grand Jury had revealed my testimony. I started laughing, and so did Charlie. We both had been called a lot of things but, neither of us had ever heard the term "camouflage agent."

Still laughing, I said to Charlie, "I think I'll let the sum bitch see the camouflage agent."

Charlie and I walked into the Sheriff's Office, where Isley was sitting with Wong. Before I could say a word, Wong looked at me and in an excited voice said, "There is something I didn't tell you, as I didn't want you to worry. You have an ulcer."

I said, "Thanks Doc, but let's talk about you."

Wong stated he was born October 4, 1919, in Honolulu, Hawaii, and received income from the estate of his deceased parents. He claimed to have attended Pacific Union College at

179

Angwin, California, and later served in the United States Army from 1944 to 1946, receiving an honorable discharge as a private first class. He advised that he received a degree as a Doctor of Naturopathy in 1953 from Central State College of Physiatrics in Ohio, and later did educational work at Madison College in Madison, Tennessee. Wong said he was asked to leave there in 1958 for medical and religious reasons. He advised that his practice of medicine there was not appreciated by local authorities. Wong said he moved to Watauga County in North Carolina in 1960, and the following year purchased land in Avery County where he constructed his clinic. He stated that shortly after his arrival in North Carolina he started diagnosing illnesses and treating patients for their ailments. He claimed most of his patients were from North Carolina, but advised a few came to him from out of state. Wong also acknowledged treating Indian patients at Lumberton, North Carolina. He stated he didn't believe in the use of narcotics, barbiturates, or amphetamines, but could write prescriptions for them if he desired.

I explained to Wong that naturopaths were not recognized by the State of North Carolina and for anyone to legally practice medicine in North Carolina they must have a State Qualification License issued by the State Board of Medical Examiners. He acknowledged he didn't possess such a license. I instructed him to discontinue his practice of medicine or he would face additional charges.

Wong posted a $1,000.00 cash bond, and his case was set for trial in the April 1965 term of Avery County Superior Court. It was subsequently continued until the October 1965 term. On October 19, 1965, I was advised by the District Attorney that Wong was hospitalized with blood poisoning in both feet and therefore his case would be continued until the April 1966 term of court. I was stationed in Raleigh in 1966 and was not subpoenaed back to court in Wong's case. I later learned Wong had been allowed to plead guilty to the charge of practicing medicine without a license and that prayer for judgment was continued. This meant that no sentence was imposed, but one could have been at a later date if it was deemed appropriate. I'll say it again, "Mountain justice."

Years later, when I told Big Glen about this case, he looked at me kind of strange and rolled his cigar from one side of his mouth to the other and said, "You done something I wouldn't have done. When that greasy Chinaman touched me, he would have been looking for a real doctor to take my size fifteen shoe out of his ass."

40

March 20, 1965, was a Saturday and the first day of spring. It was cold that morning and a few snowflakes were in the air as I sped down Interstate 40 to Morganton. I was not responding to another homicide case, safe robbery, or burglary, but I was in a hurry. Vicky was somewhat uncomfortable on the front seat beside me. Gloria was at home being watched over by a teenage girl who lived next door. I wheeled into the emergency receiving area of Grace Hospital. A few hours later, Vicky and I were blessed with the birth of a son. We named him after Dad and me, John Robert Emerson. That night, after Gloria was fast asleep, instead of dictating a memorandum to the Director, I used my old Royal manual typewriter and wrote the following:

DATE: 3-20-65
TO: The Director
FROM: S/A R.D. Emerson
SUBJECT: John Robert Emerson

The above subject escaped from custody this date after nine months confinement. He is described as a white male, 21" tall, 6 pounds 12 ounces, dark blue eyes and light sandy hair. Subject has a red complexion and reportedly is a heavy drinker consuming several bottles a day. Agent is personally acquainted with subject's mother and is requesting five days annual leave to assist her through this stressful period. Please advise.

The response to my memorandum was a telephone call a few days later from the Director in which he not only offered his congratulations, but also awarded me five days compensatory leave.

The next three months went by quickly as I continued my long hours investigating a variety of criminal cases, but I eagerly looked forward to ending my two-year tour of duty in the mountains. Vicky and I wanted a permanent duty station where we could buy a home and rear our children. On June 28, 1965, a call came from the Director advising me to prepare for a transfer about mid-July. He also wanted to meet with me at Raleigh Headquarters on Thursday, July 1. Vicky and the children accompanied me to Siler City on June 30, where we spent the night at Christian Hill. On Thursday, at precisely 9:00 A.M., I reported to the Director's office. Mr. Anderson greeted me cordially, and we talked of my two years in the Great Smokies and about some of the cases I had worked. Mr. Anderson finally said to me that when I was hired he promised me I would be transferred to Raleigh after two years at Marion. I smiled and replied that that was what I recalled. Mr. Anderson then surprised me with an offer I hadn't dreamed of. He said he was very pleased with my performance and my devotion to the law enforcement profession and therefore could have my choice of assignments. He advised I could work as an agent out of Raleigh Headquarters or as a resident agent at Siler City working a territory consisting of Chatham, Orange, and Lee counties. I was not only dumbfounded, but also temporarily speechless. After a moment, I told Mr. Anderson I was very appreciative of the opportunity to have my choice of duty stations, but before making a decision I would like to discuss it with Vicky. In an almost fatherly manner, Mr. Anderson said, "I thought you would say that. Take a few days and let me know."

I completed some administrative matters for the next couple of hours and then had an early lunch with a couple of laboratory technicians. I reviewed my pending cases, and left the office about mid-afternoon and drove to Pittsboro. Dad was not in his office, so I drove on to Christian Hill. Gloria was playing in the yard, and John was asleep in a bassinet in the kitchen where Vicky and Mom were preparing supper. Vicky could read me like a book, and knew I was excited when she glanced at me. I said, "We need to talk."

We went into the den where I told her of Mr. Anderson's offer. Her mouth dropped open and a look of shock appeared on her face. I knew she was remembering the days in Butte, the long winter in Idaho, the Minneapolis episode and the we-uns and you-uns of the North Carolina mountains. And now it seemed like a dream with us having an opportunity to select my duty station in our home county or in Raleigh, where we had started our marriage and enjoyed two wonderful years of college life.

Vicky and I giggled like teenagers, but neither of us volunteered an opinion as to which choice we should make. We decided to wait until after supper and discuss it with Mom and Dad.

Dad was late arriving home for supper, but we waited for him before we ate. After supper, Dad and I retired to the front porch and seated ourselves in the large rockers. We smoked and discussed a recent murder case he had investigated. Mom and Vicky finished the dishes, and soon joined us on the porch. John was asleep again, and Gloria was catching lightning bugs in the yard and putting them in a mayonnaise jar that had holes punched in the lid.

It was two years earlier on the same front porch where I made the decision to leave the FBI. Now there was another important decision to be made, and again we were on the front porch. I told Mom and Dad of the offer Mr. Anderson had extended to me. In the moonlight, I saw Dad smile and felt very close to him when he said he was proud that Mr. Anderson thought that much of me. Mom didn't enter the conversation, as Dad, Vicky, and I discussed the pros and cons of being stationed at Siler City or Raleigh. Dad even offered Vicky and me a couple of acres of land on Christian Hill on which to build a home if we elected to be stationed there. Dad and I discussed the advantages and disadvantages of working together. We also discussed how I would be accepted by local officers. Would the older ones still look at me as the kid who used to tag along? We also discussed my future with the SBI. Dad and I agreed that if promotions were to come, exposure in Raleigh would probably expedite them, and that if I elected to be stationed at Siler City, a later promotion in all probability would necessitate a transfer to another city. The discussion went on between Dad, Vicky, and me for a good two hours. Mom only asked a question now and then, and even took time out to give Gloria her bath and put her to bed. Late that night, Vicky and I made our decision. We believed it would be in our best interests to work out of Raleigh Headquarters. Dad agreed. The next day I notified Mr. Anderson of the decision.

Vicky and I spent the next several days looking for a home in the Raleigh area. We located one we both liked in Cary, which is a suburb of Raleigh and at that time had a population of around 4,000. We wanted our children to grow up in a small-town atmosphere. Little did we know that thirty years later, with both children grown and gone, Vicky and I would still be in the same home and Cary's population would be approaching 80,000.

41

Vicky, the children, and I moved into our new home in Cary on Tuesday, July 20, 1965. It was an extremely hot day and the heat affected me more than it normally would have, as my hair was well over my collar. After meeting with Mr. Anderson the first of July and returning to Marion to wrap up matters for my transfer, I had received a telephone call from Supervising Agent L. E. Allen, who was stationed at Greensboro. Allen, whom everyone called Bo, was well known in law enforcement circles throughout North Carolina and was very much admired as a skilled investigator. Bo congratulated me on my transfer to Raleigh and said he wanted to meet with me as soon as I was settled. Just before hanging up he said, "By the way, don't get a haircut." I knew immediately what was coming. I was scheduled for an undercover assignment, and I enthusiastically looked forward to it.

I reported for duty at headquarters on Monday, July 26, 1965, and within an hour met with the Director. He took one look at my hair and said, "I see Bo has been in touch with you." Before I could respond, he said that Bo and Special Agent E. J. Marquardt of the Federal Bureau of Narcotics were working a drug investigation at Chapel Hill and I was to assist them in an undercover role. I was excited, as Chapel Hill was only twenty miles from Pittsboro, and I was very familiar with it, as it's the home of the University of North Carolina. I had attended summer school there in 1952 and 1953.

On Tuesday, July 27, I met with Bo and Special Agents Marquardt and Ron Posey of the Federal Bureau of Narcotics. Bo and Marquardt had developed information of drug usage by the "beatnik crowd" at the university, and their objective was to determine the kinds of drugs being used and the source(s) of supply. Posey and I were to enjoy the nightlife at Chapel Hill and see what information we could glean.

Marquardt was stationed at Greensboro and Posey was stationed at Baltimore, but was on special assignment in North Carolina to work under Marquardt's supervision. Posey drove a late-model convertible and dressed as a typical college student. I wonder what my neighbors thought when he picked me up at my new home shortly before dark on July 27. The top was down on the convertible and music blared from the radio. I went out to his car wearing white jeans, a blue tee shirt, loafers, and no socks. I didn't have a gun, as I had no place to conceal it. The same was true for my credentials, but I carried my badge in the watch pocket of my jeans. Posey and I had been issued money for use in buying drugs, but any other expenses incurred had to be borne by us. Posey was an experienced undercover agent who was in his early thirties but looked to be in his mid-twenties. I could also pass as about the same age.

As Posey and I drove toward Chapel Hill, we composed our cover stories. He suggested that since neither of us were known in the Chapel Hill community, we use our true names, which would help us to avoid a slip of the tongue in conversation. We also decided that Baltimore would be Posey's hometown and Marion would be mine. If anyone demanded to see our driver licenses, the addresses would check out. We also agreed we had been friends for a couple of years, having met while attending North Carolina State University in Raleigh on the G.I. Bill. We had graduated in June and were taking the summer off, but were considering graduate school at UNC.

This was my first undercover assignment, except for the brief visit to the naturopath, and that very first night I discovered it was not for me. We made the bars, coffee houses, restaurants, and a pool room. We met and socialized with old people, young people, students, faculty members, and local residents who weren't associated with the university. In casual conversation with nice people who were in no way involved with drugs, I found it necessary to lie about my background and personal life. I abhorred living a lie, but for the next two weeks we kept up our charade. Posey appeared to enjoy it. We finally purchased a small quantity of marijuana from a waiter at a local restaurant. A few nights later, he introduced us to his source, who apparently was the main supplier for the community. He agreed to sell a pound to us. We were to meet him two nights later in front of the Post Office on Franklin Street. The next day, our investigation went down the drain. Unbeknownst to Bo Allen, Marquardt, Posey, or me; local authorities, who were unaware of our investigation, were conducting their own. They had identified the main local source of marijuana and raided his apartment. Two trunks filled with marijuana were seized, and the source was arrested. What about the waiter from whom we made a small purchase? Let's just say I wasn't pleased with the methods employed that caused the sell to be made. I couldn't have testified the idea to sell to us was entirely his own, which it had to be to avoid entrapment. The waiter's name was furnished to the agent assigned to work Chapel Hill so he could be turned into an informant. I don't know how he responded, but our case was over, and I was damned glad.

This ended my only prolonged undercover assignment. There were other opportunities in the future, but I managed to avoid them. I enjoyed conducting investigations by being truthful with people and not deceiving them. I was aware that undercover operations were necessary, but it was the first thing I had discovered in law enforcement that I strongly detested.

42

During the summer of 1965, that fraternal order of bigots known as the Ku Klux Klan had reared their ugly heads, topped by peaked dunce hats. Many of their flowing white robes appeared to have been made from bed sheets. North Carolina had several years earlier enacted a law that made it illegal for a person sixteen years of age or older to wear a mask or hood used to disguise the identity of the wearer if it was worn off the property of the wearer. This law made it easy to identify robed Klansmen. For some reason, Kluxers dressed in Klan garb just didn't look very frightening to me, especially those wearing bifocals and brogans and marching out of step. Most were harmless, honest, and law-abiding citizens who were misguided in their thoughts and beliefs. They loved to march at night around a large burning cross in a cow pasture, listening to Klan orators tell how the country was being taken over by niggers, Jews, Catholics, hippies, queers, and communists. The SBI had no interest in those passive Klansmen, most of whom had never seen a Jew, couldn't spell Catholic, and didn't know the meaning of communism. We had a great deal of interest in those who did more than attend rallies. Our mission was to identify the nightriders who burned crosses in the yards of blacks and whose standards weren't up to snuff. Of course, anyone favoring integration was a target. Sometimes, instead of a burning cross, a shotgun blast into the side of a house or a stick of dynamite exploding in a driveway would be the intimidating acts of the cowardly bigots who called themselves Klansmen. At other times, their acts were even more violent.

I'll not attempt to go into the history of the Klan in North Carolina, as this book is about my life before and during the time I was a law enforcement officer. So far the cases I have written about have been in chronological order, but now I'll attempt to set forth some of the more interesting cases not only involving the Klan, but others that had racial overtones. Bear in mind, while investigating the Klan, monitoring their rallies throughout eastern North Carolina, and developing informers within the Klan, I still had to continue to investigate murders, rapes, robberies, arsons, et cetera. I'll relate some of those cases later. I will say now that the hours I kept in Marion were banker's hours compared to those I maintained after my transfer to Raleigh.

While stationed at Marion, I didn't have to concern myself with the Klan, as very few blacks resided in the mountains. When I arrived for duty at Raleigh, I found the Klan was extremely active and growing quickly in the central and eastern parts of the state. There were Klan rallies, except during the winter, on Friday, Saturday, and Sunday nights. Another agent and I would attend and record the license numbers of the vehicles transporting the Kluxers. We were also there to attempt to avoid violence in the event black militants or white hecklers appeared on the scene. Other than myself and another agent or two, and a couple of troopers directing traffic, we were usually the only law enforcement officers present. The Kluxers knew we had our jobs to do, and I must say that we were treated with respect. There were many times the Grand Dragon of North Carolina would sit in the backseat of my car and talk about sports or current events unrelated to race as another agent and I recorded license numbers. But once the meeting started, he became a different person, as he was an eloquent speaker who could hold an audience spellbound with his rhetoric. Some rallies would have several hundred robed Kluxers and sometimes as many as a thousand spectators.

The smallest organized body of the Klan was called a Unit. In a sparsely populated rural county there might be only one Unit consisting of only twenty or twenty-five Kluxers. In a larger county there might be several Units. The FBI and the SBI had infiltrated the Klan with so many informers that sometimes a Unit would meet at their Klavern (meeting house) and there might be fifteen or twenty Kluxers present, with five or six of them being informers. The informers were unaware that there were other informers in the Unit other than themselves. This gave us the opportunity to compare the information furnished by informers against each other. I feel certain that some informers double-dipped as paid informers for both the FBI and

SBI, but whatever they received from us was damned little, as we just didn't have the funds for very much informant money. Most of our informants were dissatisfied Kluxers who were turned into informers by other agents and myself. It got to be a game with some of them, as they enjoyed meeting with us late at night behind some country church or other remote spot. Most information received from Klan informers was of limited value, as it usually was about the number of Kluxers present at a meeting, who they were, what was discussed, and who the speakers were. Klan leaders were aware there were informers in the organization, but didn't know their identities. At some meetings, Klan security personnel searched those attending looking for hidden recorders or transmitters. To my knowledge, none were ever detected. Since Klan leaders knew their organization had been infiltrated with informers, unlawful activities were not discussed at regular meetings, but those few who participated in intimidating and violent acts made their plans while sipping beer from the tailgates of pick-up trucks or in the back booth of a local tavern. Our most valued informers were those who penetrated these small groups.

Contrary to what is portrayed on television and in the movies, most information furnished by informers doesn't go down the way they think it will. I recall the first case I was involved in relating to a Klan informer. It was during the dog days of late August 1965. One of our agents down in the eastern part of the state had developed a Klan informer who had furnished him reliable information in the past. The informer's latest information was that two Kluxers from his Unit planned to dynamite a Negro church located in a very isolated part of the county. Another headquarters agent and I were dispatched to meet with the local agent and his supervising agent. The local agent believed his information was good enough to warrant staking out the church, and the supervising agent agreed. The dynamiting was reportedly to be done at night. The supervising agent made the decision that he and the local agent would be in his car, since it was not known in the county, and they would drop the other headquarters agent and me off about half a mile from the church. We were to walk to the church through a swampy area and conceal ourselves in thick underbrush where we could observe the church and the unpaved road in front of it. The supervising agent and the local agent would be backed up an old sawmill road about a mile away. It was shortly after dark on the first night of the stakeout, and we were driving down the unpaved road, and I felt good. We had reconnoitered the area earlier that day. I felt good, that is until the supervising agent said, "You boys only have two things to worry about, those damned Kluxers and snakes. This locality is invested with cottonmouths, copperheads, and diamondbacks. Be careful."

I felt my stomach turn over, as I had always been terrified of snakes. I didn't give the Kluxers a second thought, but couldn't get the damned snakes out of my mind. To make matters worse, just before we reached the drop point a rattler slithered across the road. The supervising agent took a long drag on his cigarette and said, "See what I mean." He slowed to a stop and the other agent and I quickly made our way into some nearby scrub pines. I was armed with my .357 revolver and my carbine. I also carried a canteen of water, a couple of candy bars and a five-cell flashlight. The other agent had a .38 revolver and a pump-action .12 gauge shotgun. He also had water, candy bars, a five-cell light, and a walkie-talkie for use in communicating with the other agents. Without the use of our flashlights, we made our way by moonlight to the church through semi-swampy terrain. I led the way, expecting each step to land squarely on the back of a cottonmouth. We located some high ground in the undergrowth, which provided us a good view of the church and road. We checked in on the walkie-talkie. It was not quite 10:00 P.M. and pick-up was scheduled for 4:00 A.M. We settled in for the night, but within a few minutes realized we were in trouble. Neither of us had thought about insect repellent. We were nearly eaten alive by mosquitoes over the next six hours, and to top that off, no Kluxers showed. I was so glad to get out of the area I didn't even think about snakes on the way back to the road to be picked up. If you will recall, I said earlier that not all information furnished by informers was reliable. For five consecutive nights the other headquarters agent and I kept the church under surveillance. You might think a dramatic shootout or high speed car chase ended this story. Not so! What ended the story was nothing, absolutely nothing. After five nights, we called it quits. The

192

headquarters agent and I returned to Raleigh with welts and chigger bites covering much of our bodies. The church was never dynamited or harmed in any manner. As far as I know, services are still held there and to my knowledge neither the minister nor any of the congregation knew of our presence there during those long, hot nights of 1965.

A few years later I told Big Glen about those mosquito-filled nights at the church. We were sitting in his yard under a giant chinaberry tree. Big Glen shifted in his chair, took a pull on his Tampa Nugget, and said, "I don't believe I would have come back to Raleigh without having a word or two with that informer. And when I did leave I believe he would of had a few welts on him."

43

Late October in North Carolina is that time of year when cool, crisp mornings slowly turn to warm, sunny afternoons. It's the time of year when school children leave home dressed in warm sweaters only to return later in the day with the sleeves tied around their waists. It was just such a morning, October 24, 1965, and I was kind of dragging, as I had worked the previous night and had not gotten home until well after midnight. It was 8:30 A.M. when I walked into the agent's office at headquarters, and within a minute the telephone came to life with an annoying buzz. I answered and was greeted by the very pleasant and calm voice of Sheriff Rayford Oliver of Johnston County, who was calling from his office in Smithfield. Johnston County had recently been assigned as part of my territory. Sheriff Oliver was a gentleman in every respect, quiet, easygoing, and, to use a local expression, "kind of laid back." I didn't detect any alarm in his voice when he said that we had a problem. I asked what the problem was, and was stunned when he replied that during the night the Bagley Elementary School (an all-Negro institution) had apparently been bombed, resulting in extensive damage. He said there were no injuries, as the building was not occupied at the time of the blast. Our conversation terminated when I said I would leave immediately en route to his office. As I hung up the telephone, Supervising Agent Haywood Starling walked into the office. He had worked Johnston County before it was assigned to me, and he had developed a friendship with the sheriff. I told Starling what had occurred, and without hesitating a second he said, "Let's go."

I had recently been issued a new 1965 Ford sedan, and Starling didn't say much from the passenger side as we sped well over the speed limit east on Highway 70 to Smithfield. By 9:15 A.M. we had covered the thirty-odd miles to Smithfield and walked into the Johnston County Sheriff's Department, located in the basement of the courthouse. Sheriff Oliver came out of his office to greet us, and in his unruffled manner said that about 7:30 A.M. his office received a telephone call from Mr. Bernie L. Walston, principal of Bagley Elementary School, located in the northeastern part of the county near the town of Kenly. According to Sheriff Oliver, Mr. Walston said an explosion had badly damaged the school. It was discovered by the custodian when he arrived for work. Sheriff Oliver said he dispatched Deputy Charlie Lewis to the school, and he confirmed an explosion had occurred, and that it was not accidental.

When Starling and I arrived at the school around 10:00 A.M., Deputy Lewis was talking to Mr. Walston. Starling and I started a crime scene investigation of the relatively new one-story brick structure. We determined damage was limited to one classroom, which was a combination fifth-and-sixth grade taught by Mrs. Ruth Rowe. The explosion appeared to have detonated on the floor about four feet in front of the teacher's desk, and directly in line with the third window from the east wall. The blast shattered the glass of all nine windows of the room on the east wall as well as glass in nine ventilator windows near the ceiling on the south wall. Overhead fluorescent light tubes were broken and fixtures damaged. The classroom door had major damage, with the locking mechanism and door plate being knocked loose by the blast. Plastic skylights were broken, and the teacher's desk was split in half. Masonry blocks were cracked on the north wall and books, papers, glass, tile, and other debris littered the room. From the blast area I gathered tile and concrete samples for submission to the laboratory while Starling photographed the scene.

We conducted a thorough crime scene search around the school, but located no evidence of value. There were no signs of forced entry to the building. We assumed the explosive device had been thrown from the outside through one of the classroom windows. A search for footprint impressions on the ground outside the classroom was useless, as students, teachers, and community residents had walked over the area to peer into the building.

The damage to Bagley Elementary School was discovered by school custodian Willie Black at about 7:15 A.M. when he reported to work and noticed the broken windows. He unlocked the main entrance and used the office telephone to call Mr. Walston, who rushed to the scene. The Sheriff's Department was then notified. Mr. Black said he was at the school to check on the boiler at about 8:00 P.M. the previous evening, and noticed nothing unusual.

Interviews with Mr. Walston, Mr. Black, and faculty members resulted in no information of value as to a possible motive for the explosion. All maintained they had not been active in any racial activities that may have resulted in the Klan or another extremist group perpetrating such an act.

Deputy Lewis, Starling, and I had lunch at a nearby barbecue joint and then undertook a neighborhood investigation of the area around the school. There were several homes within a couple of miles of the school, but none in the immediate proximity. At about mid-afternoon we contacted Mrs. Joyce Pugh, whose residence was located about half a mile from the school. She said that she awoke at about 1:30 A.M. and got out of bed to raise a window for more ventilation, and while doing so heard an explosion that appeared to come from the direction of the school. An elderly couple also advised that they heard what sounded like an explosion, but did not know from which direction it came, nor did they note the time. Other inquiries in the neighborhood were fruitless.

Late in the afternoon of October 25, instead of returning to Raleigh, Starling and I contacted a reliable informer whom Starling had known for several years. I had known him for only a couple of months but would subsequently develop him into not only a source for Klan information, but also a source for criminal activity unrelated to racial matters. I won't disclose where Starling and I met with the informer, as to do so could result in his identification. The informer said the Klan did not have anything to do with the explosion at the school, nor did they know who was responsible. He further stated if the local Klan learned who was responsible he would be one of the first to know and would contact us.

For the next three weeks I kept up with my other cases, but continued to pursue leads regarding the school bombing. The tile and concrete submitted to the laboratory had tested positive for nitrites, which are produced by most explosives. I must have driven several hundred miles exploring leads in Johnston, Wayne, Wake, Wilson, and other counties. All turned into dead ends. Just like any other case, as time passed, fewer and fewer leads came in until finally there were none. Sheriff Oliver and I were both disappointed, as were his six deputies who worked a county of 65,000 people and is North Carolina's second largest in square miles. The Sheriff and his deputies considered the Bagley School incident to be an ugly blemish on their county, and they wanted it resolved; however, they realized a break would have to come from somewhere.

The break came on Tuesday morning, November 16, 1965. I was in the Johnston County Sheriff's Department waiting to meet with Deputy Braxton Hinton. He and I were working on a case unrelated to Bagley Elementary School. I was early for our meeting, and radio contact with Hinton revealed it would be at least thirty minutes before he would arrive at the Sheriff's Department. About that time, Deputy Charlie Lewis came into the office and made a casual comment to Deputy Fulton Moore and me that something appeared to be deeply troubling a young white boy who was in jail. Lewis said the prisoner was Percy Lee, a sixteen-year-old whom he had arrested for violating his probation from a misdemeanor conviction. He also commented that he knew the boy very well, and had never seen him so nervous and upset. Deputies Lewis and Moore were going across the street for coffee, and asked me to go with them. Normally I would have gone, but this time I declined. I said I thought I would go to the jail and see what was troubling the young man. I left my pistol at the Sheriff's Department and rode the elevator to the third floor where the jail was located. I exchanged greetings with the jailer, and told him I wanted to talk to Percy Lee. There was a very small room near the jailer's office, which allowed for some privacy. There were two beat-up, straight-backed, wooden chairs in the room and nothing else. I waited there, and, after hearing cell doors open and close, the jailer appeared with a young man who he said was Percy Lee. The jailer left, closing the door behind him. Percy Lee was neatly dressed in jeans and a short-sleeve cotton shirt. He was of medium build with short, light hair that was nicely combed. I identified myself to him and extended my hand at the same time. He hesitated for just a second before extending his hand. His handshake was weak, and he avoided my eyes. I told him to have a seat. When he did so, I pulled the other chair close and sat facing him. I carefully explained the newly required Miranda warning to him by stating that he did not have to answer any questions or make any statements, that he had a right to remain silent and anything he did say could be used against him in court, and that he had a right to an attorney at any time he desired and if he could not afford to hire an attorney, one would be appointed for him by the State of North Carolina. I asked if he understood each of these rights and he replied with a soft, "Yes."

I could easily detect Lee was worried about something and didn't appear surprised to be interviewed by an SBI agent. It was kind of like he was expecting to be questioned. This suggested to me that he was either involved in or had knowledge of a serious crime. My usual method was to ease into an interview by obtaining physical, descriptive, and other personal data. I decided to forgo that method and to wade right in with a sink-or-swim technique. After all, I was shooting in the dark, not having any idea what secret, if any, young Percy Lee was hiding. In a firm voice I said, "Son, you know I am not here to talk to you about your probation violation. You and I both know what I am here to talk to you about, and I want you to know I am going to treat you as nicely as I would my own son. The way I see it is you can tell me you don't want to talk to me, and I'll leave now. If we are going to talk, please don't answer any of my questions except with the truth. Tell me you prefer not to answer the question rather than telling me something that isn't true. Now, I am going to ask you a very important question which I want you to think about before you answer. Percy, are you sorry for being involved in what we are going to discuss?" (Hell, I didn't know what that might be, if anything).

For some reason I wasn't surprised to hear a mumbled, "Yes."

I had broken through and immediately pressed on with a question as to how long he had been sorry. I knew I was getting closer when he responded, "Since we first done it."

I still didn't have the foggiest idea as to what Percy Lee was referring to, so I said, "Percy, I don't want to put words in your mouth, so be specific about when it was first done."

Percy Lee looked directly at me for the first time and said with a voice filled with emotion, "Since I kicked out the window and Robert Foley threw the dynamite in."

I was shocked and fought to keep my composure. I had just solved the bombing of a Negro school and had done so by interviewing a troubled young man instead of going to coffee with the deputies.

I continued the interview with Percy Lee and learned that on Sunday night, October 24, he and four other young men were at a grill in the Stancil's Chapel community of Johnston County. They left the grill and rode around for awhile with Gary Poe in his 1957 Chevrolet. Others in the car were himself, Robert Foley, Dan Smart and Tracy Phelps. Someone suggested throwing some dynamite into Bagley Elementary School to keep the niggers shook up. Robert Foley, the oldest of the group at age twenty-three, said he had some at his house. They drove to his home, where Foley got out of the car and went to an outbuilding. He returned with a stick of dynamite and a fuse. They left Foley's house and stopped at a nearby creek where they got some mud. Foley dug a hole in the dynamite with his knife, inserted the fuse, and packed mud around the hole to secure the fuse. The five of them proceeded to Bagley Elementary School, where Poe stopped the car. Poe, Smart, and Phelps remained in the car, and he and Foley walked to the rear of the school. He kicked out a window, and Foley lit the fuse and threw the dynamite into the building. He and Foley ran back to the car, and the five of them sped away. It was about 1:30 A.M.

Wrapping up the case was the next order of business, and to do it properly meant locating and interviewing each of the other suspects before they had an opportunity to contact each other. I located Starling in Raleigh by telephone and informed him of the break in the case. He arrived at the Sheriff's Department within an hour. We formed two teams. Starling and Deputy Lewis made up one team, and Deputy Hinton and I made up the other. Starling and Lewis located and interviewed Dan Smart, and Hinton and I located and interviewed Gary Poe and Tracy

Phelps. Each of the boys admitted their involvement in the dynamiting of the school, and each of them appeared sincerely remorseful.

The last suspect, Robert Foley, was considered by the deputies to be a "hard case" who was well known to their department. They believed he might possibly offer some resistance when approached.

It had been a long day, and there were four down and one to go. Starling, the two deputies, and I ate a hearty dinner at a local restaurant. It was approaching 8:00 P.M. when we located Foley at a residence near Stancil's Chapel. Starling and I interviewed him in my car. Within a few minutes, we had his confession. He was taken into custody and lodged in the Johnston County Jail.

All five subjects were charged with the felony of damaging Bagley Elementary School by the use of explosives. Their cases were consolidated for trial and, on December 7, 1965, all five entered pleas of guilty. Foley received an active sentence of seven to ten years. Each of the other four received a suspended sentence of five to seven years, and each was placed on probation for five years. They were also required to pay for repairs to the building.

I was especially proud of solving this case, as racial tensions were extremely high in the county. These tensions eased considerably when a white man went to prison for damaging a Negro school. True justice is color blind.

A few years later when I told Big Glen about this case, he cocked his head to one side and squinted at me through a half-closed left eye. He thought for a moment and said, "You did a damned fine job. I probably would have gone for coffee with the deputies."

44

July nights in eastern North Carolina can be hot, humid, and downright uncomfortable. Friday night, July 22, 1966, was one of those nights, and to make matters worse I was suffering with a terrible cold and a low-grade fever. Shortly before midnight, I was awakened from a fretful sleep by a telephone call from an officer of the Benson Police Department. Benson is a small town of 2,500 residents located in southwestern Johnston County. It is surrounded by sweet potato and tobacco farms. The officer told me a cross had been burned about an hour earlier in front of the residence of a black female minister, and it had been extinguished without incident. He also said no one was in custody and there were no suspects. I told the officer that I was sick, but hoped to be back to work in a few days and would commence an investigation as soon as I could.

On Monday morning, July 25, I was feeling much better and checked in at headquarters. Agent Everette Norton was new with the SBI, and was in training. He jumped at the chance to accompany me on an investigation, and I took him along as an observer. Our first stop, after a thirty-minute drive south on Highway 50, was at the Benson Police Department where we examined the partially burned cross. It was made of two two-by-fours nailed together and supported by a wooden stand. The upright section was seven feet in length and the cross section four feet. It had been wrapped in burlap, which apparently had been soaked in a flammable liquid. Interviews with the two officers who responded to the call and extinguished the burning cross were not productive. One of the officers was of the opinion the incident was the work of teenage pranksters.

Our next stop was at the home of the black female minister. She stated that at about 11:00 P.M. on Friday night she received a telephone call from a neighbor who alerted her to a cross burning in front of her house. She called the police department and two officers responded and extinguished the blaze. She said she had not been involved in any racial activities, but did advise that a white minister had held services at her all-Negro church the previous week, and a few days later the letters "KKK" were printed in red paint beside the front door of the church. She could think of nothing else that might have prompted the burning of the cross.

After leaving the minister's home, a neighborhood investigation, including a talk with the neighbor who spotted the burning cross, produced no information of value.

The next stop was a pay telephone near Interstate 95. I placed a call to a local Klan informer whose first words were, "I thought ya'll would be ringing me up." I wanted to meet with him, but he thought it was too dangerous. I didn't even have to tell him what I was calling about, as he said, "All I can tell you is that three Kluxers did the cross burning in front of the nigger preacher's house. I don't know who two of them was, but one was Guy Coombs and his car was used. That's all I can find out." Before the informer hung up, I learned that Coombs was employed at a local gasoline station.

On July 28, I returned to Benson accompanied by Agent Norton. We were waiting at Coombs's residence when he arrived home from work. Coombs was short, slightly built, and soaked to the bone wouldn't weigh 120 pounds. He had bright red hair above his ears, but was completely bald on top. He had a pointed chin, and when I first looked at him I didn't think he had any eyebrows, but they were just so thin and lightly colored they were hard to distinguish. Coombs had beady eyes that set so far back in his head I couldn't tell what color they were.

Coombs was interviewed in my vehicle after I advised him of his Miranda rights. The interview was from 4:30 P.M. to 5:15 P.M. During that time Coombs's answer to every question was more of a whine than a response. He was scared and extremely nervous. I went straight to the point, but still remembering my old ONI training, left Coombs with an out. I said, "Guy, we know you and your car were at the cross burning this past Friday night. We also know you are a member of the Klan. Now what we want is only the truth so if you deny being there then I can't believe anything else you tell me. My question is this: Was burning the cross your idea?"

I knew he was going to deny it being his idea but in so doing he acknowledged being a party to it. He said, "It weren't my idea, but my car was used to haul the cross, but I didn't do the driving. I rode in the car, but I didn't light the match to the cross. But I was there." When pressed as to the identity of the others involved, Coombs said he wouldn't answer any other questions without seeking advice from a source whom he would not identify. The interview was terminated, but Coombs agreed to meet with us again at 7:30 P.M. after he had talked to his confidant. At precisely 7:30 P.M., another meeting was held with Coombs. I knew what was coming, and I might as well have been home having dinner. Coombs advised he had been instructed not to have any further conversation with us.

For the next ten days I worked on this case whenever I had the opportunity, but developed no new information. On August 8, I met with District Attorney Archie Taylor and briefed him on the details of the investigation. Mr. Taylor advised he would send a bill of indictment to the grand jury at the next term of Johnston County Superior Court charging Coombs with the burning of a cross. Mr. Taylor was of the opinion that once Coombs was indicted he would be more cooperative and perhaps furnish the names of the others involved in hopes of receiving leniency. I agreed with Mr. Taylor.

What a mistake we made! Mr. Taylor sent a bill of indictment to the grand jury on August 23, and I testified before them that same date. The grand jury is made up of eighteen citizens who hear state witnesses and then decide if there is probable cause for the person(s) named in the bill of indictment to be tried. It takes only twelve of the eighteen members for a true bill to be returned. In this case, the grand jury returned the bill of indictment as "Not a true bill," which meant they didn't believe the state had probable cause to try Coombs. Why? A deputy told me several members of the grand jury were known Kluxers and others were Klan sympathizers. In the dozens and dozens of times I have testified before state grand juries, this was one of the few times an indictment was not handed down.

A few years later, when I told Big Glen about this case, his only comment was: "Hell, that state grand jury wouldn't have indicated that sum bitch if he had been videotaped lighting a match to the cross."

45

Racial tensions were extremely high in North Carolina in 1966, especially in the eastern part of the state. They were almost to a boiling point in the small towns and rural areas where blacks outnumbered whites in many communities. In order to avoid embarrassment to those involved in the story that follows and the town where the incident took place, I shall not divulge the true identities of the individuals nor will I identify the town.

It was 7:00 P.M. in early October 1966 when I answered the telephone at my residence. The call was from the chief of police of a small town a short drive from Raleigh. He said his department had received a complaint an hour earlier from an eighteen-year-old white female who claimed a black male had burglarized her residence the previous night and raped her. The chief requested my assistance. I said I would be there as soon as possible, as I knew first degree burglary and rape were both capital crimes.

Shortly before 9:00 A.M. I arrived at the police station. The chief greeted me less than enthusiastically and related the following:

At 6:07 A.M. a telephone call was received at his department from Jane Woody, mother of Polly Ann Woody, an eighteen-year-old white female. Ms. Woody said a black male had broken into the home occupied by her and her daughter, and that her daughter had been raped. Officer Benny Cates responded to the call and talked briefly to the victim. She claimed she was asleep in one bedroom and her mother in another. At about 4:00 A.M., she awakened to find a black male standing beside her bed. He said he wouldn't hurt her if she didn't resist him. He did not have a weapon, but she was very frightened and therefore submitted to sexual intercourse with him. She said that after he left she awakened her mother, and they walked together to a neighbor's home where they telephoned the police. She claimed they walked back to their residence and, while waiting for the police to arrive, the black male drove by the residence in a station wagon and stopped momentarily in front of the house before driving on. After officer Cates arrived at the Woody residence, he was talking to Ms. Woody and Polly Ann when the conversation was interrupted by Polly Ann pointing out a passing white Mercury station wagon that she said was operated by the man who raped her. Officer Cates ran to his patrol car but was unsuccessful in an effort to overtake the vehicle; however, a couple of officers with the department were familiar with the vehicle and knew the owner to be a forty-three-year-old black male named Alfred Cardy.

The chief wanted me to conduct a crime scene search at the Woody residence before evidence was contaminated or destroyed. I immediately proceeded to the residence, but found no one at home. I figured the victim and her mother were probably at the hospital for a rape examination. Photographs were made of the outside of the home, with special emphasis given to the dining room window that the chief said was the point of entry. Directly under the window, the soil was of a soft, sandy loam that contained several impressions, which were approximate one inch square in size. They appeared to have been made by the high heels of ladies' shoes. No other impressions were noted. Examination of the window screen disclosed it had been ripped open at the lower left corner of the window, but the hole was not large enough for me to work through to do a latent fingerprint examination of the outside of the window and the window sill. I pulled the screen open further, which allowed me to examine a windowpane that was broken where the latch secured the top and bottom windows together. The latch was in the locked position! My latent fingerprint examination failed to detect any prints or fabric marks at the apparent point of entry. Strange, to say the least! I wouldn't enter the residence without a witness present, so I drove back to the police station.

The dispatcher on duty informed me that the chief was interviewing the victim in his private office. I knocked and then opened the door and entered. The office was occupied by the chief, the victim, and the town's only female officer. As soon as I entered, the chief excused the female officer, and without even introducing me to the victim said to her, "Wouldn't you rather talk to me alone about what happened?"

205

She responded with a nearly inaudible, "Yes."

The chief turned to me and said, "Would you please interview Ms. Woody, who is waiting outside?"

I was furious, and was right on the verge of telling the chief if he wanted to conduct his own investigation it was fine with me, but not to request my assistance in the future. Before I spoke, I stopped myself and thought of how Dave Planton, my old ONI mentor, would have handled the situation. He certainly would not have made a rash decision that might have played right into the hands of the chief. In my mind I tried to picture how Dave would have reacted, and I did what I thought he would have done. I said, "Chief, I'll be glad to interview her."

Ms. Jane Woody, age forty-seven, was sitting in a chair near the dispatcher's office. She was nodding and saliva was easing out of the corner of the her mouth and dripping onto her dirty, wrinkled blouse. She was ugly as homemade sin and reeked of terrible odors, some of which were stale beer and vomit. It took some doing, but I finally got through an interview with her, as she was under the influence of alcohol and as Big Glen would say, "Just as tight as a tick."

She claimed to have been divorced for ten years and said she and her daughter lived together on Happy Sack Road. She claimed to have gone to bed at about 10:00 P.M. the previous night while her daughter, Polly Ann, attended a local fair with a girl-friend. She did not hear Polly Ann when she came home, and did not awaken until about 5:30 A.M. when Polly Ann roused her and said a Negro man had been in the house. She claimed her daughter said she was afraid to resist him and had submitted to him sexually.

Ms. Woody also said her daughter claimed she and her boyfriend had seen the Negro man a few nights earlier at a local convenience store and had had a casual conversation with him, and that he drove a light-colored station wagon and his first name was Alfred. She said that after having sex with the Negro man, her daughter said they went to the kitchen where they drank water and talked briefly, at which time he told her he entered the house through the dining room window. She said Polly Ann unlocked the back door for the man to leave and then awakened her. She and Polly Ann walked to a nearby neighbor's house, where a call was placed to the police department. They walked back home and while waiting outside for the police to arrive the Negro man drove slowly by and said something that they couldn't understand. When officer Cates arrived, they were talking to him in the yard when the Negro drove by again. Officer Cates ran to his car and tried to overtake the station wagon but failed to find it.

After I finished my interview with Ms. Woody, I walked alone down the street to a small café. I took a seat in a back booth and ordered only coffee. I sipped it while deep in thought. Why the hell had the chief called me for assistance and then given me such a cool reception? Why did he insist on interviewing Polly Ann Woody without me being present? In my mind I had the answer to the first question. The chief didn't want my assistance, but someone had caused him to request it. That person could have been the mayor, district attorney, town manager, or even a local judge. But how would any of them have known about the incident so early in the morning? Then it hit me like a ton of bricks. The former chief, who had retired a few months earlier, was at the police station when I arrived. He had been a good chief and the personnel of his department loved him. He highly regarded the SBI and a good working relationship had existed between the two departments for many years. Many of the officers of the department were unhappy with the new chief, who was not one of them, as he came from another department in a distant city. A telephone call from an officer to the old chief could have resulted in him contacting a source who prompted the new chief to request SBI assistance. I figured the new chief was out to prove himself and didn't believe he needed anyone to help him conduct an investigation involving an open-and-shut case of burglary and rape.

I walked back to the police station and arrived just as the chief finished his interview with Polly Ann Woody. As they came out of his office, I got my first good look at her. She may have been eighteen years old, but looked twice that. She was not unattractive, but she had that hard look I had seen so many times when interviewing whores in Idaho. She flopped in a chair next to her mother and lit a cigarette.

The chief took his time acknowledging my presence, but finally motioned his head toward his office. I followed him inside. He didn't say anything, but handed me a statement obviously written by him, but bearing the signature of Polly Ann Woody. It told of her first meeting the suspect two nights earlier at a convenience store and next seeing him beside her bed about 4:00 A.M. earlier that day. She claimed he said he wouldn't hurt her if she didn't resist, and she therefore submitted to sexual intercourse and other sexual acts with him. Much of the lengthy statement went into explicit detail to describe the sexual acts with filthy language which, in my opinion, was unnecessary. I noticed the statement mentioned that while not engaged in sexual activity, they smoked cigarettes, visited the bathroom, and sat at the kitchen table and drank water from a container from the refrigerator. She claimed the suspect told her his name was Alfred, and said he entered the house through the dining room window. Polly Ann's statement also disclosed she unlocked the back door and let the suspect out when he was ready to leave. The remainder of her statement contained essentially the same information that was furnished by her mother. The chief didn't offer me a copy of the statement.

I told the chief that I hadn't completed the crime scene search, as I didn't have a witness present so I could enter the house. I volunteered to drive Polly Ann and her mother to their residence so I could finish my work there. The chief immediately said he would also go along. This certainly didn't surprise me, as I knew the chief didn't want me talking to Polly Ann.

At the Woody home I obtained the sheet from the bed where the alleged rape took place, and I also obtained the panties Polly Ann claimed to have put on after the rape. I also recovered Winston and Chesterfield cigarette butts from an ashtray in Polly Ann's bedroom. I noticed Polly Ann's brand was Winston. I found a pair of ladies' shoes under the bed. They had heels about one inch square with soil on the bottoms. I asked Polly Ann when she had last worn them. She wasn't stupid, as she immediately said she put them on after the Negro left to go outside and examine the dining room window.

I conducted a latent fingerprint examination of the inside of the window at the alleged point of entry. Both Ms. Woody and Polly Ann stated they had not recently touched the window or the surrounding area where entry was reportedly gained. A palm print and one fingerprint of value were obtained from the windowsill. Two latent fingerprints of value were obtained from the glass water container, which was still on the kitchen table. Prior to leaving the Woody residence, I shocked Ms. Woody and Polly Ann when I took their inked fingerprint and palm print impressions.

After leaving the Woody residence, I dropped the chief off at the police station and drove directly to the SBI laboratory with the evidence I had gathered. I filled out the paperwork for each item and requested the appropriate examination of each.

It had been a long and tiring day, and as I ate dinner at home Vicky could detect something was wrong. I told her of the day's events and my firm belief that neither a rape nor a burglary had taken place. I also told her of the chief's unusual behavior and his apparent desire to have the suspect charged—even before the physical evidence could be examined and the suspect interviewed. I wanted to see what the laboratory tests revealed. Hell, the suspect wasn't going anywhere, and even if he did he could be found.

Our dinner was interrupted by the ringing of the phone. I answered and was surprised to hear the voice of Homer Hasner, a police officer from the town where I had spent the day. He had the reputation of being a damned good officer. He told me that shortly after I left town the chief had also left on personal business and would not be back for several days. Hasner also said that Polly Ann Woody had taken warrants for Alfred Cardy charging him with first degree burglary and rape. He said Cardy had been arrested and was being held in the county jail without privilege of bail. Hasner wanted me to interview Cardy.

The following morning I contacted Hasner at the police station, and he rode with me to the county jail. Cardy was a muscular six feet two inches and weighed two hundred pounds. He was forty-three years of age and had a dark complexion, short hair, and a neatly trimmed mustache. He was scared, and had every reason to be so. I informed Cardy of his Miranda rights and then told him in very plain language that I wasn't there to trick or deceive him in any way. I said I was there for only one purpose, and that was to determine if he had committed the crimes for which he was charged. He told me he was raised in the area, but had lived in Baltimore all of his adult life and had only recently returned to live with his mother, who was in poor health. He said he had heard stories of how blacks were mistreated in southern courts, and he was afraid it was going to happen to him. I told Cardy the color of his skin didn't mean anything to me and if he thought I was part of the system he had heard about, then why was I there? I could just make up a confession and say that was what he had told me. Cardy thought for a few moments and his shoulders sagged as he looked at me and said, "Here's what happened."

For the next two hours, I took copious notes as I listened to Cardy and questioned him in detail. He told of first meeting Polly Ann Woody and her boyfriend a few nights earlier at a local convenience store, where he had become friendly with the white man who owned the store. He claimed that later that night, actually about 2:30 A.M., he accompanied the store owner to the Woody residence where Polly Ann's mother, Jane Woody, got into the car with them. The store owner drove back to his store, where he went inside to get some cigarettes, soft drinks, and whiskey. He remained in the car with Ms. Woody and had casual conversation with her. He was aware she had been drinking, but didn't consider her drunk. He claimed she told him that after the store owner took her home he could later come to her house to see her. When the store owner returned to the car, he got out and drove his own station wagon to his mother's house. He went to bed, but got up about 6:30 A.M. and drove to the Woody house. He was admitted to the house by Jane Woody and agreed to pay her ten dollars for sex. He didn't have any money, but she agreed to sex anyway with his promise to pay later. Polly Ann Woody was asleep in another bedroom.

Cardy said that after having sex with Jane Woody he left but returned shortly after noon that same day and was admitted to the house by Polly Ann Woody. She said her mother was there but was passed out drunk in her bedroom. He claimed to have talked to Polly Ann for fifteen or twenty minutes, and she invited him to come back that night. He said he didn't return that night, but came back during the early morning hours of the following day. He knocked on the back door and was admitted into the house by Polly Ann, who again said her mother was there, but drunk. He claimed to have talked to Polly Ann for a few minutes prior to having voluntary sexual relations with her in her bedroom. He also claimed the two of them smoked cigarettes while they sat on her bed and talked (I noted during his interview he smoked Chesterfield). He said that when they left Polly Ann's bedroom they went into the kitchen and sat at the kitchen table and drank water from a glass jar that had been in the refrigerator. Cardy advised that when he was ready to leave, Polly Ann opened the back door and let him out. He steadfastly denied breaking into the Woody house, and insisted his sexual activities with Polly Ann were completely voluntary on her part. He could offer no explanation as to why she would want to accuse him of burglary and rape, except she was possibly influenced by her mother who was angry that he hadn't paid for the sex he had had with her.

After completing my interview with Cardy, I obtained a set of his inked finger and palm prints.

A couple of days later, I received the results of tests conducted on the evidence I had submitted to the laboratory. The bedsheet failed to show the presence of seminal stains, but did reveal human hair having the characteristics of the Negroid race. The panties failed to show the presence of Negroid hair, but did reveal acid phosphatase, which is an ingredient of seminal fluid. The palmprint at the alleged point of entry was identified as the right palmprint of Polly Ann Woody. The latent fingerprint at the alleged point of entry was identified as the right thumbprint of Jane Woody. The two latent fingerprints from the water jar were identified as the right middle finger and left thumb of Alfred Cardy.

The day I received the laboratory report I located the district attorney, who only had limited knowledge of the case. I briefed him fully and after I did so he said, "Conduct no more investigation. I'll hold a preliminary hearing day after tomorrow in Recorder's Court, and you can testify as to your findings. I am well acquainted with Jane and Polly Ann Woody and their reputations. I know they are capable of anything."

The preliminary hearing was before a rather large audience. After all, a black man had been accused of raping a white woman and this was in the deep south in 1966. Segregated courtrooms were a thing of the past, but not so on this day. Black spectators seated themselves on one side of the courtroom, and whites seated themselves on the other and in the middle section of seats. After trying a couple of frivolous misdemeanor cases, the district attorney called the cases against Alfred Cardy. Polly Ann Woody was the first witness for the state, followed by Jane Woody. Their testimony was essentially the same as was furnished by them during the investigation. Cardy now had an attorney and a strong cross-examination by him brought out some inconsistencies in their testimony, but nothing he could hang his hat on.

I was the next witness for the state. After answering the usual questions as to my name, education, occupations, et cetera, I was asked if I had conducted any investigation regarding the defendant and the charges against him. When I replied in the affirmative, the district attorney asked me to relate the results of my investigation. Silence engulfed the courtroom as the attention of those present, including attorneys waiting for their cases to be called, focused on me. I was uninterrupted as I carefully and deliberately recounted the details of my investigation, including the results of the laboratory examinations. When I completed my testimony, the district attorney looked at the judge and stated that he had no further questions. Cardy's defense attorney turned to the judge and very deliberately said, "Your Honor, I have no questions."

The judge took only a few minutes to rule there was not probable cause to bind Cardy over for grand jury action and dismissed the charges against him. I had never experienced such a feeling before. For nine and one-half years my investigations had resulted in persons being found guilty of crimes because they were guilty. I felt good after those convictions, but proving a person to be unjustly charged with two capital crimes gave me a feeling of satisfaction unmatched at that time in my career.

A few weeks after the hearing, a letter was received by SBI Director Walter Anderson. He forwarded a copy to me. It was a letter of commendation from Cardy's attorney and a copy of it appears on a following page. In order to conceal the identity of those involved in this case and the identity of the town, I have blacked out small portions of the letter and letterhead of the attorney's stationery. I wish I could identify the writer of the letter, as his name would be immediately recognized by many North Carolinians.

Years later, when I told Big Glen about this case, he looked at me with that lopsided grin and said, "There's one thing for damn certain and that is ain't no lawyer ever paid me a compliment."

ATTORNEYS AT LAW

███████ NORTH CAROLINA

TELEPHONE ███████

October 18, 1966

Mr. Walter Anderson
Director
State Bureau of Investigation
Justice Building
Raleigh, North Carolina

Dear Mr. Anderson:

Approximately two weeks ago a nineteen year old white girl obtained a warrant charging a negro man with first degree burglary and rape (both capital crimes). Special Agent Robert Emerson came to ██████████ and conducted an investigation at the scene of the alleged crime. This investigation was conducted on Sunday. Mr. Emerson obtained fingerprints from the alleged point of entry and from various objects in the house. The Chief of Police did not see fit to allow him to discuss the alleged crime with the prosecuting witness, but he did obtain a detailed statement from the defendant. He also obtained shoe impressions from around the house.

The prosecuting witness's testimony at the hearing on October 10, 1966, was vague and full of inconsistencies, but she did relate enough to bind the defendant over for Grand Jury action. This young girl and her mother probably have the worst reputations of any two women in the ██████████ area. Mr. Emerson then testified as to his findings. His findings were based on the most competent and thorough investigation that I have seen in my years of practicing criminal law. The physical evidence proved beyond any reasonable doubt that the prosecuting witness broke the window and her fingerprints and shoe impressions showed that she had completely fabricated the alleged crime.

The purpose of this letter is to commend your department and Special Agent Emerson for a job well done. The State of North Carolina saved the expense of a lengthy trial and an innocent man was exculpated. Special Agent Emerson's diligent efforts are a complete contradiction to the alleged attitude of law enforcement officials. He proved beyond any reasonable doubt that the purpose of law enforcement is to obtain the truth and not merely to obtain a conviction. At the hearing I was proud of our State Bureau of Investigation, Special Agent Emerson and our system of criminal justice. Please accept my sincere appreciation and congratulations.

Yours truly,

BY: ████████████████████

October 18, 1966 letter commending author's actions during burglary and rape investigation.

46

The North Carolina State Fair was first held at Raleigh in 1853 and featured agricultural exhibits. It has been held annually since that time, except for a few years when such things as the influenza epidemic of 1918 prohibited it. The fair still has a basic agricultural theme, but has grown to attract exhibitors of all types and provides entertainment for the entire family. Top stars of movies and television perform daily at the fair arena. The 1996 attendance figure for the ten-day event was 759,429. In 1966, it was a six-day event that attracted nearly half a million people. It also attracted that bigoted bunch of clowns I called Kluxers, but were officially known to our files as the United Klans of America, Inc., Knights of the Ku Klux Klan. They had a booth at the fair where they handed out racial literature, talked to anyone who would listen, and attempted to recruit members. The SBI had the responsibility to monitor activities at the booth and to attempt to avoid confrontations between the Kluxers and other fairgoers. We were also there to enforce the laws of the State of North Carolina.

The 1966 fair started on Monday, October 10. Several of our agents alternated duty at the Klan booth during the week, and things ran smoothly with no significant incidents occurring. I was involved in the alleged rape and burglary case of Alfred Cardy, and therefore missed being initially assigned to the fair detail. After completing the Cardy investigation, I received word from Supervising Agent Starling that I was to work security at the Klan booth with him and agent Gary Griffith from 4:00 P.M. to midnight when the fair closed on Saturday, October 15.

I arrived at the fairgrounds a few minutes before my scheduled time and parked near the Wake County Sheriff's command center. I wandered through the crowd until I located the Klan booth. Starling and Griffith arrived at about the same time, and we exchanged hellos and good-byes with the agents we relieved. Before they departed, we learned there had been no problems that day. It was 4:00 P.M. and the fair was to officially close at midnight. I thought if we could get by the next eight hours without any incidents, it would be a remarkable week, considering the precarious environment in which the Klan had placed itself.

Starling, Griffith, and I took turns going to dinner. Starling was first, and upon his return Griffith went. It was approaching 7:00 P.M. when I left and made my way through the crowded midway to the White Plains Methodist Church booth where I ordered a barbecue plate. As I walked slowly back toward the Klan booth, I could detect tension in the air. Carnies were short tempered, exhibitors were tired, and people who had worked all week at the fair were ready to go home. As Big Glen would say, "Most people had a short fuse."

Starling, Griffith, and I stayed close to the Klan booth and kept our eyes on the Klansmen and those who stopped by the booth. From time to time the Grand Dragon of North Carolina, R. J. James, would come over and talk to us. He was very personable and seemed to appreciate our presence near the booth. He appeared to want to avoid any confrontations and certainly didn't want any bad publicity. I had a feeling things had gone too well, and I was right.

At about 11:40 P.M., I was standing in a semi-darkened area on the east side of the booth, Starling was on the west side, and Griffith was mingling with the crowd in front. A loud and heated argument erupted near the front of the booth between the North Carolina Grand Knight Hawk and a white male of college age who was with a white female. I had seen the Knight Hawk at Klan rallies where he acted as master of ceremonies, but didn't know him nor had I even spoken to him. Griffith was near the argument and quickly identified himself to the couple and instructed them to move on. They immediately complied. I had started to the confrontation, but Griffith had broken it up before I got there. I eased back to my position beside the booth and a moment later noticed the Knight Hawk walk from the front of the booth to an unoccupied automobile parked near where I was standing. The Knight Hawk didn't see me. He was not wearing his Klan robe, but was dressed in casual clothes with a cardigan sweater. I watched closely as he reached with his right hand across his waist to his left side and remove a holstered revolver from under the sweater. He then opened the left front door of the automobile and tossed the holstered revolver on the front seat. The Knight Hawk immediately returned to the front of the booth where other Kluxers were congregating. I looked around and saw Starling nearby. I stepped from the shadows and motioned to him. He came over, and I told him what I had seen. Starling had a flashlight, and he shined it through the automobile window. On the front seat was the holstered revolver. The Knight Hawk noticed us at the automobile and hurried over. In response to my questions, he said the revolver belonged to him and the automobile was owned by a friend of his. Starling opened the door of the automobile and recovered the revolver, which was a .38 caliber Smith & Wesson containing six rounds of ammunition. I didn't know what the reaction of the Grand Dragon and the other Kluxers would be, but I knew a violation of North Carolina law had taken place in my presence. I turned and faced the Knight Hawk and told him he was under arrest for carrying a concealed weapon. To my surprise neither he, the Grand Dragon, nor any of the other Kluxers present voiced any objections. I didn't even handcuff the Knight Hawk and he voluntarily walked with me to the Sheriff's command center, but no magistrate was there. I told the Knight Hawk I would have to transport him downtown to the courthouse where a magistrate was on duty. He requested to go back to the Klan booth where he could obtain some money from the Grand Dragon so he could post a cash bond. I complied with his request, and then transported him to the magistrate's office. I signed a warrant charging him with carrying a concealed weapon, and the Knight Hawk posted a one-hundred-dollar cash bond for his appearance in Recorder's Court on October 25. I then gave him a ride to the local motel where the Kluxers were staying.

The North Carolina Grand Knight Hawk appeared in Recorder's Court on the specified date without an attorney and represented himself. He entered a plea of not guilty. Starling and I testified as to our observations and actions and were both unsuccessfully cross-examined by the Grand Knight Hawk. He then testified in his own behalf. He claimed that after engaging in the argument with the young white male, he obtained the revolver from the automobile and started to put it on but changed his mind and put it back on the front seat of the automobile. He claimed that at no time was it concealed.

The judge apparently believed me, as the Grand Knight Hawk was found guilty. He received thirty days suspended and the payment of court costs and twelve months good behavior. The revolver was confiscated and turned over to the SBI for official use.

I have told of this case because the North Carolina Grand Knight Hawk was the highest ranking Klan officer I ever arrested. On other occasions I arrested Unit officers of the Klan, including members of their Security Guard force, but they were not state officers.

Years later when I told Big Glen about this case he said, "I don't believe I would have driven the Grand Knight Hawk to his motel. I would have let him walk or call a cab."

47

It appears to me that today there are mainly two types of armed robberies. Those committed by amateurs trying to obtain enough cash to buy a little dope, and those perpetrated by professionals. Instead of working for it, professionals would rather forcibly take from others their honestly made hard-earned cash and, if necessary, kill for it. Back in 1966, drugs were just beginning to be a problem, so armed robberies were still carried out mostly by professionals. Along with homicides, I always afforded them top priority of the offenses I investigated. It was a challenge to me to attempt to identify and apprehend persons responsible for putting weapons in the faces of innocent people and demanding their money. Regardless of what wording was used during a robbery, the message was always the same . . . give me what is yours or die.

I found that most criminals who successfully pulled an armed robbery didn't stop with one. They became addicted to the adrenaline highs they experienced during the robberies and like habitual gamblers they were always looking for a big score. The case that follows is that of armed robberies in Johnston County that led to the ghettos of Baltimore, Maryland.

Movies and television seldom show investigators dictating reports, filling out evidence forms, or performing other administrative tasks necessary to properly prepare their cases for trial. I was deeply engaged in those duties at SBI Headquarters on the morning of February 10, 1966, when I was interrupted by a telephone call from Sheriff Oliver of Johnston County. He and I had become good friends and any request from him for assistance was handled by me as promptly as possible. As soon as I answered, he said, "Bob, L.T. Sloan's Store was robbed a few minutes ago, and I need your help." Sheriff Oliver gave me directions to the store, which he said was about five or six miles south of the town of Zebulon on Highway 39. I left paperwork scattered on my desk and at about 11:30 A.M. pulled into the driveway of the store. A couple of sheriff's vehicles and a trooper's car were parked near the front door. L.T. Sloan's Store is what we refer to in the south as a country store, stocked with basic grocery items, cigarettes, chewing tobacco, a few hardware goods and a large soft drink box. There were a couple of gasoline pumps outside. It's a place where farmers gather for rook, gossip, and politics on cold winter evenings.

The first deputy I saw when I entered was Charlie Lewis, who I knew worked that area of the county. He motioned me over to the side of the room and told me that Mrs. Sloan, a white female in her early forties, was held up by several black males who had pistol whipped her. She was going to seek medical attention but wanted to furnish as much information as possible before leaving the store.

I introduced myself to Mrs. Sloan, who was seated at the rear of the store in a cane-bottomed chair. I noticed she had fresh scalp wounds and splotches of dried blood were on the shoulders of her blouse. She forced a smile when I said I would conduct my interview with her as quickly as possible. In a remarkably calm manner she furnished the following information:

She was alone in the family store at about 10:30 A.M. that day when she heard a vehicle arrive and stop at the south side of the building. Two black males entered the store through the front door and one through the rear door. One of the men who had entered through the front door asked her where the grape drinks were located. She told him they were in the center section of the drink box. At about that time, all three of the men pulled pistols from their clothing and pointed them at her. The one who had asked about the drinks said, "We want your money."

He then pointed at the cash register and said, "You open it real smooth." She did as the man had instructed and put the money in a paper bag. The amount totaled about $500 in currency and a lot of coins.

The second man who had entered by the front door spoke to the one who had entered by the rear door and said, "You take care of her." The one who had entered the rear door pulled some cord from his pocket, grabbed her, and attempted to tie the cord around her. She struggled, and the other two men came to his assistance. All three of them proceeded to strike her about the head and upper body with their pistols as they continued to try to restrain her with the cord. One of the men, she believed he had the bag with the money, went out the back and drove the car to the front of the store. The other two men abandoned their efforts to tie her up, fled out the front door, and got into the car, which left at a high rate of speed heading north on Highway 39.

Mrs. Sloan said that when the two men ran out of the front door, she saw the car they got into had a license plate on the front. She did not recall the color of the plate, but did note it had the letters FZ followed by the numbers 3225. She wrote FZ-3225 on a piece of paper and then called the police department in Zebulon to report what had happened. Mrs. Sloan handed the piece of paper to me, and I retained it for evidentiary purposes. As for a vehicle description, she could only recall that the car was either partially tan or all tan in color. She described the three black males as:

1. The subject who entered through the front door, did most of the talking, and took the money from her as early thirties, medium height, 140 pounds, dark complexion, unmasked, no gloves, no glasses, and wearing a dark hat and dark coat. He held his pistol in his right hand, and it had short square barrel. He had no noticeable accent.
2. The second subject who entered the front door was in his twenties, five-eight to five-ten, with a medium build and medium complexion. He, too, was unmasked and didn't wear gloves. He was casually dressed with a dark hat. He held his pistol in his right hand and it also had a short square barrel.
3. The subject who entered the back door was recalled to be in his thirties and of medium height and weight. He wore a dark hat and no gloves or mask. He was armed with a pistol, but she didn't recall in which hand it was held.

As soon as I completed my interview with Mrs. Sloan, I rushed outside to my car, where I used the radio to contact the Highway Patrol dispatcher in Raleigh. I furnished information regarding the robbery to him including a description of the suspects, their vehicle and direction of travel and the all-important *front* license plate. I requested an immediate all points bulletin

(APB) with a caution that the subjects should be considered armed and dangerous. The APB was immediately broadcast throughout the state.

I went back inside the store and used the telephone to call headquarters. One thing I knew for certain was that North Carolina only issued one license plate, and it was to be displayed on the rear of the vehicle. Agent John Boyd answered the telephone. John was a ballistics expert and polygraph examiner and, when not in court, spent most of his time in the office. He was well-known throughout the state and very well-liked by those who knew him. I told John about the robbery and the front plate information. I requested that he contact the Department of Motor Vehicles (DMV) to determine what eastern states issued two plates and that a teletype be sent to those states requesting registration information for license FZ-3225. As soon as I finished, John said, "Consider it done."

Deputy Charlie Lewis and I walked out to my car so we could monitor my radio. We smoked, talked and were soon joined by deputies Braxton Hinton and Howard Olive. We discussed the robbery and all agreed there had to be a local connection, as a daring daylight robbery in a rural area of Johnston County by out-of-state black subjects was not only unusual, but also unheard of. Highway 39 is not a major artery, but a rural paved road running from the Virginia border through the North Carolina counties of Vance and Franklin and ending in the Johnston County town of Selma. It was not a highway a person would find themselves on by mistake. I suggested that deputies Hinton and Olive work north on Highway 39, checking at houses and other country stores to see if they could develop any information. Charlie Lewis and I would work south on Highway 39.

The first stop Charlie and I made was at the residence of Bess Glosson, who lived about 500 yards south of L.T. Sloan's Store. She recalled that about 10:00 A.M. that day she saw an automobile traveling south on Highway 39. It slowly passed Sloan's Store and the driver used her driveway to turn around and drive back toward the store. She couldn't see the occupants well enough to identify or describe them, but did remember the car was beige in color and was a four-door model with a radio antenna on the right side. She recalled it had a license plate on the front which was mostly yellow in color. She didn't recall ever having seen the vehicle before, and didn't know whether or not it stopped at the store.

Charlie and I continued to work the area south of Sloan's Store and Braxton Hinton and Howard Olive continued working north. I wanted desperately to catch those responsible for robbing and pistol whipping a very courageous woman whom I considered fortunate to be alive. I still felt very strongly there was a local connection to the robbery, and I intended to do my best to determine what it was. Charlie and I had missed lunch, so late that afternoon we stopped at a greasy little grill, and we each had a couple of hot dogs and a Pepsi. We continued working well into the night but no one, including several informants Charlie had in the area, knew anything. We finally called it a day, and I arrived home at 11:30 P.M. Vicky was still up and warmed dinner for me as I told her about the robbery.

The next day was Friday, February 11, and I was at headquarters at 8:30 A.M. reviewing teletype messages received from the District of Columbia and those eastern states that issued two license plates. Only Maryland scored a hit. Their DMV message reflected Maryland license plate FZ-3225 was issued to Ernest Phillips, 910 West Franklin Street, Baltimore, Maryland, for a 1956 Cadillac.

A teletype inquiry to the Baltimore Police Department regarding Ernest Phillips resulted in their reply that he was a black male, age forty-two, five-seven, and 165 pounds. His arrest record extended back to 1942 and included four assaults, the unauthorized use of an automobile, and a larceny. On September 19, 1959, he was detained and released to the FBI.

I responded with a teletype back to Baltimore requesting they conduct investigation reference subject Phillips, and if he was employed, to accertain if he worked on February 10. I also requested efforts be made to determine a complete description of his current motor vehicle. I then placed a telephone call to Sheriff Oliver and brought him up to date on the Baltimore lead. The Sheriff and I agreed that unless something new developed we could only wait to see what the Baltimore police could find out.

On February 15, a teletype from Baltimore stated subject

Phillips had moved seven months ago from the West Franklin Street address, his current whereabouts were unknown, and a description of his automobile was unavailable. I read the teletype a second time and became absolutely furious. While working other investigations for several days after the robbery, my mind had never been completely free of it and I wanted the sum bitches who pistol-whipped Mrs. Sloan. Hell, I hadn't just gotten off the turnip truck so I pretty well had figured out what had happened in Baltimore. My request for information regarding subject Phillips had probably been assigned to a rookie officer who didn't know a pimp from a prostitute, or it had been handed to some worn-out detective who was about to retire and just didn't give a damn. I made up my mind then and there that if enough information could be obtained to justify a warrant for Ernest Phillips, I was going to Baltimore come hell or high water.

The SBI published a weekly bulletin of criminal activity that was disseminated to all sheriff and police departments in the state. I had the Sloan Store robbery information included in the next bulletin, and it paid handsome dividends. On February 18, Sheriff Oliver received a telephone call from William Jones, Chief of Police in the town of Scotland Neck, North Carolina. Chief Jones reported that on February 10, at 8:30 P.M., he and officer B.R. Poteat stopped a beige-colored 1962 Oldsmobile bearing Maryland license plates FZ-3225. Chief Jones advised the vehicle was operated by Ernest Phillips, who was accompanied by two other black males. According to the chief, Phillips had a Maryland driver's license showing an address of 1719 West North Avenue in Baltimore. He also had a Maryland registration for the vehicle but it did not appear to be properly filled out. Chief Jones advised that Phillips was issued a citation for improper registration and posted a twenty-five-dollar cash bond for his appearance in Mayor's Court on February 11. He failed to appear.

After talking to Sheriff Oliver, I made arrangements with Chief Jones for a copy of the citation to be forwarded to me to be held as evidence. I was convinced more than ever that Ernest Phillips and his accomplices had gone into hiding shortly after the robbery as it had gone down at 10:30 A.M. and they were stopped only about eighty miles away at 8:30 P.M. I also knew

Highway 258 ran through Scotland Neck, and it was an alternate and less-traveled route back to Baltimore for anyone wanting to avoid I-95, which was more heavily patrolled.

Sheriff Oliver, Charlie Lewis, and I discussed all the information we had regarding Ernest Phillips and the Sloan Store robbery. The three of us were in agreement that it was time to take warrants for him. Since the robbery had taken place in the area of the county assigned to Charlie, he said he would like to take the warrants and did so on February 19. Justice of the Peace Nathan Lassiter issued two felony warrants for Ernest Phillips charging him with armed robbery and feloniously assaulting Mrs. L. T. Sloan.

Arrangements were made for deputies Braxton Hinton and Charlie Lewis, accompanied by Mrs. Sloan, to drive to Baltimore on Monday, February 21, and meet me at the Robbery Division of the Baltimore Police Department. Charlie was to have with him the two felony warrants for Ernest Phillips. I was tired and planned to have a restful weekend with the family and start my drive to Baltimore early on Monday morning. Agent E.B. Pearce had agreed to make the trip with me. The restful weekend was not to be. I was called out on a murder case at 12:30 A.M. on Sunday, February 20. I worked on the case and didn't get home that night until 9:00 P.M. The details of that case will be in the next chapter.

On Monday morning, February 21, I filled out evidence sheets for the material collected in the murder case that had to be submitted to the laboratory for examination. It took awhile to complete the paperwork so Pearce and I were late leaving for Baltimore for our scheduled rendezvous with Mrs. Sloan and the deputies. We made up the lost time by driving well over the speed limit and limiting our stops. It was about 2:00 P.M. when we walked into the Robbery Division to find Charlie, Braxton Hinton, and Mrs. Sloan already there. The deputies, Pearce, and I met with Captain of Detectives George Mooney, Lieutenant Carlton Mann, and Detectives Brooks and Smith. We laid out our case to them, and they listened attentively and from time to time politely interrupted with questions. All the information in their files regarding Phillips was made available to us, but the only additional item of interest was that he was born December 27,

1924, in Wilson, North Carolina. Pearce, the deputies, and I were all aware that Wilson was less than twenty miles from Sloan's Store.

The deputies and Mrs. Sloan waited at the Robbery Division while Pearce and I were escorted by Detectives Brooks and Smith to the Baltimore Office of the FBI. We received a cordial welcome and within a matter of minutes had a copy of Ernest Phillips's FBI record and a 1958 mug shot showing a very distinctive crescent-shaped scar in the center of his forehead. His FBI record contained numerous arrests for the offenses of burglary, larceny, receiving stolen property, escape, and a 1958 arrest at Henderson, North Carolina, for a liquor law violation.

When we returned to the Robbery Division, subject Phillips's mug shot was mixed in with half a dozen others of black males from the files of the Baltimore Police Department. All were displayed to Mrs. Sloan, who immediately identified the photograph of Phillips as that of the subject who entered the store through the rear door and attempted to tie her with cord. Her identification of the photograph and the two felony warrants from North Carolina resulted in a Maryland fugitive felony warrant being issued for Phillips. Detective Brooks was assigned to work with Pearce and me, and Detective Smith was to work with the deputies. A list was made of old addresses for Phillips, car dealerships he had done business with, and other lead material obtained from arrest reports and DMV records. Brooks and Smith divided the leads, and Mrs. Sloan was escorted to a nice hotel where rooms were reserved for us. After a pleasant meal at the hotel restaurant, Pearce and I left with Brooks in his unmarked car and the deputies left with Smith. I can't say about Smith, but Brooks didn't once refer to a map during the several hours we worked with him. He expertly snaked his way through traffic as we worked out leads in some of the roughest and toughest sections of Baltimore. Smith and the deputies did likewise, as we maintained radio contact with them. By midnight our leads were exhausted and so were we. The hotel was a welcome sight.

The deputies and Mrs. Sloan got an early start the next morning for their return trip to Johnston County. Pearce and I returned to the Robbery Division and met with Lieutenant

Mann. He assigned another detective to work with us to check out a couple of automobile dealerships that had been closed the previous night. These inquiries were fruitless. It was approaching mid-afternoon before Pearce and I started our trip back to Raleigh.

I was dead tired when I walked into the house a few minutes before 10:00 P.M. Vicky unpacked my luggage while I told her of my trip. Before she could finish, the telephone rang and I answered. It was Charlie Lewis, and he was very excited as he said, "They've just hit again at Farmer's Plantation!" I asked who had been hit, and what the hell was Farmer's Plantation. Charlie replied that it was a country store located on Highway 39 a few miles from L.T. Sloan's Store, and it had been robbed a few minutes earlier by some black males just as Mrs. Sloan was robbed. I told Charlie I was on my way, but before leaving home I placed telephone calls to Starling and Pearce. Both said they would meet me at the scene.

As I sped through the night along the twisting roads of Johnston County, I didn't notice my fatigue as adrenaline was pumping into my system. I didn't know what to expect at Farmer's Plantation, but if Ernest Phillips and his gang had pulled another robbery I knew it would be a very long night.

There were several vehicles parked at Farmer's Plantation when I arrived shortly after 11:00 P.M. including those of deputies Charlie Lewis and Braxton Hinton. A couple of state troopers were parked beside the store. When I entered, Charlie escorted me behind the wooden counter where he introduced me to Leonard Marsh, a thirty-eight-year-old white male who was seated on a stool sipping on a Coke. He was the clerk on duty in the store when it was robbed. He furnished the following information:

He was alone in the store about 9:40 P.M. when three black males entered through the front door. He did not see or hear a vehicle drive up and did not know how they arrived at the store. The first to enter said, "I want a half pound of bologna and a half pound of cheese." He started behind the meat counter to get the bologna, but as he did the one who ordered it pulled a sawed-off double-barrel shotgun from under his coat and said, "Come out from behind there or I'll kill you. Go to the back of the store."

He did as told, and when he got to the back of the store one of the men said, "Lay face down and put your hands behind you."

Another voice said, "Don't shoot him unless you have to." After he was on the floor, they used cord that they had with them to tie his hands and feet. While he was being tied, one of them asked how to open the cash register. He did not immediately reply, until he heard what he thought was the hammer being cocked on a shotgun. He then told them to just turn the key that was sticking out of the register. After he was tied with the cord, one of the men took his wallet containing his driver's license, personal papers, and twenty to twenty-five dollars in currency. About the time his wallet was taken, he heard the cash register open and a moment later heard the front door close. A few seconds later he heard the front door open. It was his wife, and she found him at the rear of the store and untied him. He called the Sheriff's Department and reported what had happened. His wife had driven to the store and had just stopped her car as three black males came out. She hadn't noticed what they looked like or how they were dressed, but did recall they got into a white automobile and headed north on Highway 39.

Leonard Marsh described the subject who held the shotgun on him as a black male who appeared to be in his thirties and about five-ten and 150 pounds. He had a small goatee and a half-circle scar in the center of his forehead. He didn't wear a hat or gloves but did wear a tan topcoat.

I went to my automobile and obtained the photograph of Ernest Phillips that had been obtained from the FBI in Baltimore. I placed it with the photographs of several other black males that I obtained from other cases, which were in the trunk of my car. I returned to the store and displayed the assortment of photographs to Marsh. Without the slightest hesitation, he picked out the photograph of Ernest Phillips as the subject who held the shotgun on him. Marsh could only describe the two subjects with Phillips as black males, as he said he couldn't take his eyes off the one holding that sawed-off double barrel. Marsh said the register contained about one hundred dollars, which the thieves took.

While I interviewed Marsh, Starling made notes, and by the time I finished he had returned to his car and contacted the

Highway Patrol dispatcher in Raleigh and had an APB broadcast regarding the robbery. Starling also had a teletype sent to the Baltimore Robbery Division reference the robbery, which was apparently perpetrated by subject Ernest Phillips.

Pearce dusted the cash register for latent fingerprints and obtained two prints thought to be identifiable. He then proceeded to take the inked fingerprint impressions of Leonard Marsh and those of the store's owner who had arrived on the scene. Their inked impressions were taken for elimination purposes, only in the event any identifiable prints from the register might be theirs instead of prints left by the perpetrator who entered the register. It was later determined that Pearce had obtained identifiable prints but both were those of Leonard Marsh.

When Pearce and I finished inside the store, we went outside to find that Starling had very efficiently organized a search using deputies, troopers, and various other officers who had arrived on the scene. Just as I was, Starling was convinced Phillips and those with him were "laying low" not too far away. Starling had a full-scale manhunt underway and was coordinating it with precision. It covered portions of Johnston, Wake, Wilson, Nash, and Franklin Counties. Deputy Hinton got into the car with Pearce and they joined the search. Charlie got a .12 gauge shotgun from his car, and I retrieved my M-2 carbine from the trunk of my car and racked a round into the chamber from the thirty-round magazine and placed the selector on full automatic. Charlie got into the car with me and we joined the search. We figured those we were hunting wouldn't be easily taken. But hell, that didn't turn out to be a problem, as again the search was negative. I got home at 4:00 A.M. after driving the last few miles with the window down on the driver's side of the car so the cold February night air would keep me awake. I was asleep by the time my head hit the pillow, but was up at 7:30 A.M. and back in service an hour later.

I drove to the town of Wilson, a tobacco and farming community of 30,000 located about twenty miles east of Highway 39 where the two robberies had taken place. I wanted to check birth records in Wilson, as we had learned in Baltimore that Phillips was born in Wilson on December 27, 1924. The birth certificate of Ernest Phillips was located and it only reflected his parents to be Ed Phillips and Annie Williams Phillips of Wilson County. A search of county tax records, voter registration files, and other courthouse records were negative in regard to Ed or Annie Williams Phillips.

The following day, February 24, I was back in Johnston County and shortly before noon completed some additional inquiries at Farmer's Plantation. I drove south on Highway 39 and stopped for lunch at a small downtown café in the Johnston County town of Selma. After lunch, I decided to drop by the police station to see Chief Percy Moore. He had been a lawman for many years, and was noted for his friendliness and good humor. I had many dozens of photographs made in the SBI laboratory from the one obtained from the FBI in Baltimore. I wanted to leave several of the photographs with Chief Moore. I found the Chief in his office, and he smiled as he said, "What brings the SBI out of Raleigh on such a cold day?" I took a seat, lit a cigarette, and told him I was working on the two armed robberies on Highway 39. He was aware of the details of both and asked only a few questions. I told him about the trip to Baltimore, and when I finished I showed him a photograph of Ernest Phillips. He took one look at the photograph and said in a voice just above a whisper, "I know him." I nearly jumped out of the chair. The chief looked at me with a serious expression as he said, "I know him as Dish Phillips. He grew up in eastern Johnston County. His father was Ed Phillips and his mother was named Annie. They moved from this area and went north before World War II. Dish comes back to visit from time to time. I saw him a couple of weeks ago on the street here in Selma. He was with a younger black male. I talked to Dish for a minute or two, and he said he was living in Baltimore and was here on vacation."

In response to my questions, Chief Moore said he didn't know what type of vehicle Phillips was driving, where he was staying, or who he was visiting. I left several photographs of Phillips with Chief Moore for use by his department and requested that he and his men use extreme caution if they attempted to apprehend Phillips.

I drove on to Smithfield and, after informing Sheriff Oliver of the information received from Chief Moore, I completed some follow-up investigation on the homicide I had worked on Sun-

day, February 20. It was late in the afternoon before I could resume the investigation regarding Ernest Phillips. By that time,
all of Sheriff Oliver's deputies knew of Phillips's Johnston County background and information regarding him was circulating
throughout the county. People were frightened, and many were
openly arming themselves while others were covertly doing so.
I figured it was just a matter of time before someone was killed
if Phillips and his accomplices weren't apprehended.

A late dinner of country ham at The White Swan, my favorite Johnston County restaurant, was followed by a radio message to meet Deputy Glen Cobb at the police station in the town
of Clayton. I had worked with Glen before and found him to be
a very capable officer who relied heavily on informants and common sense. He loved working serious crimes, despised a thief,
had no interest in frivolous misdemeanor cases, and loathed paperwork. He was a damned good investigator who knew most of
the county's residents or their families, and most of them knew
him.

It was approaching 10:00 P.M. when I met Glen at the police
station in Clayton. He said he had received information that
Ernest Phillips was related to a black female named Susie Wilson who lived on Archer's Lodge Road. Glen got into my car and
directed me to Susie Wilson's residence, which was in an isolated location. I drove slowly past the small unpainted frame house,
and Glen and I were both satisfied there was no vehicle parked
in front or behind the house. If there had been, we would have
radioed for backup. There was a light on inside the house. I
parked in the grassless yard, and Glen and I made our way to
the front door past a barking hound dog. Glen tapped on the door,
which was soon opened by an elderly black woman. Glen shined
his flashlight on himself and said, "Aunt Susie, it's Glenn Cobb."

She immediately recognized him and said, "Why Mr. Cobb,
do come in."

A small black and white television was playing loudly on a
short table in the corner of the room. There was no one else in
the room, which was excessively hot from the heat of a wood-
burning stove. Ms. Wilson took a seat in a rocking chair, which
faced the television. Glen walked over to the small portable set
and turned it off. He looked down at Ms. Wilson and asked her

who else was in the house. He and I were both satisfied when she said, "Not nary a soul."

Glen looked directly into the face of Ms. Wilson, and in a very gentle voice told her that what he was going to ask her was very important. She nodded. Glen said, "Aunt Susie, what can you tell me about Ernest Phillips?"

Ms. Wilson hesitated for only a brief moment and then spoke very deliberately. "Mr. Cobb, one time years and years ago, I was married to Ernest Phillips's grandfather, but I ain't no blood kin to Ernest. He come by here three Sundays ago and visited me a few minutes. He said to me he was living in Baltimore but wouldn't give me no address. There was two others with him that I ain't never seen before. Ernest said they were all on vacation and had been staying down the road a little piece with Sarah Peacock."

Glen asked Ms. Wilson what type car Ernest was driving, but she said she didn't know nothing about cars and could only remember it was light colored. He walked back over, turned the television on, and as I started to the front door I saw Glen slip a few bills to "Aunt Susie." He didn't do it for the information we received, he did it because he felt sorry for her. Glen was that type of person. He could be as tough as nails or gentle as a lamb.

Glen and I walked outside and stood beside my car and talked about what we had learned from Susie Wilson. The cold night air felt good after being inside her well-heated house. It was late, and most of the deputies were off duty. I used my radio to see if there was an SBI agent who was still working and not too far away. Agent Everette Norton was in southern Wake County, and immediately answered my radio call. I directed him to a location where Glen and I waited, parked off the shoulder of Archer's Lodge Road. I figured it best to have another agent along if we stumbled on Phillips and those with him. Glen was familiar with the residence of Sarah Peacock and told Everette and me it was just a tenant shack located beside a tobacco field about one hundred yards off the hard surface road. As we were talking, I opened the trunk of my car and retrieved my M-2 carbine. Glen had only his revolver with him, so I handed my .12 gauge sawed-off shotgun to him along with half a dozen shells.

Before locking his car, Everette got his .12 gauge pump shotgun from it and then got into the car with Glen and me. Following Glen's directions, I drove on Archer's Lodge Road past the narrow dirt road leading to the home of Sarah Peacock. The house was dark, and we didn't see a vehicle at the residence, but we all agreed one could be hidden in some nearby woods. I turned around several hundred yards down the road and out of sight of the house. We decided on a simple plan. We would drive slowly back without lights and ease right up to the house with the front of the car facing the front door. I would switch on the headlights and the house would be illuminated. I would conceal myself in the darkness to the left of the car, and Glen was to conceal himself in the darkness on the right side of the car. Everette was to dash around the house and cover the back door. It was a simple plan, which should have worked to perfection, but didn't. Everything went as planned, except Glen called time and time again without a response from inside the house. Finally, Glen came over to where I was concealed behind a steel barrel used for burning trash. He said, "I can just make out some smoke coming from the chimney. They are either in there or Sarah's drunk again."

I flipped the safety off the M-2 carbine as Glen and I walked to the front door. We stood on either side of it as Glen rapped loudly on the door with his flashlight. A light came on inside and the door opened just slightly. I could see a middle-aged black female dressed in a flannel shirt and jeans standing just inside the door. She had difficulty keeping her balance. Glen said, "Sarah, this is Glen Cobb. Are you drunk again?"

Sarah Peacock looked at Glen and said, "Mr. Cobb, I ain't drunk, but I have had a drink or two." Glen asked her who else was in the house, and she said that no one else was there and then added, "Come on in and see for yourself." We did and found she was correct. Glen then attempted to question her about Ernest Phillips, but all he could get out of her was that he had been by to see her two days earlier.

Everette and I chatted back and forth over the radio as we drove back to Raleigh. Our chatter helped to keep us both awake. I arrived home at 2:30 A.M. to find Vicky was awake, as little John was sick with the croup. She had given him medication prescribed by his pediatrician and had just finished rocking him to sleep. A cool air vaporizer made the house seem uncommonly damp, but it didn't make much difference as I fell into bed completely worn out.

On February 25, Deputy Glen Cobb contacted me by telephone and said he had interviewed Henry and Millie Lynch, a black couple of the Wilson's Mills community in Johnston County. Glen stated they claimed Ernest Phillips, accompanied by three younger black males, visited at their residence on the afternoon of February 22. They said Phillips was driving a 1962 white Buick, and he and his companions left in the Buick about dark, and they have not seen them since. Glen advised that the Lynch residence was only a few miles from Farmer's Plantation.

On February 28, I received a letter from Captain Mooney of the Baltimore Robbery Division. He brought me up-to-date on what Baltimore detectives had done regarding their efforts to apprehend Ernest Phillips. They had not been successful, but had learned he had a girlfriend named Mildred Martin who lived at Route 3, Louisburg, North Carolina. I was elated, as Highway 39 in Johnston County leads directly to Louisburg, which is in Franklin County and about twenty-five miles north of L.T. Sloan's Store. I figured Phillips and those with him could have gone into hiding at the Martin residence after the robberies. Maybe Phillips's base of operations had finally been located.

I called Sheriff Oliver and told him of the Louisburg lead. He immediately dispatched Deputy Fulton Moore to meet me in Raleigh. Fulton rode with me to Louisburg, where we contacted Franklin County Sheriff J.W. Camp and SBI agent Lin Harton, whose territory included Franklin County. I briefed Lin and Sheriff Camp on the Johnston County robberies and how we had developed Ernest Phillips as a suspect and him reportedly having a girlfriend, Mildred Martin, at Route 3, Louisburg. Sheriff Camp said he was acquainted with Mildred Martin, who lived a couple of miles east of town. He stated she was a black female about forty years of age and lived alone in a nicely kept home. Sheriff Camp readily agreed to direct us to her residence. I drove my car with the sheriff beside me and Lin and Fulton following in Lin's car. There were no vehicles at the Martin residence, so we didn't slow down as we drove past. We stopped about a mile away and the four of us talked. We all agreed it would be best not to interview Mildred Martin, as she might tip off Phillips that we were onto him, which would make his apprehension more difficult. Sheriff Camp said that he and his deputies would check by the Martin home regularly, and if a suspicious vehicle was there he would contact me by radio or telephone, and while I was en route he would organize his deputies for a raiding party. I was more than pleased with Sheriff Camp's enthusiasm and knew I could depend on him to keep a close check on the Martin residence.

Oh March 1, I was back in Johnston County to pursue a lead developed by Selma Chief Percy Moore. He had learned Phillips's car was repaired at a local garage. I located the garage and interviewed a black mechanic named Edward James. He advised he knew "Dish" Phillips and about three weeks previously Phillips came to the garage and told him his car was broken down at Sarah Peacock's house on Archer's Lodge Road. James said he went to the location and towed Phillips's car to the garage where he repaired the transmission. Garage records revealed only that the vehicle was a 1962 Oldsmobile and was repaired on February 9. The bill totaled $82.75, and was paid in cash. James recalled the car was beige in color and had out-of-state license plates. He also recalled that while the car was being repaired, Dick Massey came to the garage and made an inquiry about it. He said Massey was a black male who lived in the nearby Red Hill community.

On March 1, I located Dick Massey at his residence a few miles from Selma. He stated that about three weeks earlier he stopped his car near the residence of Sarah Peacock to assist three black males whose vehicle was broken down. He gave them a ride to Selma, where the one who apparently owned the vehicle, and who said his name was Steve, went to a garage where Edward James worked. Massey said the two men with Steve were younger than Steve, and one said his name was Tracy. The other said his was Harris or Harrison. Massey said that while the car was being repaired, he allowed Steve and his two companions to visit in his home and at the home of his sister, Carolyn Massey.

Pauline Massey, wife of Dick Massey, was present during his

interview and both of them identified a photograph of Phillips as the person who called himself Steve. They described Harris or Harrison as having a dark complexion, about twenty years of age, five-eight, slender build, and wearing dark glasses. Tracy was described as having a medium complexion, late twenties, tall, and slender with a short goatee. He also wore dark glasses. Dick and Pauline both recalled that all three of the men were armed with pistols.

Carolyn Massey, sister of Dick Massey, a thirty-four-year-old black female who lived in a shack about a mile from her brother, was interviewed on March 1. She could add little to the information furnished by Dick and Pauline, except that the men identified themselves to her as Jim, Spain, and Spade. She identified a photograph of Phillips as the one known to her as Jim. She also said that all three of the men carried pistols and one of them, she didn't recall which, had two pistols. When asked what they did at her house she replied, "We just laid around and drank whiskey before they left with my brother."

It had been another long, two-packs-of-cigarettes day when I arrived home. I crept into the kitchen and noted the wall clock we had received as a wedding present pointed to midnight. Vicky had been in bed, but not asleep. She got up and came into the kitchen and asked if I was hungry. I told her I was famished. Vicky made a thick ham and cheese sandwich, which I washed down with a tall glass of chocolate milk. As we prepared for bed, she asked, "Find him yet?" When I shook my head, she said, "I hope it's soon."

The next day, March 2, found me at headquarters trying to get caught up on my paperwork and reviewing my notes in the Phillips case to see if any leads had been overlooked. I had lunch with a couple of other agents and returned to the agent's room at headquarters and was deeply involved in dictation when I was interrupted about 1:30 P.M. One of the secretaries said I had a call from Sheriff Oliver. When I answered, he said, "Two of my deputies just arrested Ernest Phillips and three of his gang and are bringing them in." I told the sheriff I was on my way. Agent Pearce was in the agent's room and heard my end of the conversation. I was excited as I turned to Pearce and told him about the arrests. The two of us dashed to my car, and I weaved it through downtown traffic until we reached Highway 70 and from there to Smithfield I didn't dare glance at the speedometer. I screeched to a stop at the Sheriff's Office and Pearce and I hurried inside. Sheriff Oliver was not his calm, easygoing self. I asked where Ernest Phillips and the others were and he said, "Upstairs in jail." I told him it would be best if they were kept separated. He replied that they were all in the same cell, but he would have them separated where they couldn't communicate with each other. I knew that being together in the same cell for only a short time was going to result in them collaborating to furnish identical information on how and why they were in Johnston County. I asked Sheriff Oliver, who had made the arrests, and he replied, "Charlie Lewis and Fulton Moore." I could see Charlie, Fulton, and Glen Cobb going through a car parked in one of the spaces reserved for the sheriff's vehicles.

Pearce stepped outside and returned with Charlie, who grinned nearly ear to ear when I congratulated him. I asked Charlie to tell Pearce and me about the arrests. He related the following:

At about 1:10 P.M., he answered the telephone at the Sheriff's Office, and it was a call from Buddy White who operated a service station on Highway 39 about six miles north of Selma. White stated a late-model Chevrolet, dark blue, bearing Maryland license plate CE-4253, had just left his station, and was occupied by four black males. He said he watched the car turn off Highway 39 and head toward the Red Hill community.

Continuing, Charlie said he and Fulton drove to the area looking for the car and noticed it parked at the residence of Odell McLeod. He and Fulton parked about 500 yards away where they couldn't be seen from the house. They waited for only a few minutes before the car was driven away from the McLeod home. After it traveled a short distance on the state paved road, they overtook it and pulled it over. Fulton went to the driver's side of the car and he went to the passenger's side. Fulton checked the driver's license of the subject operating the car and determined him to be Ernest Phillips. Fulton placed Phillips under arrest on a charge of armed robbery, got him out of the vehicle, and handcuffed him. One of the other occupants of the car attempted to hide under a coat in the backseat. When he did so, he and Fulton ordered all the subjects out of the car and searched each of them and the car. One of them, later identified as Anthony Boyer, had a fully loaded .25 caliber pistol in his pocket. A .380 caliber pistol was also found in the car, as was a sawed-off .12 gauge double-barrel shotgun. Other deputies soon arrived on the scene and Phillips and the other subjects were transported to the Johnston County jail and the car to the sheriff's parking lot.

By the time Pearce and I had finished our interview with Charlie, other deputies had completed a thorough search of the automobile and personal effects of all four subjects. The vehicle was determined to be a 1964 Chevrolet Impala, and no registration card could be located for it. An owner's manual in the glove compartment reflected the owner to be Eugene L. Sullivan of Randallstown, Maryland. Three sets of current Maryland license plates were located in the car's trunk. The plates were CZ-2713 and dealer plates AO-59 and AO-71. A registration card attached to back of one of the AO-59 plates disclosed it was issued to Park Circle Motor Company in Baltimore.

Pearce and I examined the two pistols and the sawed-off shotgun and made notes of their manufacturers and serial numbers. We also noted several feet of window sash cord had been recovered from the glove compartment and it appeared to be identical to that used to tie Leonard Marsh and in the attempt to tie Mrs. Sloan.

The personal effects of one subject, later identified as Jimmy Coats, disclosed a slip of paper with the handwritten name of Lillie Martin and two telephone numbers beside her name, a post office box number, and the town Louisburg, North Carolina. The personal effects of subject Boyer (who had the loaded pistol in his pocket) and the other subject who had been identified as Tony Small, revealed nothing of interest. This was not the case for Ernest Phillips, as the following items were among his personal effects and were of interest to us:

1. A slip of paper with the handwritten name of Mildred Martin, Louisburg, North Carolina, and the same post office box number and telephone numbers, as were on the slip of paper of subject Coats.
2. A check on a Baltimore glass and mirror company payable to a

Baltimore liquor store in the amount of six dollars and dated February 26, 1966. This item was hidden in the shoe of subject Phillips.

3. An American Oil Company credit card issued in the name of Roger Player, 1011 Fort Avenue, Baltimore.

4. Two Maryland temporary registrations dated January 19, and February 2, 1966, for a 1962 Oldsmobile bearing plates EX-3325.

Immediately after the examination of the weapons and other items recovered from the subjects, I placed a telephone call to Lieutenant Mann of the Baltimore Robbery Division. I briefed him on the arrest of Ernest Phillips and subjects Coats, Boyer, and Small and informed him of the serial number of the 1964 Chevrolet. I also furnished to him a listing of the personal effects of subject Phillips. Within an hour, Mann called back and said the automobile was reported stolen in Baltimore on February 26, and the check found in Phillips's shoe was taken in the robbery of a Baltimore liquor store. He also said the oil company credit card was taken in another Baltimore armed robbery. Lieutenant Mann advised he would make necessary arrangements for travel to Smithfield and planned to arrive on March 4.

Even though Phillips and the other three subjects were in jail, there was still a hell of a lot of work to be done to properly prepare their cases for trial. The first order of business was a lineup. Sheriff Oliver dispatched a deputy to transport Mrs. Sloan and Leonard Marsh to the Sheriff's Office. While he was gone, Pearce and I selected five black male prisoners from the jail to appear in a lineup with Phillips and those arrested with him. Of course, none of those appearing in the lineup could be in restraining devices, so security had to be exceptionally tight to guard against an escape attempt by any of those in custody. At 4:30 P.M. we held our lineup in the grand jury room of the Johnston County courthouse. Mrs. Sloan was the first to view the lineup, and she immediately and positively identified Phillips as the subject who entered the back door of the store on February 10 and participated in her robbery. She identified Boyer and Small as possibly being the other two subjects. Leonard Marsh picked out Phillips and Coats as being two of the

239

subjects who robbed him on February 22.

Based on the identifications of Mrs. Sloan and Leonard Marsh, Charlie Lewis obtained warrants for Boyer and Small charging them with the robbery and felonious assault of Mrs. Sloan. Charlie also obtained warrants for Phillips and Coats charging them with the armed robbery of Leonard Marsh. Bail was set at $30,000 for Phillips and $10,000 for each of the other subjects.

Immediately after the lineup, subject Phillips was interviewed by Agent Pearce and myself. Phillips was five-seven in height and weighed 170 pounds. He had a thin mustache, short hair that was receding, and the half-moon-shaped scar in the center of his forehead was very pronounced. I informed Phillips of his Miranda rights, and, after he acknowledged he understood them, Pearce and I proceeded to conduct our interrogation. He claimed to have lost the paperwork on the car he was driving, and that he had purchased it three days earlier in Baltimore. He maintained he picked up the three men with him when he saw them hitch-hiking in Virginia and didn't know their names. He stated he didn't know anything about the weapons found in the car, and didn't know they were in there. Phillips acknowledged being in Johnston County for a few days on a previous trip and returning to Baltimore on February 10. He said on that occasion two other young men were with him, but he only knew their first names to be Howard and Herman. He said they borrowed his 1962 Oldsmobile several times and it was possible they pulled a robbery but, if so, he was not aware of it.

I couldn't see any reason to continue Phillips's interrogation as he was a hard ass, and to obtain a confession from him was going to take some doing. Something was needed to influence him to acknowledge his participation in the robberies. Perhaps one of the other subjects would talk.

Pearce and I interrogated subjects Small, Boyer, and Coats separately on March 2, and each of them furnished essentially the same information. Each claimed the three of them hitch-hiked from Baltimore to Washington and into Virginia, where they were picked up by Phillips, whom they didn't know. All three denied ever having previously been in North Carolina. Boyer stated the pistol found on him was for protection. They denied knowledge of the other weapons.

Pearce and I terminated our interrogation well before midnight to avoid any claim that their rights had been violated. It was approaching 1:00 A.M. when we left Smithfield, as we met with Sheriff Oliver and Charlie Lewis and a couple of other deputies to plan our next move. No decisions were reached, but I told Sheriff Oliver I would be back in a few hours. It was 2:00 A.M. when I arrived home, and 8:30 A.M. when I started the drive back to Smithfield. Pearce was on another assignment. On the way to Smithfield, I decided on an approach to use that might get one of the subjects to tell the truth. Coats, Boyer, and Small were all young toughs whom those of us in law enforcement referred to as "hard cases." I figured the source most likely to come forward with the truth, if properly prompted, was the ringleader, Ernest Phillips! And I had a method figured out to do it.

Coats and Boyer both had extensive criminal records, but Baltimore had not been able to locate a record for Small, who claimed no previous arrests. He was twenty-three years of age and must have lived a fairly clean life to avoid having a rap sheet. I judged him to be the weakest link in the chain, and if I did, then maybe Ernest Phillips did also.

When I arrived at the Sheriff's Office, I found Sheriff Oliver, Charlie Lewis, and Fulton Moore waiting. I told them I had a plan, and then explained it to them. I said that for a short while after their arrests all the subjects were in the same cell, where they obviously agreed on the hitch-hiking story. But they were soon placed in separate cells, where they could not communicate with each other, but could see each of the others being taken from the jail for interrogation. I said I felt this caused each of them to worry and be concerned over what the others had said, and if they had withstood the pressure of interrogation. I told Charlie I wanted him to go to the jail and bring Small to the interview room located in the Sheriff's Office. I told him that he and I would close the door to the room and sit in there with Small for an hour. We would talk about hunting, fishing, basketball, or anything that came to mind except the robberies. We would not ask Small a question about anything. Since the room was small with no ventilation, we wouldn't smoke. As soon as we had closed the door, Fulton was to go to the jail and bring Ernest Phillips to the

Sheriff's Office and have him sit in a chair positioned far enough away so he could not hear our conversation in the interview room with the door closed but could see and hear us with the door open. I then told Charlie and Fulton I would handle things after that. We positioned the chair, and Charlie escorted Small to the interview room where I was waiting. Charlie closed the door as I motioned for Small to have a seat. I gave Small an artificial smile and said that I hoped he had had a good night's sleep and enjoyed his breakfast. Charlie looked at me as if I had lost my mind. I then talked to Charlie about his war experiences, and even talked to Small about the Orioles. Time passed slowly, but I knew it was passing even slower for Ernest Phillips, who was waiting outside. Finally, it was time. I told Small that we had checked with Baltimore and learned that he was truthful when he said he had no record there. I stood up and opened the door. I pretended not to notice Phillips seated across the room. I offered Small a cigarette, which he accepted.

I put my Zippo to it and said to Small in a voice I knew Phillips could hear, "Deputy Lewis is going to have to take you back to jail now, but I want you to know I really appreciate you being truthful with us." I then extended my hand to him, and with a look of surprise on his face, Small shook it. As Charlie led Small away, I walked to the vending machine down the hall and got a Pepsi.

When Charlie returned, I had him bring Ernest Phillips into the interview room. I again informed him of his Miranda rights, and he again acknowledged that he understood them. I said, "Ernest, I really don't care whether you tell me anything or not. But listen to me and I'll tell you a thing or two." I then went into detail about when, where, and whom he knew and had visited in Johnston and Franklin counties, including the automobile repairs in Selma. I told him about the 1964 Chevrolet being stolen in Baltimore and the check from his shoe and the credit card being stolen in separate robberies in Baltimore. I went into detail of the robbery of L.T. Sloan's Store and how Mrs. Sloan had been badly beaten without cause, but how she had nevertheless been able to write down his license number and been able to identify him from the lineup held the previous day. I then put the icing on the cake, "Ernest, even the boys with you say they are being truthful. I just hope they don't shift too much blame to you and make you out to be the leader of a gang who has led them astray. If you want to talk to me, then I'll listen. If not, then I'll let the others do all the talking."

I tried to appear not to care one way or the other, but my insides were in knots. I pulled out a pack of cigarettes and offered one to Phillips. He took a long drag and exhaled smoke through his nostrils and said, "Let's talk." I called Sheriff Oliver into the interview room and Phillips furnished the following information:

On February 10, he was in Johnston County in his 1962 Oldsmobile. With him were Herman Brock, a twenty-two-year-old black male who lived on Brookfield Avenue in Baltimore, and another black male with the last name of Mayo and who was an escapee from the Maryland Penitentiary, where he was serving a murder sentence. Mayo had a brother named Ralph and the two of them hung around a poolroom at Fulton Avenue and Baker Street in Baltimore. On the morning of February 10, he, Brock and Mayo went to a country store on Highway 39 just south of the town of Zebulon. He entered the store by the back door and Brock and Mayo went in through the front door and held up the lady clerk with their pistols. After they took the money from the cash register, Brock and Mayo pistol-whipped the lady. He did not hit or touch her. The three of them got into his car, and he drove to Louisburg to the residence of Mildred Martin. On the way they divided the money, which totaled about five hundred dollars. They stayed there for a few hours and then used back roads for the return trip to Baltimore. That night he was stopped by the police in Scotland Neck and received a traffic ticket.

On February 22, he was back in Johnston County driving a 1962 Buick. With him were Jimmy Coats, Anthony Boyer, and Tony Small. They had been drinking and decided to rob a store. It was about 10:00 P.M. when he drove to a country store a few miles north of Selma on Highway 39. There was a sawed-off shotgun in the car that belonged to him. He waited in the car while the three boys went inside the store. They all had pistols, and one of them had the shotgun. A car stopped at the store just as the boys came out. There was less than one hundred dollars taken in this robbery. They drove back to Baltimore and left the Buick parked on the street, as it was stolen from a Baltimore dealership. The .380 caliber pistol found in the 1964 Chevrolet is his and the shotgun was the one used in the robbery on February 22. On February 26, the 1964 Chevrolet was stolen by him from a Chevrolet dealership in Baltimore, and on February 28, he drove it as a getaway car while Coats, Boyer, and Small pulled robberies at a liquor store and an insurance office in Baltimore. He acknowledged the check found in his shoe was stolen in the liquor store robbery, and the gasoline credit card was taken from an employee of the insurance company.

Based on the information obtained from Phillips, there was little difficulty encountered in obtaining confessions from Small, Coats, and Boyer regarding their involvement in the robbery of Leonard Marsh and the two Baltimore robberies.

On the afternoon of March 3, Lieutenant Mann and Detective Montgomery arrived from Baltimore. All four subjects reiterated their confessions to them regarding the liquor store and insurance company robberies. Using the information obtained from Phillips, the Baltimore officers upon return to that city were able to identify the two subjects who participated with Phillips in the robbery of L.T. Sloan's Store. They were Herman Brock, age twenty-three, and Alfred Mayo, age twenty-two. It was obvious Mrs. Sloan's identification of subjects Boyer and Small as being involved in her robbery was not correct. The charges against them for assaulting and robbing her were dismissed but both were charged with the robbery of Leonard Marsh and bail for each was set at $10,000. Warrants for Brock and Mayo were obtained, charging them with the felonious assault and armed robbery of Mrs. Sloan. Copies of these warrants were forwarded to the Baltimore Robbery Division.

Subjects Phillips, Coats, Boyer, and Small appeared before Justice of the Peace Nathan Lassiter on March 7, 1966, and attorneys were appointed for each of them. In a hearing before Mr. Lassiter on March 8, probable cause was found against Phillips for the felonious assault of Mrs. Sloan and the armed robberies of her and Leonard Marsh. Phillips's bail was set at $30,000. Probable cause was found against subjects Coats, Boyer, and

Small for the armed robbery of Leonard Marsh, and bail for each was set at $10,000.

Subject Phillips was tried in the April 1966 term of Johnston County Superior Court for the felonious assault and armed robbery of Mrs. Sloan. He was found guilty of both charges and the following day was tried with subjects Coats, Boyer, and Small with the armed robbery of Leonard Marsh. I was on the witness stand the better part of two days, most of which I underwent stringent cross-examination by four very capable defense attorneys. The jury returned guilty verdicts in the Leonard Marsh case. Subject Phillips was sentenced to thirty years in the case involving Mrs. Sloan and thirty years in the Leonard Marsh case, with the sentences to run concurrently. Subject Coats received twenty to twenty-five years, subject Boyer fifteen to twenty-five years and subject Small ten to twenty-five years.

A week or so prior to the trials in Johnston County, subject Alfred Mayo was apprehended by Baltimore police after a shootout. He was charged in that city with seven counts of armed robbery and one count of murder, as a victim was killed during one of the robberies. In view of the numerous felony charges he faced in Maryland, his extradition to North Carolina was not pursued.

On July 28, 1966, subject Herman Brock was apprehended by Baltimore police but was not extradited because of the Maryland charges against him and because of Mrs. Sloan's reluctancy to undergo the emotional experience of a second trial.

You would think this would be the end of this case. Not so! Subjects Coasts and Boyer were both awarded new trials based on technical flaws in their original trials. Both were tried again in the April 1967 term of Johnston County Superior Court and both were found guilty of armed robbery. Coats received eighteen to twenty-five years, and Boyer received fifteen to twenty-five years.

The investigation I have just written about was lived by me on a daily basis from February 10 through March 8, 1966. Many of the hours spent on this case were taken away from my family. Some men are addicted to alcohol, some to gambling, and others to drugs or women. I was addicted to solving crimes, especially those of armed robbery and murder. I can't explain why, but I just couldn't stop working those cases until they were resolved or there were absolutely no leads remaining. I lived on cigarettes, coffee, soft drinks, and energy that's been a long time gone.

Years later when Big Glen and I discussed this case he said, "I guess those Baltimore holdup fellows thought they could come down here and stick up folks and then meander back to the big city. I'll bet they have second thoughts now that they're our guests at the state pen in Raleigh."

48

When I arrived home at 1:00 A.M. on Saturday, February 19, 1966, I was bushed from the long hours of investigating the robbery of L.T. Sloan's Store. I was badly in need of rest, and planned to relax with the family before leaving for Baltimore early on Monday morning. I slept late on Saturday morning and later in the day did some honey-do chores. That evening, Vicky prepared a delicious steak dinner, complete with pecan pie for dessert. I played with little John and Gloria before putting them to bed. A quiet evening of television followed, and ended with the 11:00 P.M. news. Vicky and I were sound asleep when we were startled by the jingle of the telephone at 12:30 A.M. Vicky uttered an infrequent expletive. It was Deputy Howard Olive calling from Johnston County. He said, "Bob, sorry to wake you but we need your help. Julian Pike was shot from ambush tonight. He died in the driveway of his home. We haven't made an arrest." In response to my question as to the location of the Pike home, Howard said it was in a rural area of the county a few miles from the town of Four Oaks. He said he would meet me at the Four Oaks police station, and an hour later I was there.

Howard was not alone, but was with Deputy Dailey Stewart. Howard got into the car with me, and we followed as Dailey led the way to the Pike home. As I drove, Howard related the following:

Julian R. Pike, a fifty-six-year-old farmer, lived with his wife in a nice brick home about 3 miles southeast of Four Oaks. His wife had attended a baby shower earlier that night and returned home between 9:30 and 10:00 P.M. She discovered her husband lying on the driveway of their residence near the back door. She drove to the nearby residence of their daughter, who summoned an ambulance. The ambulance was dispatched from Underwood Funeral Home in Smithfield, which is owned by V.J. Underwood, Johnston County Coroner, who accompanied the ambulance to the scene. Coroner Underwood examined Mr. Pike and declared him dead as a result of gunshot wounds. His body was transported to Underwood Funeral Home and the Sheriff's Department was contacted. Coroner Underwood had in his possession a spent bullet found on the ambulance stretcher. He and Dailey went to the funeral home, examined the body of Julian R. Pike, and noted several apparent bullet wounds that appeared to have been inflicted by a small-caliber weapon. He and Dailey then proceeded to the Pike residence, where a large crowd of friends and relatives had gathered. A search of the area resulted in the recovery of four .22 caliber cartridge cases on the ground near where the victim's body had been. They also recovered five .22 caliber cartridge cases beside a large oak tree about forty yards from where the victim was apparently killed.

In addition to the above, Howard advised he was personally acquainted with Mr. Pike and knew he enjoyed an excellent reputation and apparently had no known enemies. He considered robbery the motive as Mr. Pike's wallet was missing.

It was 2:00 A.M. when I followed Dailey into the driveway of the Pike residence. I immediately knew a crime scene search for footprints or tire impressions would not be possible because of the many vehicles and crowd of people around the house. I noticed a large blood-stained area on the driveway, and Howard said it was where the victim's body had lain. I took a tape measure from my evidence kit and made some measurements. The blood stains were twenty-one feet from the back door of the victim's home and 142 feet from the large oak tree where the five cartridge cases were found. I noted that a person concealed behind the tree would have a clear field of vision to where the victim was found. The five cartridge cases found at the tree and the four found near the victim's body indicated to me that he apparently was shot first from the tree and then the perpetrator(s) came up close and fired additional shots into the body before taking Mr. Pike's wallet. I didn't make photographs of the scene that night, but returned and did so a few days later during daylight hours.

The victim's wife was being comforted by relatives and friends and was too distraught for an in-depth interview from me. I elected to interview the couple's thirty-three-year-old daughter, Lizzie Pike Whitfield, who lived only about 300 yards away. She was very upset and was struggling to control her emotions. She agreed to an interview and answered my questions in a soft voice interrupted by occasional sobs. She furnished the following information:

She was the wife of Bunn Edward Whitfield and was an elementary school teacher. She and her husband had been separated for about ten months. She lived just a few hundred yards from the home of her parents, and the only other occupant of her household was her brother, Alton Dell Pike, age twenty-four, who stays with her at night. He was not there on the night of February 19, as he was on duty with the National Guard. Other than her parents, the only other person residing at their home was her twenty-year-old sister, Jean Bell Pike, who was a college student and was not at home on the night of February 19. At about 8:00 P.M. that night, her father drove his automobile to her home. He was alone, as her mother was attending a baby shower in the community. Her father watched television until about 9:30 P.M. and then put on his coat, got his flashlight from the table, told her goodnight and walked out to his car for the short drive home. About ten or fifteen minutes after he left, she heard what sounded like firecrackers popping in the direction of her parents' home. She looked out the window and saw headlights come on in the road near her parents' home. The vehicle left at a moderate rate of speed and passed on the road by her house. It was dark, and she could not see the occupant(s) nor could she describe the vehicle other than that it was an automobile. She didn't think much of the incident as she believed it was some mischievous teenagers shooting firecrackers. A few minutes after 10:00 P.M., she heard a car horn at her home and opened the door and found her mother there in a state of hysteria. Her mother said her father was lying on the driveway, was not conscious and was hemorrhaging badly. She called for an ambulance, got into the car with her mother, and drove quickly to where her father was facedown on the driveway with a lot of blood on and around him. She didn't know he had been shot until the coroner examined her father when he arrived with the ambulance.

She was separated from her husband, Bunn Whitfield, who resides with his sister and brother-in-law, Mr. and Mrs. Wallace Harrington, in Johnston County near the town of Benson. She and Bunn had had marital problems for several years prior to their separation. She believed most of the problems resulted from his resentment of her education, her making her own money, and her not being financially dependent upon him. He disliked her family and was offended by her devotion to her father. He was jealous of her father and believed her love for her father was greater than her love for him. Bunn acted strange on occasions and didn't hide the fact that he was unfaithful to her and claimed to love another woman.

After their separation, she was harassed by being followed by her husband's friends, and sometimes he would drive back and forth slowly past her home. On one occasion, he followed her in his automobile and struck her car in the rear forcing her off the road.

At about noon on February 19, she was in Benson to make a bank deposit. As she started to drive away from the bank, Bunn pulled his car next to hers. He asked some questions about insurance and about filing income tax. Bunn then asked if she was going to live with him again. She told him she was not, at which time he said, "Lizzie, you will have tears as long as icicles before long. I'll kill the person who made you feel toward me the way you do. I won't do it, but I'll have it done. We will die together."

In addition to the above, Mrs. Whitfield advised she returned home and had not seen her husband since she left Benson. She also stated she understood her father's wallet was missing, but she didn't consider robbery the motive for him being killed as he never carried much money on his person. She also said his coat and flashlight were inside the house, which indicated he had arrived home after leaving her house and had gone back outside when he was killed.

The interview of Mrs. Whitfield was followed by the interviews of neighbors and other relatives of the victim. No information of value was obtained. It was approaching 5:30 A.M. when Howard, Dailey, and I pulled into a truck stop on I-95 just south of Benson. We ate a hearty breakfast with strong, steaming coffee as we discussed our case. Howard needed to be off for a couple of hours to attend to some personal business. I figured we needed the assistance of another agent, so at about 6:30 A.M. I placed a telephone call to Pearce at his home in Raleigh. I briefed him on the case, and he readily agreed to meet Howard at the Benson police station at 9:00 A.M. Daily and I were going to attempt to locate and interview Bunn Whitfield.

At 7:00 A.M., Dailey and I arrived in my car at the residence of Wallace Harrington at Route 3, Benson. I went to the front door and knocked. The door was opened by a white male in his mid-thirties who was about six feet in height and weighed approximately 275 pounds. He had short red hair and a light complexion, spotted with freckles. He was dressed in jeans and a short-sleeve plaid shirt. I identified myself and asked if Bunn Whitfield was there. He said, "That's me."

I said I had a matter that I would like to discuss with him and would like to do so in my car. He didn't ask what the discussion was going to be about, and walked with me to the car where I introduced him to Dailey. Bunn got into the back, and, when he was comfortably seated, I informed him of his Miranda rights. He acknowledged that he understood his rights, but still didn't ask why he was being interviewed or what it was about. After some introductory questions, I told him that his father-in-law, Julian Pike, had been shot to death at his home the previous night. There was absolutely no change in his expression, nor did he ask how it happened or whether it was an accident, murder, or suicide. He didn't show any emotion regarding Mr. Pike's death, and didn't express any anger or concern when I said we were checking on his activities for the previous day and night. Bunn said, "I ain't got nothing to hide."

Bunn Whitfield stated that shortly after noon on February 19, he saw his wife near the post office in Benson and briefly spoke to her about some car insurance and filing income tax. He said they didn't argue, nor did he threaten her or anyone else. He claimed to have stayed around Tom's store in Benson for the remainder of the afternoon and early evening. He then drove to his sister's home and ate supper with her and her husband. He said he then borrowed his brother-in-law's truck and went to Benson and bought a headlight for his car. He claimed to have driven back to this sister's home and installed the headlight in his car and at about 9:00 P.M. drove it to the home of his brother, Elmer Whitfield, who lived just a few miles away. He said he assisted his brother in the installation of a washing machine and didn't leave the premises until about 12:15 A.M., when he drove back to his sister's home.

Bunn Whitfield voluntarily consented for his automobile to be searched, but nothing of an evidentiary nature was discovered. When questioned as to what firearms he owned, he said he had a .25 caliber pistol in the house. At my request, he went inside and returned with it. I retained it for a possible ballistics examination. When questioned about a .22 caliber weapon, Bunn stated he sometimes borrowed a .22 rifle from his brother, Elmer, which he used in rabbit hunting. He said he last borrowed the rifle about a month previously and had returned it about a week ago. No one was at home at the time, so he left it in the corner of Elmer's bedroom, and a day or so later told him about returning the rifle.

I wanted to check out Bunn's story, so I told him I appreciated his cooperation and would like for him to remain at his sister's home where I could locate him later for a formal statement. Bunn said he would be there for the remainder of the day.

Dailey knew the location of Elmer Whitfield's home, and, following his directions, we were there in just a few minutes. Elmer appeared to be in his mid-forties. He and his family lived in a small, rural home at Route 2, Four Oaks. He seemed to be genuinely surprised to hear of the death of Julian Pike. He answered my questions in a forthright manner without the slightest hesitation. Past experience led me to believe he was one of those rare individuals who just wouldn't lie for himself or anyone else.

Elmer stated that on the night of February 19 he was at home the entire time, except for a few minutes around midnight when he drove to Benson to buy some cigarettes. He said that prior to making the trip for cigarettes he had installed a washing machine for his wife. That he was assisted by his son, Nathan Whitfield, and his brother, Kermit Whitfield. He stated he last saw his brother, Bunn Whitfield, in downtown Benson on the afternoon of February 19. He said that to the best of his knowledge Bunn was not at his house on the night of the 19th. Elmer advised he owned a .22 caliber semi-automatic rifle, which was in his bedroom closet. I requested him to produce the rifle but a search of the house failed to locate it. Elmer said he was unaware of Bunn ever borrowing the rifle, nor did he recall Bunn ever saying anything about leaving the rifle at his home.

Immediately after the interview of Elmer Whitfield, Dailey and I entered the bedroom of nineteen-year-old Nathan Whitfield and awakened him. He was asked if he had seen his uncle, Bunn Whitfield, the previous night. He replied that Bunn arrived at his home between 7:30 P.M. and 8:00 P.M. and remained there without leaving until about midnight. I told Nathan that his information was not consistent with that furnished by his father. He became excited and immediately changed his story. He said his uncle Bunn came by about 10:00 P.M. and stayed for only fifteen or twenty minutes and then left in his 1956 Pontiac.

I wanted Nathan Whitfield out of the friendly confines of his home. I took his father aside and told him Nathan had told two different stories about Bunn's whereabouts on the previous night. I said I wanted to interview him in my car instead of his own room. Elmer responded by saying he wanted his son to tell only one thing, and that was to tell only the truth. He agreed that I should continue the interview in the car.

When Nathan Whitfield was settled on the backseat of my car, I informed him of his Miranda rights. He was scared, and his voice quivered when he acknowledged that he understood his rights. I told him we were investigating the murder of Julian Pike, and then I went straight for the jugular. "Nathan, I only talked to you for ten minutes in the house and received two different stories about last night. If you didn't kill Julian Pike, then let's have the truth and let's have it now!"

Nathan dropped his head, and I thought I detected a slight choking in his throat. He said in a barely audible voice that his Uncle Bunn had stopped by his house about 10:00 P.M., and he rode to Benson and back with him. That during the trip his uncle said to him, "I just had someone take care of Julian Pike."

After Nathan made the statement regarding the comment he attributed to Bunn Whitfield, I called Elmer Whitfield to the car and had Nathan reiterate the statement to him. I then told Nathan I would like for him to accompany Deputy Stewart and me to the SBI office in Raleigh. He agreed to do so. I drove to the police station in Benson and found Pearce and Howard Olive waiting there. I briefed them on the latest developments in the case, and we made a change in plans. Nathan got into the car

253

with Pearce and Howard for the trip to Raleigh, while Dailey and I picked up Bunn at his sister's home.

Pearce and Howard arrived at headquarters about 10:00 A.M. and commenced their interrogation of Nathan Whitfield. Dailey and I arrived a few minutes later and started our interrogation of Bunn Whitfield. I had just started to get warmed up in my interrogation of Bunn, when I was interrupted by a tap on the door of the interview room. It was Pearce, and he motioned with his head for me to step into the hallway. After I closed the door behind me, Pearce said that Nathan had confessed to being involved in the murder of Mr. Pike. I followed Pearce to the room where Nathan was waiting with Howard Olive. Pearce asked Nathan to tell his story to me, and he said that two or three weeks ago his uncle, Bunn Whitfield, talked to him about dropping off a Negro man near the home of his father-in-law, Julian Pike. The Negro man, nicknamed "Piggy," was to kill Mr. Pike. At about 10:00 P.M. on February 19, his uncle came to his home and said that "Piggy" was outside and was ready to be dropped off. He went outside with his uncle and they got into his father's car, with him behind the wheel and his uncle on the backseat. "Piggy" got into the car on the passenger side of the front seat. "Piggy" had a .22 caliber semi-automatic rifle which belonged to his (Nathan's) father. He drove to the Pike residence and stopped the car on the road near the driveway and "Piggy" got out. He and his Uncle Bunn drove back to his home, where Bunn got into his car and left. His father didn't know of the plan to kill Mr. Pike, and didn't know that his car and rifle were used in the murder.

I returned to the interview room where Bunn was waiting. Up until that time he didn't know that we had talked to Nathan and was unaware that he was in the adjoining room. I took a few seconds trying to think of a way to give Bunn some justification in his own mind for what he had done. I knew in the Johnston County area where Bunn grew up that stealing was a despicable crime and was absolutely not tolerated. Making whiskey, fighting and other offenses against the peace and dignity of the state were acceptable, but stealing was taboo. I said to Bunn, "Nathan is in the next room and has told us about the two of you dropping 'Piggy' off last night to shoot Mr. Pike with Elmer's rifle. What I would like to hear from you is why it was done."

I knew robbery wasn't the motive and was probably something "Piggy" did on his own. I continued, "Mr. Pike's wallet was taken, which indicates he was killed for a small amount of money. I have also heard he may have caused the break-up of your marriage. Bunn, was Mr. Pike killed for his money or for what he did to your marriage?"

Bunn let out a deep sigh and a low moan escaped from deep inside him. He said that several days ago he thought of doing away with his father-in-law, Julian Pike. He discussed it with a local Negro called "Piggy," who worked on Edgar Seagrove's farm. He didn't know "Piggy's" real name. He had Elmer's .22 caliber rifle. On the afternoon of February 19, he happened to see "Piggy" at Tom's Store in Benson. "Piggy" said he was ready and to pick him up after dark in Benson in the alley beside the potato house. "Piggy" was to do the job for $200, which he was to pay after Mr. Pike was killed. At about 8:00 P.M. he drove to the alley where "Piggy" was waiting. He gave the rifle and a box of cartridges to "Piggy." As he drove toward Elmer's house, "Piggy" loaded the rifle. When they arrived at Elmer's home, "Piggy" remained outside and out of sight while he went inside. He was in the house for about an hour, during which time he asked his nephew, Nathan, to do the driving. Elmer was busy installing a washing machine and may not have known he was there. Nathan agreed and told his father he wanted to use his car for a quick trip to Benson. Nathan drove his father's car with "Piggy" beside him on the front seat. He was in the back seat. Nathan stopped the car near the driveway to Mr. Pike's home and "Piggy" got out with the rifle. He and Nathan were supposed to ride the roads in the area and pick up "Piggy" after he had done the job. After "Piggy" got out of the car with the rifle, Nathan kind of panicked and drove back to his house. He got into his car and drove to his sister's home. He didn't know "Piggy" had actually killed Mr. Pike until I had talked to him that morning. If Mr. Pike was robbed, it was something "Piggy" did on his own. It was not in the plans. He believed his wife cared more for her father than she cared for him, and was more devoted to her father than to him. He believed Mr. Pike had turned his daughter against him, and if Mr. Pike was out of the way, maybe his wife's love for him would return. This was why he wanted Mr. Pike killed.

We transported Nathan and Bunn to Smithfield, where they were charged with murder and lodged in the Johnston County jail without privilege of bail. A telephone call to Deputy Fulton Moore who lived in Benson revealed he knew "Piggy," but didn't know his true name. He said he could easily find out. A few minutes later, Fulton called back and said "Piggy's" real name was Joseph McNall. A murder warrant was taken for McNall and a search for him was immediately undertaken by the Benson police, sheriff's deputies, and highway patrol troopers. About 4:30 P.M., trooper D. M. Cole advised by radio that he had "Piggy" McNall in custody near Benson.

I elected to interview "Piggy" with Fulton Moore as my witness, as he was personally acquainted with "Piggy" and was on good terms with him. The interview was conducted at the Benson police station. I carefully explained "Piggy's" Miranda rights to him, and after he acknowledged he understood them, he agreed to be interviewed.

When I looked across the table at "Piggy," I didn't see a killer for hire, but rather a twenty-nine-year-old short, stocky Negro with a very dark complexion. He was a typical Johnston County field hand whose previous brushes with the law had been a misdemeanor conviction for breaking and entering, and a liquor law violation. I started "Piggy's" interrogation with irrelevant questions and then eased into his whereabouts of the previous night. He lied very smoothly, and I allowed him to do so until I believed he thought he had Fulton and me convinced that he didn't know anything about the death of Julian Pike.

I let him down very hard when I said in a very casual voice, "They gave you up, 'Piggy'. Bunn and Nathan have already told us how they dropped you off last night at Mr. Pike's house with Elmer Whitfield's .22 rifle. The question now is not whether you shot Mr. Pike, but whose idea was it for him to be shot?"

"Piggy's" eyes darted from side to side as if he was cornered and looking for a way out. I saw Fulton shift in his seat ready to spring into action if "Piggy" bolted. I prodded "Piggy" some more. "Did you talk Bunn and Nathan into dropping you off so you could kill and rob Mr. Pike and split the money with them?" I knew this was not the case, but it was something he could sincerely deny and at the same time put the blame of the plan to kill Mr. Pike where it rightfully belonged. "Piggy" accepted a cigarette from me, and with Fulton and me also smoking, through a thick, blue cloud of smoke, he told the following:

About four or five days ago, Bunn Whitfield talked to him about killing Mr. Julian Pike. At first he told Bunn he wouldn't do it, but finally Bunn offered to pay him $200 to do the job. Yesterday afternoon he had happened to see Bunn at Tom's store in Benson. Bunn again offered him $200 to kill Mr. Pike. He had been drinking, and agreed to do it. Bunn said he would pick him up shortly after dark in the alley near the potato house in Benson. He waited in the alley for Bunn, who arrived in his Pontiac at about 8:00 P.M. Bunn was alone, and he got into the car with him. Bunn had a .22 caliber rifle that belonged to Elmer Whitfield. Bunn handed the rifle and a box of bullets to him, and he loaded the rifle while Bunn drove to Elmer's home. Bunn went inside, and he stayed in the car. About an hour later, Bunn came out with his nephew, Nathan Whitfield, who got behind the wheel of Elmer's car. He got in beside Nathan on the front seat with the rifle and the extra bullets. Bunn got into the back. Nathan drove to the home of Mr. Julian Pike, and stopped on the road near his driveway. He got out with the rifle and the box of bullets. Nathan and Bunn drove off. They were to ride the roads and pick him up after he had killed Mr. Pike. His plan was to make some noise outside the house, and when Mr. Pike came out to see what it was he was going to shoot him. He was out of the car for only a few minutes and was standing by a big tree behind Mr. Pike's house when a dog started barking. Mr. Pike came out the back door and stood in the driveway. He aimed from behind the tree and shot Mr. Pike about four times. Mr. Pike didn't fall, so he ran up close to him and shot him three or four more times. Mr. Pike fell facedown. He ran into the woods behind the house and walked for several miles. He was in the woods all night, and at about 8:00 A.M. went to a farmhouse and paid a man to drive him to Benson.

"Piggy" insisted he didn't rob Mr. Pike. He also said he hid the rifle and extra bullets near a large pine tree in the woods not far from Mr. Pike's house. I didn't believe "Piggy" when he said he didn't rob Mr. Pike, but I didn't disagree with him, as I wanted to stay on his good side so he would lead us to the rifle. I told "Piggy" I wanted to believe him and would like for him to point out the place where he had hidden the rifle. He agreed to do so, and I drove with Pearce beside me and "Piggy" in back between Fulton and Howard. Dailey followed in his car. "Piggy" directed me to a location about half a mile from the Pike residence, where I stopped the car beside the road. Following "Piggy's" directions, we made our way through the woods for about a quarter of a mile to where "Piggy" pointed to a tall pine tree. He said the rifle and bullets were hidden under some brush near the tree. He was right, as when we moved the brush aside we discovered a .22 caliber semi-automatic rifle with six unfired cartridges in the magazine and one unfired cartridge jammed in the chamber. Also recovered was a box containing sixteen unfired Federal .22 caliber cartridges.

Prior to leaving the area, "Piggy" again sat in the back seat of my car between Fulton and Howard. Pearce was beside me on the front seat as I drove over roads in the community behind the Pike residence. It didn't take long before "Piggy" identified a farm home where he paid a man to take him to Benson. Fulton knew the home to be that of Byron Dixon. "Piggy" was taken to Smithfield, where he was placed in the Johnston County jail without the privilege of bail.

On the evening of February 20, Pearce and I met with Mr. V.J. Underwood, the Johnston County Coroner. He stated that earlier that day he transported the body of Julian R. Pike to Wake Memorial Hospital in Raleigh, where an autopsy was performed by Dr. L.J. Kent, Pathologist. It disclosed that Mr. Pike suffered five gunshot wounds, with the fatal wound perforating the right lung and heart. There were two gunshot wounds to the lower facial area and two wounds passing through the left arm. The bullet that penetrated the heart was recovered, and it was received from Coroner Underwood along with the bullet found on the ambulance stretcher. The victim's shirt was also received from the Coroner. All items were placed in separate evidence containers, which we initialed and dated. Howard Olive and I had done the same with the empty cartridge cases found at the scene. Howard, Pearce, and I scratched our initials on the rifle recovered in the woods behind the Pike residence, and we initialed and dated the box of cartridges found with it.

Before leaving Smithfield on the night of February 20, Pearce and I met with Howard Olive, Fulton Moore, and Dailey Stewart. Since Pearce and I were scheduled to leave the following morning to meet with Baltimore officers regarding the robbery of L.T. Sloan's Store, we discussed what loose ends needed to be tied up in the Pike case. It was agreed that I would submit all physical evidence to the laboratory the next morning before leaving for Baltimore. Fulton was to contact Byron Dixon to determine if he was the person who gave "Piggy" a ride to Benson. Howard Olive was an excellent woodsman, and he and Dailey said they would return to the location where the rifle was recovered and attempt to backtrack "Piggy's" route from the Pike residence in hopes of locating Mr. Pike's wallet. Pearce and I left Smithfield with hopes of a good night's rest before leaving for Baltimore.

I arrived home at 9:00 P.M. The children were asleep, and Vicky was ironing some shirts for my Baltimore trip. I was extremely tired, sad that a good man had been murdered, but satisfied with the investigation, which had resolved the case within a matter of hours and resulted in three people being charged with the crime. After a sandwich, a glass of milk, and a large slice of cake, I sat in my easy chair in the den while Vicky continued to iron. I told her about the case, and when I finished she looked at me with a puzzled expression on her face. She said, "A man killed another man whom he didn't dislike for $200 on credit?" I nodded as she said, "Be careful and don't let it happen to you."

After Pearce and I returned from Baltimore, we learned that Byron Dixon had identified "Piggy" as the person he had driven to Benson on the morning of February 20. We also learned that Howard Olive and Dailey Stewart had backtracked "Piggy's" route and had located Julian Pike's wallet in a shallow creek about 300 yards from where the rifle was recovered. It contained his driver's license and other personal papers but no money.

A few days later, I received the ballistics report which stated the bullet which caused the fatal wound was fired by the rifle I submitted as evidence as was the bullet from the ambulance stretcher. What surprised me most in the report was that the bullet that penetrated the cheek of the victim had passed through the collar of the victim's shirt and was fired from a distance of approximately five inches. "Piggy" had apparently attempted to apply the coup de grace to his fallen victim.

On March 20, 1966, a preliminary hearing was held at Smithfield for Bunn Edward Whitfield, Nathan Whitfield and Joseph "Piggy" McNall. All subjects were represented by attorneys. Justice of the Peace Nathan Lassiter found probable cause against each defendant and they were bound over without privilege of bail to the next term of Johnston County Superior Court. Their cases came to trial in the April 4, 1966 term of court. The District Attorney allowed Nathan Whitfield to plead guilty to being an accessory before the fact of a felonious assault. He received a sentence of 10 years, which was suspended, and he was placed on probation for five years. Joseph "Piggy" McNall plead guilty to murder in the first degree and received a life sentence. Bunn Edward Whitfield plead not guilty to a charge of accessory before the fact of murder. After a lengthy trial, in which I testified over a period of two days, he was found guilty and sentenced to life imprisonment.

You would think the case would be over, but not so. Bunn Edward Whitfield was paroled January 16, 1981, and was released from parole January 29, 1986. I didn't know until I did some research for this book that Joseph "Piggy" McNall escaped from the prison system April 3, 1975, and as of this writing has not been apprehended.

Years later, when I told Big Glen about this case he said, "With inflation and all, I wonder if 'Piggy's' price for a contract killing has gone up? Maybe he now takes MasterCard."

49

Friday, May 12, 1967, was one of those lazy, warm spring days sporting a beautiful Carolina blue sky. It was really too nice a day to have been working, but I was up to my neck in paperwork from a recently completed homicide investigation. At 9:25 A.M. the telephone rang in the agent's room and I answered. An unidentified male voice said, "A black man is going to rob the bank at Bunn this morning." Pearce was across the room, and I caught his eye and motioned for him to pick up on an extension. I told the caller that I didn't understand what he had said. He repeated that the bank at Bunn would be robbed that morning and then hung up. Pearce and I dashed quickly down the hall to the SBI Director's office and informed him of the call. He instructed us to immediately alert the local FBI office and then proceed to Bunn. I placed the call to the FBI office and it was answered by Don Murray, senior agent of the Raleigh resident agency. He advised he would notify the local sheriff's department. I knew FBI policy prohibited agents from participating in bank stakeouts. I told Murray to inform the sheriff's department that if Pearce and I got to the bank before it was robbed that we would be inside when the robbery went down. As Pearce and I hurried out the door for my car, we met agent Everette Norton as he was entering the building. I didn't say why, but told him to come with us. The three of us jumped into my car and I burned up the road on the twenty-five-mile trip to Bunn. On the way we told Everette about the anonymous telephone call.

Bunn is a small, sleepy farming community located in Franklin County. In 1967, it had only a few hundred residents, and I'm not sure if it had a traffic light. But it did have a small branch office of First Citizens Bank and Trust Company. At approximately 10:05 A.M., I parked on the main street half a block from the bank leaving Everette in the car as backup. Pearce and I had our coats unbuttoned for quick access to our weapons in the event we walked in on a robbery in progress. As we walked in the front door we were both relieved to see that everything appeared normal. Two female tellers were on duty at their teller windows and an elderly gentleman was leaving after completing his business. We could see the branch manager at his desk in the bank's small office. Pearce and I both identified ourselves to one of the tellers, and I asked to see the manager. His door was open, and he heard my request and came out of his office and examined our credentials. He then introduced himself as Bill Avent. As we shook hands, I said we needed to speak to him in private. Behind the closed door of his office, we explained to Mr. Avent that we had received information that the bank would be robbed that morning, but we could not vouch for the reliability of the information. Mr. Avent responded by informing us that local officers had received a tip that the bank was to be burglarized Saturday night, May 6. They had kept the bank under surveillance that night and the following night and nothing had happened. Mr. Avent chose to keep the bank open, and Pearce and I volunteered to remain in the bank. I returned to the car and asked Everette to remain there as backup as Pearce and I were going to stay in the bank. I retrieved my sawed-off, double-barrel .12 gauge shotgun from the car but left it in the olive drab army case while walking back to the bank. While I was gone Pearce had briefed the two tellers, Mrs. Strong and Mrs. Judd, on the information we had received. He and Mr. Avent had also decided on a plan. Mr. Avent was to take the place of Mrs. Strong at her teller window, and she would wait in the vault. If a black male came into the bank, Pearce was to stand at the teller window talking to Mr. Avent while pretending to be a customer. The robber would in all probability go to Mrs. Judd's window, and Pearce would terminate his pretext conversation with Mr. Avent and turn to leave, at which time he would execute some of his martial arts training on the unsuspecting bank robber. I was to conceal myself in the bank's office with the shotgun and spring into action as things unfolded. We had been in position for about twenty minutes, during which time Mrs. Judd waited on several regular customers before a black male entered the bank alone. He appeared to be in his early twenties, five-nine, 150 pounds, smooth complexion with no facial hair. He was wearing a dark golf style cap, which buttoned over a short bill. He also had on

262

a blue cardigan sweater with black vertical stripes. He went to Mrs. Judd's teller window and asked for change for a five-dollar bill. He received the five ones from Mrs. Judd and left via the front door. All of us remained in our positions and the same subject returned in about ten minutes. As soon as he stepped through the door I knew a robbery was about to go down. I could feel the adrenaline kick in as I eased the safety off on the shotgun. The subject walked straight to Mrs. Judd's window and pulled a brown paper bag and a semi-automatic pistol from under his sweater. He handed the paper bag to Mrs. Judd with his left hand and held the pistol on her with his right hand. He told her to fill up the bag. Pearce terminated his pretext conversation with Mr. Avent at the next teller window and turned to walk behind the robber. As Pearce turned away from the teller window, the robber quickly turned to face Pearce and at the same time pointed the weapon at him. Pearce had no choice but to raise his hands and I heard him say, "Okay."

The robber reached into Mrs. Judd's teller window with his left hand and took the paper bag from her. He turned to his left to back toward the door. That's when I made my move.

I came out of the office and pointed the shotgun at the robber and said, "Police officer—hold it!" I was about fifteen feet away and knew I could cut the robber in half at that range. However, I had no sooner gotten the words out of my mouth when I realized I couldn't shoot. Several feet behind the robber was a large plate glass window which faced the street. Standing on the sidewalk at the window were a farmer, his wife and their two children. I knew my sawed-off shotgun with #4 buckshot would scatter and not only take out the robber but probably some of the farmer's family. The robber had turned to face me, and as he did so pointed the pistol directly at me. I saw his hand jerking as he pulled hard on the trigger, trying to get the weapon to fire. For some reason, it wouldn't shoot.

He bolted out the front door with Pearce and me close behind. He turned in the opposite direction from where Everette was parked and ran down the sidewalk a short distance before running across a vacant lot to an open field. His long, graceful strides quickly lengthened the distance between us. Pearce pulled his revolver and fired two warning shots followed by a command to, "Halt." I stopped running, dropped to one knee, and fired the right and then the left barrel of the shotgun. Mine weren't warning shots, but I was too far away to inflict a serious or fatal wound. The shotgun blasts either stung him good or scared the robber into dropping the paper bag containing the bank's money, totaling $8,758. After crossing the open field, he stopped and turned to face us before entering a wooded area. He pointed the pistol in our direction, but it still wouldn't fire. Pearce and I were nearly 100 yards from the robber and a couple of shots from each of our snub-nosed .38's sent the robber scurrying into the woods.

Federal, state, and local officers from near and far converged on the town of Bunn, where a command post was set up to coordinate a massive manhunt. Bloodhounds from the Prison Department were brought in, as was an observation plane from the Highway Patrol. The search continued all afternoon and well into the night. About 10:30 P.M., Franklin County Deputy Lonnie Hunt spotted a subject fitting the robber's description walking along Highway 56, two miles west of the town of Franklinton and about twenty miles from Bunn. Deputy Hunt took the subject into custody and returned him to Bunn, where Pearce and I positively identified him. He was twenty-year-old Charles Eller Woods from Columbia, South Carolina. He plead guilty June 5, 1967, to federal bank robbery charges and received a sentence of fifteen years. How he arrived in Bunn is still a mystery, as is the identity of the anonymous caller.

It has been said that your entire life flashes past when you stare death in the face. Not so for me. My only thoughts were that I wished the farmer and his family weren't on the sidewalk.

Years later, when I told Big Glen about this case his only comment was, "Death was on a holiday. It just wasn't your time or the robber's."

50

I answered the telephone at my residence a few minutes before 11:00 A.M. on Sunday, December 17, 1967. The caller was Harold R. Farmer, Smithfield Chief of Police. Little did I know this call was to forever change my life. Chief Farmer said a four-year-old girl was missing and presumed kidnapped. He requested my investigative assistance. I told him I would leave within a few minutes and would meet him at his office. I thought of Gloria and little John, and Vicky must have detected the concern on my face. As I put on a dress shirt and knotted my tie, she asked me what had happened. I told her a four-year-old girl in Smithfield was missing and may have been kidnapped. I heard Vicky catch her breath before she said, to me, "Please find her."

Earlier that morning it had been well below freezing, but it didn't take my two-year-old Ford long to warm up as I drove on Highway 70 toward Smithfield at a rate well above the limit. Years earlier I had learned from my dad that the quicker an investigation is undertaken, the better the chance of solving it. I hadn't been called out the previous day or night and had gotten a good night's sleep. I didn't know, as I stopped at the Smithfield police station, that I would soon need all the energy and mental toughness I could muster combined with the common sense learned in Chatham County, the interrogation techniques acquired from ONI, and my FBI training.

It was about 11:30 A.M. when I shook hands with Chief Farmer in his office. I had a seat beside his desk and took a stenographer's shorthand notebook from my briefcase. As the chief talked, I made notes while interrupting him from time to time with questions. He related the following:

At 10:10 P.M. on Saturday night, December 16, a telephone call was received by police dispatcher Bill Norton. The caller identified himself as Jay Atwater. He claimed to have stopped a few minutes earlier at the Charcoal Inn Restaurant on Highway 301 in Smithfield and went inside for only a few minutes, leav-

265

ing his stepdaughter in his automobile. He said that when he returned to the vehicle she was gone, and he could not find her. In response to the dispatcher's questions, Atwater advised that his stepdaughter was four years of age and named Patricia Ann Guthrie but was called Patty.

Chief Farmer advised that Sergeant Ted Marshall was dispatched to the scene along with auxiliary officers Leland Crowder and J.B. Pickett. A thorough search of the area in and around the restaurant failed to locate the missing child, and therefore the search was expanded with additional officers being called in as well as prison department personnel with bloodhounds. Still, there was no trace of Patty Guthrie.

The chief stated that Sergeant Marshall had learned that Jay Atwater (not his real name) was on parole after serving time for armed robbery and kidnapping, and that he was married to Patty's mother, Mable Atwater, but had been separated from her for several weeks. Mrs. Atwater was living in Durham, and Patty in Smithfield with her maternal grandmother, Mrs. Rebecca Hargrove. Chief Farmer said that Sergeant Marshall had learned that Atwater planned to visit his wife in Durham, was going to take Patty with him, and had stopped at the restaurant to use the rest room before leaving town. The chief also advised that Mrs. Atwater and Patty's father, Jack Guthrie, had both been notified of Patty's disappearance, and both had arrived in town and were available to be interviewed. I told the chief I wanted to interview Mrs. Atwater and for someone to contact the local parole officer, as I wanted him as a witness when I talked to Jay Atwater.

Mrs. Atwater was at the Smithfield police station, so as soon as I finished talking to Chief Farmer I interviewed her. She was a petite, attractive lady who appeared to be in her mid-twenties. There was redness in her eyes that I assumed was from prolonged weeping. She was very distraught, but answered my questions in a subdued voice and a polite manner. She supplied the following information:

She was divorced from Jack Guthrie, who lives in Raleigh and is employed there as a mechanic. One child, Patricia Ann Guthrie, was born of the marriage on October 18, 1963. Everyone calls her daughter Patty. She and Patty's father divorced and on December 24, 1966, she married Jay Atwater, who was originally from Johnston County and was working at a local manufacturing plant in Smithfield. Jay was on parole from the North Carolina Prison Department, having served several years for armed robbery and kidnapping. She didn't know much about the crime except that Jay was in the army when it happened. In early November 1967, she and Jay separated, and she went to Durham, North Carolina, to live with Jay's mother, Betty Grayson, who was also on parole for murdering her second husband. Jay remained at Smithfield, where he continued to live in a house they had rented on Brogden Road. She did not take Patty with her to Durham, but left her in care of her mother, Mrs. Rebecca Hargrove, who lived on South Fifth Street in Smithfield. Actually, Patty stays there at night but is kept by her cousin, Mrs. Mildred Monroe, during the day.

Mrs. Atwater advised that on Thursday, December 14, she wrote a letter to her husband requesting that he drive over with Patty to Durham on Saturday for a visit with her and his mother. She said she didn't mail the letter until Friday, and was not sure he would receive it in time to make the trip. She therefore contacted him by telephone on Friday night and asked him to come to Durham the next day and bring Patty with him. He indicated he would probably do so. She expected them to arrive on Saturday, but they didn't show.

At about 12:30 on Sunday morning, her mother telephoned and told her Patty was missing. She left Durham shortly after receiving the call and drove to Smithfield, where she contacted her husband who told her of the circumstances regarding Patty's disappearance. She, her husband and a cousin, Samuel Hargrove, drove the thirty miles to Goldsboro, North Carolina, to see if Patty could possibly be at the home of her paternal grandparents, Mr. and Mrs. John Guthrie. Patty was not there, and they had no knowledge of her whereabouts.

The only explanation Mrs. Atwater could offer for the trip to the Guthrie residence in Goldsboro was that Patty had stayed with them from time to time, and she and her husband could think of no other place to look for her. She said she knew of no one who would want to harm the child, and that to her knowledge neither she nor her husband had any enemies.

I commenced my interview with Jay Dorn Atwater, a twenty-six-year-old white male, at the Smithfield police station at 12:38 P.M. on December 17, 1967. Fred E. Gardner, State Parole Officer, was a witness to the interview. Atwater was of medium height and build and had a smooth olive complexion. He had short brown hair and wore horn-rimmed glasses, which gave him a very academic appearance. I informed Atwater of his Miranda rights and after he acknowledged he understood them, and after declining to have an attorney, I asked him to first tell me about himself and then about what occurred the previous night. In a monotone, void of expression or emotion, he related the following:

He was born in Johnston County, and after attending public school he enlisted in the army. He hadn't been in the service but a couple of years when he and another person robbed a gasoline station in Raleigh and took the attendant with them and later released him unharmed. The two of them were apprehended and convicted, and he served four and one-half years before being paroled a couple of years ago. He returned to Johnston County and became employed as a millwright. In December 1966 he and his wife, Mable, were married. They have no children of their own, but his wife has a four-year-old daughter, Patty, by a previous marriage to Jack Guthrie. He, Mable, and Patty lived in a rented house on Brogden Road just south of Smithfield until early November 1967, when he decided he didn't want to be married anymore. He and Mable separated, and she went to Durham to live with his mother, Betty Grayson. Mable planned to study to be a nurse's aide. Patty remained in Smithfield with Mable's mother, Mrs. Rebecca Hargrove. She also stayed sometimes with her father's parents, Mr. and Mrs. Ben Guthrie, in Goldsboro. Patty's father, Jack Guthrie, lives and works in Raleigh.

During the latter part of last week, Mable wrote a letter to him, which she followed with a telephone call, requesting that he bring Patty and visit her and his mother on the weekend. On Saturday, the 16th, he slept in until nearly noon and remained around the house on Brogden Road until mid-afternoon. He then decided to make the trip to Durham. He filled the tank on his 1965 Chevrolet station wagon and late that afternoon drove to the residence of Rebecca Hargrove on South 5th Street in Smithfield. Mrs. Hargrove was there, but said Patty was at the home of Mable's cousin, Mildred Monroe. He and Mrs. Hargrove drove to the home of Mildred and Alfred Monroe where they picked up Patty. He then dropped off Mrs. Hargrove back at her home and proceeded to his house on Brogden Road and arrived there about 6:00 P.M. No one else was there. They went inside, and he got a change of clothes for Patty and some canned goods to take to his wife. His parole officer is Mr. Bond, who lives in Raleigh. He placed a telephone call to his residence in order to receive permission to leave the county. The call was answered by a young man, whom he assumed was Mr. Bond's son. He was told that Mr. Bond was in the shower and to call back in a few minutes. A short time later he called back, and the same young man answered and said that Mr. Bond had gone out for the evening and would not be back until later that night. He decided to ride around with Patty and show her Christmas lights and decorations. He planned to try to call Mr. Bond later that night. He and Patty left the house about 6:30 P.M. in his station wagon. He drove with her on the front seat beside him. She was fascinated by the lights and decorations, so they rode around Smithfield and the town of Selma for about three hours or so. During this time he didn't see anyone he knew, nor did he stop anywhere except to obey traffic regulations. Shortly before 10:00 P.M. his bowels became upset so he drove into the parking area of the Charcoal Inn Restaurant on Highway 301. Patty was sitting on the front seat beside him, and he told her he had to go inside the restaurant. She was sleepy, but nevertheless asked him to bring her a Coke. She lay down on the front seat and he covered her from the neck down with his coat. He went inside to the rest room and had a bowel movement. He then came out of the rest room and got a glass of water and took four aspirins. He got a Coke for Patty and walked back outside to his station wagon. Patty was not in the vehicle and his coat was partially on the front seat and partially on the floorboard. He looked around the parking area for Patty but didn't find her. He went back inside and called the police. He had no idea what happened to her.

Near the end of Atwater's interview, he reluctantly acknowledged to me that he had recently become very depressed and had considered suicide. He said he strongly considered it after he awakened on the morning of the 16th, but would not elaborate on why he was depressed or why he was considering suicide. He also acknowledged that shortly after he and his wife separated he had obtained a pistol, but later let someone else have it. He wouldn't identify the person who received the pistol from him. Armed with this information, I excused myself from the room and made my way to the dispatcher's office, where I placed a call to Judge M.R. Wooten, Chairman of the North Carolina Board of Paroles. Judge Wooten lived across the street from me, and he and I were friends. I told Judge Wooten about Patty's disappearance when she was last known to be with parolee Jay Atwater. I also told him about Atwater's alleged suicidal tendencies and his admission that he had recently been in possession of a pistol. Judge Wooten was about to leave with his family to visit relatives at Clinton, North Carolina, but said he would detour by Smithfield and come by the police station to see what progress had been made in the case, if any.

After I finished my interview with Atwater, and while waiting for Judge Wooten to arrive, I obtained from Jay Dorn Atwater voluntary written authorization to conduct searches of his residence and station wagon and to seize anything considered of evidentiary value, and to conduct any type laboratory tests deemed appropriate on his station wagon and his residence and/or the contents of either.

I finished with Atwater at 3:00 P.M. at which time he was taken into custody by Parole Officer Fred E. Gardner on authority of a temporary parole revocation signed by Judge Wooten. He was lodged in the Johnston County Jail.

No matter how hard I had tried to confuse, upset, or offend him, I couldn't find a chink or a dent in Atwater's armor. I knew I had just talked to the coldest son of a bitch I would ever encounter. I was convinced he was responsible for Patty's disappearance, but I was in the minority as his wife and some other family members believed in his innocence and thought I should be looking elsewhere for the person(s) who kidnapped her. I couldn't explain it, but I knew Jay Dorn Atwater was responsible for whatever had happened to Patty, and I feared the worst. I also knew if I was wrong that precious time was passing without my investigative attention being devoted to developing other leads which might result in Patty's safe return. I looked at the photograph of little Patty that had been received from a relative. I had never seen a more beautiful child. She appeared to be a little angel with dark hair, long lashes, and a smile that would steal your heart away. I wanted more than anything in the world to find her, and made up my mind that sooner or later Jay Dorn Atwater was going to tell me where she was. I was going to play by the rules, but I was going to use every legally acceptable interrogation technique I had ever learned and intended to employ all the technical SBI assistance I needed. As I looked at Patty's photograph again, I could almost hear her crying out for help. I was going to find Patty, and Jay Dorn Atwater was going to lead me to her. I made that promise to Patty and myself.

I placed a telephone call to the residence of Myron McBryde in Raleigh. A few months earlier, he had replaced Mr. Anderson as Director of the SBI. I explained to him the details of the case and said that I needed the services of a chemist to conduct some luminal tests for blood. Mr. McBryde immediately replied he would personally send Chief Chemist W.S. Best to Smithfield and said if I needed additional laboratory assistance, or the assistance of other agent personnel, to call him back regardless of the hour.

I drove alone to a nearby restaurant and nibbled at my food in silence. As I planned the next steps in the investigation, my mind would wander occasionally to thoughts of the beautiful little girl in the photograph who was cradling a doll in her arms.

I returned to the police station to find Jack Guthrie waiting for me. He was obviously concerned and emotionally upset. He asked me if there had been any progress in the effort to locate Patty or determine what had happened to her. I shook my head negatively, and then proceeded to interview him. He stated that on Saturday, the 16th, he was with a friend named Wallace Poston until about 7:00 P.M., when he dropped Poston off at his home in Raleigh on Cooper Road. He advised he then went to the Continental Lounge on Western Boulevard and had one beer before driving to his nearby trailer at College View Trailer Park. He arrived there about 8:30 P.M. and remained there alone. About 6:00 A.M., he was awakened by Raleigh police officers who informed him Patty was missing and wanted to know if she was there. He dressed and drove to Smithfield. Jack Guthrie stated he didn't know the whereabouts of Patty and knew of no one who would want to kidnap her. He appeared to be a man stricken with grief and barely able to endure the pain of his daughter's mysterious disappearance.

After talking to Jack Guthrie, I walked into Chief Farmer's office and told him about the written authorization I had received from Jay Atwater to search his vehicle and residence. I said I wanted to do it while it was still daylight. Chief Farmer assigned Sergeants W.A. Young and Ted Marshall to assist me. The three of us rode in my car to the Johnston County jail, where Atwater was released to our custody. He was handcuffed and transported to his residence on Brogden Road, a half mile southeast of I-95. The dwelling was a one-story, white-frame structure with seven rooms. From his bedroom closet I recovered a pair of workboots and an army field jacket he claimed to have worn the previous day. From a clothes hamper I recovered a pair of gray work trousers and a long-sleeve gray shirt. A search of the remainder of the house and out buildings disclosed nothing considered of evidentiary value.

Atwater was returned to the Johnston County jail, and when I returned the two sergeants to the police station, I found Chemist W.S. Best waiting for me. He was accompanied by Technical D.C. Matheny. Atwater's station wagon had been taken to the local Ford agency where Best, assisted by Matheny, conducted luminal tests (which have to be done in darkness) for the presence of blood. The tests were conducted on the vehicle and contents and disclosed what Best stated were small traces of blood on the right front floorboard of the station wagon and small traces on the right side of the rear seat. Several other minute spots of blood were also detected on a quilt located behind the rear seat. The quantity of the blood was not sufficient to determine if it was of human origin or some other group.

With the discovery of the blood in Atwater's vehicle, I decided to confront him again. I thought that if I didn't get a confession from him I would at least give him something to worry about. Back to the jail I went where I saw Deputy Braxton Hinton. I asked him to sit in as a witness while I interviewed Atwater, and he readily agreed to do so. I again informed Atwater of his Miranda rights and this time his interview lasted only from 10:00 P.M. to 10:38 P.M. He was as cold and unemotional as when I first interviewed him earlier that day. When I told him we had found blood in his station wagon and on the quilt, he just looked at me without any change of expression, shrugged his shoulders, and said he didn't know how it could have gotten there. He failed to respond to anything I said. After he was returned to his cell, and while Hinton and I were walking to our cars, I told Hinton that the brief interview with Atwater had cemented my conviction that Atwater was responsible for whatever had happened to Patty. When Hinton asked me why, I said, "Don't you think an innocent man would have welcomed seeing us and would have immediately asked if Patty had been found? He didn't ask about being released and just glared at me when he came into the room. He knows where Patty is, and sooner or later I'm going to know."

I followed Hinton in my car to a local restaurant where we had coffee and hamburgers. I arrived home at midnight. Vicky was in bed, but got up when I came in. We talked for an hour as I tried to unwind. I slept little and was up before 6:00 A.M. Less than an hour later I was on my way back to Smithfield. I decided I could use the assistance of another agent, so when I got to the police station I placed a call to Director McBryde and requested the help of Agent W.F. Crocker. In less than an hour he was there.

While waiting for Crocker's arrival, I reviewed the Smithfield police report of the incident and detected something of which I was not aware. A Smithfield policeman, off-duty officer C.M. Stone, was in the Charcoal Inn Restaurant when Atwater reported Patty was missing. When Crocker arrived, we went for coffee and I went over the case in detail with him. He listened attentively and occasionally stopped me to ask questions. He studied the photograph of Patty with the doll, and I could tell he was disturbed. Crocker was a good, hard-working agent who damn sure didn't watch the clock. He and I had successfully worked together before, and I felt fortunate to have him with me. We started with an interview with Officer Stone who furnished the following information:

On Saturday the 16th, around 9:30 P.M., he stopped for a cup of coffee at the Charcoal Inn Restaurant. He was off-duty and wearing civilian clothing. He had been in the restaurant for about ten minutes when he saw a green station wagon drive into the parking lot and stop on the north side of the driveway. The station wagon had arrived from the direction of the town of Selma. A white male immediately got out of the vehicle from the driver's side and walked into the restaurant. He was wearing a gray shirt, gray trousers, and glasses. He walked to a table in the dining room where several teenage boys were sitting. He apparently asked directions to the men's room, as he immediately walked to the rear of the restaurant where the rest rooms are located. He came out in about five minutes and ordered a Coke. He drank about half of it and then took the bottle with him as he walked outside. He was gone for about thirty seconds before he came back inside. He asked the owner if there was a telephone available, as his child had been kidnapped. The owner said there was a telephone in the rear of the restaurant and the subject went to use the telephone and returned a few moments later. He accompanied the subject outside, and they searched the area but to no avail. Sergeant Marshall arrived within a few minutes and took charge.

In addition to the above, Officer Stone advised he clearly saw the station wagon when it entered the parking lot, and there didn't appear to be anyone else in the vehicle. He also advised he could see the station wagon from where he was sitting in the restaurant, and didn't see anyone get out of the vehicle while the subject was inside, nor did he see anyone approach the vehicle.

Crocker and I returned to the police station where he and I again reviewed the police report and also examined the written statement obtained from Patty's grandmother, Mrs. Rebecca Hargrove, and a statement from Alfred Monroe, from whose home Mrs. Hargrove and Jay Atwater picked up Patty. Information in their written statements was consistent with that previously furnished to me by Chief Farmer.

At 12:30 P.M. on Monday, December 18, 1967, I again informed Atwater of his Miranda rights, and Crocker and I began his interrogation at the Johnston County Sheriff's Department. I had finally won the confidence of Mrs. Atwater, and from time to time I brought her into the interview room where she would

274

plead with her husband to be truthful with us. Nothing worked. Jay Dorn Atwater wouldn't bend, much less break, under our intense questioning. At one point during his interrogation, I displayed the photograph of little Patty to him in which she was holding the doll. He looked at the photograph for what seemed to be a long time and my hopes grew until his eyes shifted to meet mine, and he calmly said he would like to have a copy to keep with him. Out of the corner of my eye I saw Crocker stiffen in his chair and then relax. Crocker was known to have a quick temper, and I knew he was fighting to maintain self-control as he realized a screw-up could jeopardize any case we might have against Atwater and might prevent Patty from ever being found. After sparring with Atwater for a good two hours, I had Officer Stone to come into the room. He told of his observations at the Charcoal Inn Restaurant on Saturday night, and stated upon stopping his vehicle Atwater immediately got out and did not take the time to cover anyone with his coat who may have been lying on the front seat. Stone also said no one got out of or approached the station wagon while Atwater was in the restaurant. What was Atwater's reaction to Stone's statements? Nothing—absolutely nothing. He just didn't respond until Stone had left the room. I asked him to explain to us why Stone would say such things if they weren't true. His response was that he didn't know and that he only knew he was being truthful. That gave me the opportunity to ease the question to him I had been holding back, "If you are being truthful then you wouldn't mind taking a polygraph test, would you?" It was 3:15 P.M. when he looked at Crocker and me and said he would take the test.

At 3:30 P.M., Crocker and I left Smithfield with Atwater in my car. A telephone call to Raleigh had assured us Agent Pearce, who recently had been assigned to the laboratory as a polygraph examiner and ballistics expert, would be available for us. So as not to offend Atwater and give him an excuse to back out of taking the polygraph examination, Crocker and I didn't discuss the case with him on the way to Raleigh. It was difficult to do, but we acted as friendly as possible toward him. We arrived with Atwater at SBI Headquarters at 4:25 P.M. While Atwater was detained in another office, Crocker and I briefed Pearce on the details of the case. He made notes and listened to all we had to

275

say. He then decided on the questions he would use in the examination. At 5:15 P.M., Pearce again informed Atwater of his Miranda rights, and after he acknowledged he understood his rights and said he didn't want an attorney, Pearce administered a series of polygraph tests to Atwater while Crocker and I watched through a two-way mirror in the adjoining observation room. At the completion of the examination, Pearce went to his office and Crocker and I followed. Pearce studied the polygraph charts for a few minutes before he said that in his opinion Atwater had not been truthful when he denied knowledge of Patty's whereabouts and was not truthful about the events at the Charcoal Inn Restaurant. I looked at Crocker and said, "She's dead, and that son of a bitch did it." He nodded. Crocker and I went back into the interrogation room, where Atwater was still seated in the polygraph chair, but the instrument had been disconnected from his person. Crocker and I pulled up folding chairs close to Atwater. I knew I was about to commence my final interrogation of Jay Dorn Atwater. I was going to give it everything I had, and if a confession was not forthcoming, then I would have been defeated as I wouldn't know how to approach him again.

I moved my chair directly in front of Atwater so close our knees were nearly touching. Thick cigarette smoke filled the room. I was well into my third pack of the day. I looked at Atwater and said, "Jay, there's not much need of me saying so, as you know as well as I do that you didn't pass the polygraph test. In other words your answers about Patty's disappearance were not truthful."

For the next thirty minutes I didn't stop, and I didn't ask a question. It seemed as if some higher power was controlling me as words, phrases, expressions, and sentences flowed freely from me that were foreign to my usual manner of speaking. I didn't berate Atwater, but told him I knew Patty was dead and that he had killed her. I told of many things in her childhood she would never experience and then proceeded to adolescence and womanhood. I was on my knees begging and pleading for him to tell me where she was. My eyes were misty as I looked eyeball to eyeball with Jay Dorn Atwater and whispered the question, "Is she in the water?"

Atwater shook his head negatively and said in that unemotional voice of his, "She's in the ground, where I buried her. Will there be much publicity?"

I fought to control myself, and apparently did a good job of it, as I said, "Jay, I'm glad it's over and I know you are. Tell us all that happened Saturday night and then let's find Patty. She deserves a Christian burial." He related the following:

On Saturday, December 16, 1967, he and Mrs. Hargrove picked up Patty at the Monroe residence. He then dropped off Mrs. Hargrove at her home and drove with Patty to his home on Brogden Road. He was in his Chevrolet station wagon. He planned to go to Durham to see his wife and take Patty with him. After he and Patty arrived at his home, he tried to contact his parole officer by telephone in order to get permission to leave the county for the trip to Durham. He didn't make contact with him. He then decided to have sex with Patty. He undressed her and put her on the bed. He had intercourse with her, but didn't climax. Patty screamed and struggled, and her vagina was torn up badly and was bleeding. He got a washcloth and a bedspread and cleaned the blood off Patty and dressed her. He then got his shovel from behind the house and put it and Patty in his station wagon. He drove toward Goldsboro, passed by the community of Brogden, and turned right on a rural paved road. He drove for a couple of miles before he located a dirt path that led through a trash dump area. He drove up the path about thirty yards and stopped. He got out and took the shovel with him. He went about ten yards into the woods where he dug Patty's grave. He went back to the station wagon and led Patty by the hand to the grave. He used his hands to choke her to death. He placed her in the grave and covered her with dirt. He then spread pine needles over the grave so it wouldn't be detected. He drove about two miles to a bridge where he stopped and threw the bedspread and washcloth into the river. He rode around for a while, returned to his house, and put the shovel back where it belonged. He then drove to the Charcoal Inn Restaurant where he reported Patty missing.

I looked at Atwater and said, "Jay, please draw a map to help us find Patty." His expression still hadn't changed, and in that unemotional voice I had heard so often for two days, he asked

277

for paper and pen. Crocker handed both to him and Atwater sketched a crude map from his residence to where he said the body was buried.

Crocker and I stepped out of the interrogation room and for the first time I realized I was soaking wet from perspiration. I looked down at my left hand and saw a cigarette held between my fingers. I also had one between my lips. I was completely exhausted, as was Crocker. Those who have never participated in an interrogation will never know how much they can drain you physically as well as mentally. I was ecstatic over having obtained Atwater's confession, but saddened to hear how little Patty had died and the horrible suffering she experienced before her death. Crocker and I shook hands, and as we did so, I said, "Let's take him back to Smithfield and at the appropriate time I'll see if he will lead us to the body."

Crocker and I arrived with Atwater at the Johnston County Sheriff's Department at 8:35 P.M. It had started to rain and as I stopped my car near the sheriff's office, I turned to face Atwater who was beside Crocker on the back seat. I said, "Jay, Patty is in the cold ground and it's raining harder. It's time to bring her home. Will you please show us where she is?"

In that same tone I had heard for two days, Atwater agreed to lead us to the body. I went into the sheriff's office and found Braxton Hinton on duty. I told him Jay Atwater had confessed to killing Patty and had agreed to lead us to the body. I said I was going to wait in the car with Atwater and Crocker and I wanted him to notify Coroner V.J. Underwood and Chief Farmer. Within thirty minutes, Coroner Underwood, Sergeant Yow, and Officer Joe Gerrell of the Smithfield Police Department arrived at the sheriff's office. I drove slowly out of the parking lot, followed by a sheriff's department vehicle, a Smithfield police car, and an ambulance from Coroner Underwood's funeral home. It was raining harder. Following Atwater's directions, I drove southeast of Smithfield on rural paved road 1007 for a distance of approximately sixteen miles to the intersection of rural paved road 1224, where he directed me to turn right. I followed this road for a distance of 2.1 miles, where Atwater pointed to a wide dirt path leading into a pine forest. While the remainder of the group followed a respectable distance behind us, Crocker and I followed Atwater's directions and escorted him about seventy-five yards up the path into the pine thicket. He had us to turn to the right and we walked eighteen paces to a spot in the thicket that looked no different from the rest of the area. Atwater pointed to the ground and said, "She's there." Crocker and I shined our flashlights on the spot, but couldn't tell it had ever been disturbed. As the other members of the group arrived, we realized no one had thought to bring a shovel. Without a word being exchanged between us, Crocker and I dropped to our knees in the cold rain that was slowly falling. I brushed back pine needles and saw freshly disturbed soil. Crocker and I dug gently with our hands into the soft, wet earth to a depth of about two feet. Suddenly, I touched the lifeless form of four-year-old Patty. Carefully, the soil was moved aside to disclose the doll-like features of a beautiful child lying on her back as if asleep. I gently lifted Patty from her grave and placed her on a canvas stretcher. Director McBryde had arrived on the scene along with several other officers. As I looked around I knew those present had seen death many times and thought they had become hardened to it, but there was not a dry eye among them.

Deputy Hinton came over to me and said that we had crossed out of Johnston County and were in Wayne County. He had already used his radio to notify the Wayne County Sheriff's Department in Goldsboro of our location and requested that the Wayne County Coroner be dispatched to the scene. In less than an hour, Wayne County Coroner I.T. Still arrived, accompanied by deputies Isaac Ennis and Robert Day. I briefed Coroner Still and the two deputies. Coroner Still ordered an autopsy of the body of Patricia Ann Guthrie, and released it to Coroner Underwood to be transported to Wake Memorial Hospital in Raleigh.

It was 2:00 A.M. on Tuesday, December 19, 1967, when I turned into my driveway. Vicky heard me open the front door and hurried to meet me in the foyer. She thought I had been hurt, as I was soaked to the bone and muddy from head to toe. I glanced into the living room and saw our Christmas tree and the presents under it. I suddenly realized it was just six more days until Christmas, but little Patty would never see her fourth Christmas on this earth. I could see that Vicky was talking to me, and I forced myself to listen to the words. I assured her I was not injured and, as she made coffee, I told her about Jay Dorn Atwater and little Patty. We talked for a couple of hours and then I showered. I slept less than three hours before I got up, ate a light breakfast, and drove to Raleigh Headquarters, where I met Crocker. We talked briefly with the Director, and then the two of us drove in my car to Goldsboro where I signed a warrant issued by Justice of the Peace R.P. Young, charging Atwater with the murder of Patricia Ann Guthrie. We drove back to Smithfield, where I signed a warrant issued by Justice of the Peace Nathan Lassister, charging Atwater with the rape of Patricia Ann Guthrie. I served both warrants on him at the Johnston County jail at 3:30 P.M. on December 19, 1967. He later waived preliminary hearings on both charges and was bound over without privilege of bail to await grand jury action in Wayne and Johnston Counties.

About 4:00 P.M. on the 19th, Jackie Guthrie, Patty's father, was intercepted by a deputy sheriff in the Johnston County Court house en route to the jail to "visit" Atwater. The deputy found a fully loaded pistol concealed on Guthrie. Crocker and I were notified, and we held a discussion with Sheriff Rayford Oliver. He stated that feelings were extremely hostile in the local community against Atwater and that he would feel much better if he was transferred to Wake County for safekeeping. At Sheriff Oliver's request, I placed a telephone call to resident Superior Court Judge James H. Pou Bailey and explained the situation to him. He said he would immediately issue an order authorizing Atwater's transfer to the Wake jail and would notify Wake County Sheriff Robert J. Pleasants. Since Crocker and I were returning to Raleigh, Sheriff Oliver requested us to deliver Atwater to the Wake County jail. We agreed to do so, and, after placing Atwater in the car, I again informed him of his Miranda rights. Crocker and I had agreed we wouldn't ask Atwater any questions and would avoid talking to him. We rode along in silence for several miles without a word being spoken. Finally, Atwater came out with this statement to us:

"After killing Patty, I thought about going on to Durham and killing my wife. I had planned to kill my wife for several months and was going to dispose of her body where it would never be

280

found. I love my wife and I also hate her part of the time. While having intercourse with Patty, I was thinking about my wife. While I was digging Patty's grave, I was crying all the time. If I had not told you where her grave was, you would never have found her. Do you think you would have convicted me if I had not confessed?"

Neither of us answered his question. As Crocker and I were leaving the Wake County jail, he said to me that he wished he had better words to describe Atwater other than, "He is one cold-blooded son of a bitch."

Atwater was subsequently sent to a state mental hospital where he was observed over a period of sixty-six days. He was found to be sane and capable of distinguishing between right and wrong. His IQ was determined to be 121. The average IQ ranges from 90 to 115.

Atwater's murder trial began in Wayne County Superior Court at Goldsboro on Monday, August 5, 1968. I was there well before court convened, as I knew I would be one of the first witnesses to appear before the grand jury. When I entered the courtroom, I was shocked to see the size of the crowd waiting for court to open. District Attorney Archie Taylor saw me and motioned for me to follow him. He led me to a small anteroom off a halfway behind the judge's bench. Mr. Taylor, in a very calm manner, informed me that Jackie Guthrie was sitting in the courtroom directly behind the defense table, and that he had received information he was armed with a pistol. I told Mr. Taylor there was only one way to find out and told him I would be right back. I walked into the courtroom and immediately spotted Jackie Guthrie. I went over to where he was sitting and said that I needed to talk to him for a minute and asked him to come with me. He followed me into the anteroom where Mr. Taylor was waiting. I told Jackie that Mr. Taylor was the district attorney who would handle the prosecution of Jay Dorn Atwater and that he had prepared long and hard for the trial and fully expected for Atwater to receive the death penalty. I also told Jackie I had done my best to compile a strong case against Atwater, and I too felt he would receive the death penalty.

I said, "Jackie, if you have a gun, please give it to me now so that you won't be back in this same courthouse facing a murder charge." He reached into the back pocket of his trousers and pulled out a .25 caliber semi-automatic pistol, which had a cartridge in the chamber and a full magazine.

He handed the weapon to me. I looked at Mr. Taylor, who said, "Give it back to him after the trial." Jackie returned to his seat in the courtroom. You may ask why I didn't charge Jackie Guthrie with having a concealed weapon. Do you think Mr. Taylor would have prosecuted the case against him? Not on your life!

Monday and part of Tuesday were taken up with jury selection. Testimony got underway on Tuesday afternoon. I had never before primed myself for a trial as I had for this one. I had gone over and over my notes and reports until I had everything committed to memory, including all dates, times, distances, directions, and what was said and done by whom. I was on the witness stand for a day and a half being examined and cross-examined, and I never had to refer to a note. The defense had two very prestigious attorneys, but theirs was a losing battle. The case went to the jury on Friday, August 9, 1968, and they were out for only seventeen minutes before returning a verdict of guilty of murder in the first degree! Judge Joseph W. Parker sentenced Atwater to die in the gas chamber at the state penitentiary in Raleigh on September 20, 1968.

As with any death sentence, the appeals go on and on and they did so in this case. On August 17, 1970, Atwater stood trial in Johnston County Superior Court for the rape of Patricia Ann Guthrie. I again testified over a period of two days. The case went to the jury on Wednesday, the 19th, and this time the jury was out one hour and ten minutes before returning a verdict of guilty of rape without a recommendation for life imprisonment. This made the death penalty mandatory, and Judge James H. Pou Bailey sentenced Atwater to be executed in the state's gas chamber at Raleigh on November 13, 1970, between the hours of 10:00 A.M. and 3:00 P.M. The never-ending appeals process was again set into motion.

Atwater was never to be executed for the rape and murder of little Patty Guthrie. North Carolina's death penalty was declared unconstitutional, and Atwater's death sentences were therefore changed to life imprisonment. He lives today!

When I heard Judge Parker sentence Jay Dorn Atwater to

The author, pictured left, and agent W.F. Crocker digging for the body of four-year-old Patty Guthrie.

die on that hot August day in 1968, I knew my days in law enforcement had come to an end, as there was nothing left for me to accomplish. I had continued to work and work hard after Crocker and I deposited Atwater in the Wake County jail eight months earlier. I had received a lot of recognition and was promoted to Assistant Supervising Agent. I continued to successfully investigate homicide cases, armed robberies, and other felonies, but I knew I would never again be confronted with a challenge comparable to the Atwater case. I was thirty-five-years-old but going on sixty. I considered Jay Dorn Atwater the epitome of evil. I had talked the talk, walked the walk, and danced with the devils. Four months later I resigned to enter the world of corporate security. May little Patty rest in peace.